"*Gospel Truth* has deepened my understanding of Jesus and given me hope that Jesus scholarship may spur some exciting (if divisive) changes within Christianity during the years to come. Whatever your faith, this volume is likely to forever change the way you regard the man beneath the halo."

—*New Age Journal*

"Exciting and entertaining . . . a responsible and comprehensive account of the current scholarly and cultural controversy about Jesus."

—Marcus Borg, Hundere Distinguished
Professor, Oregon State University, and
author of *Meeting Jesus Again for the First Time*

GOSPEL TRUTH

The New Image of Jesus Emerging from Science and History, and Why It Matters

RUSSELL SHORTO

RIVERHEAD BOOKS, NEW YORK

Riverhead Books
Published by The Berkley Publishing Group
A member of Penguin Putnam Inc.
200 Madison Avenue
New York, New York 10016

Book design by Marysarah Quinn
Cover design by Tom McKeveny
Cover art: Andrea del Verrocchio, *Doubting Thomas*, sculpture. Orsanmichele, Florence, Italy; Alinari/Art Resource, NY

First Riverhead hardcover edition: March 1997
First Riverhead trade paperback edition: April 1998
Riverhead trade paperback ISBN: 1-57322-659-9

The Penguin Putnam Inc. World Wide Web site address is
http://www.penguinputnam.com

The Library of Congress has catalogued the Riverhead hardcover edition as follows:

Shorto, Russell.
Gospel truth : the new image of Jesus emerging from science and history, and why it matters / by Russell Shorto.
p. cm.
Includes bibliographical references.
ISBN 1-57322-056-6 (alk. paper)
1. Jesus Christ—Rationalistic interpretations. 2. Jesus Christ—History of doctrines—20th century. 3. Jesus Christ—Biography—History and criticism. 4. Jesus Christ—Historicity. 5. Jesus Seminar. I. Title.
BT304.95.S56 1997 96-43749 CIP

Printed in the United States of America

10 9 8 7 6 5 4 3 2 1

For Anna and Eva

ACKNOWLEDGMENTS

Probably the only thing more foolish than taking on a subject so vast and fraught with peril would be to try doing it alone. As it happens, many people helped me with this book. First I would like to thank Edward Beutner, scholar, priest, and walking parable, for his many wisdoms and kindnesses; my agent and friend, Anne Edelstein, for making it happen, and for tolerating the occasional raving phone call; my editor, Mary South, whose sharp but delicate touch improved the manuscript greatly; and my father, Anthony Shorto, for turning a visit to Israel from a research trip into a life experience.

I am also grateful for the assistance of Char Matejovsky and Bob Schwartz of the Westar Institute; Zvi Greenhut, Miki Waisman, and the Israel Antiquities Authority; Drew Kadel and the staff of Union Theological Seminary

Library; John Henricksson, Robert Cwiklik, and Tim Paulson, who read the manuscript at various stages and offered excellent insights; and the ministers and priests who gave me a sense of how historical Jesus material is at work at the church level, including Blayney Colmore, Edward Hasse, Wade Renn, Richard Watts, Marianne Niesen, Edwin Bacon, James Karpen, and John Paulson.

My first exploration of this field was for a magazine article on the Jesus Seminar; I want to thank Art Cooper, editor-in-chief of *Gentleman's Quarterly,* and Lisa Henricksson, executive editor, for giving the article a home on what to some might have seemed alien soil. Thanks also to Bishop John Shelby Spong, Dick Staub, Catherine Kurs, Stacy Davids, and Scott Woodward; to Maura Strausberg of the Gallup Research Library; and to Judy Kuker for giving me a push at the crucial moment. A special thanks to Elaine Pagels and the students in her spring 1996 "Jesus in Contemporary and Ancient Debate" seminar at Princeton University, for giving me the opportunity to air the approach I take in this book and for enriching it with their questions and insights.

Of course I am grateful to all of the scholars who devoted time to guiding me along the more precipitous slopes in their field, especially John Dominic Crossan, Marcus Borg, Paula Fredriksen, Robert Funk, Stephen Patterson, and N. T. Wright.

I owe my wife, Marnie, something beyond mere thanks, but in a book words are the only thing on offer.

CONTENTS

INTRODUCTION
1

CHAPTER 1
JESUS RULES
7

CHAPTER 2
IN THE BEGINNING
17

CHAPTER 3
A MOTHER RELIGION GIVES BIRTH TO TWINS
49

CHAPTER 4
GREEKNESS
65

CHAPTER 5
THE BIG DIPPER
81

CHAPTER 6
"SOME FABULOUS YONDER"
109

CHAPTER 7
MIRACLES
123

CHAPTER 8
NEW GOSPELS
145

CHAPTER 9
MURDER MYSTERY
167

CHAPTER 10
"THE MOST WRETCHED OF DEATHS"
197

CHAPTER 11
RESURRECTION
213

CHAPTER 12
THE HISTORICAL JESUS GOES
TO CHURCH
231

CHAPTER 13
THE CASE AGAINST
251

CHAPTER 14
OPEN SPACES
269

NOTES
275

BIBLIOGRAPHY
289

INDEX
297

INTRODUCTION

Sometime around 5 B.C.E., a Palestinian Jewish couple named Miryam and Yosef did something quite unremarkable: they had sexual intercourse. Miryam later gave birth to a son, whom they called Yeshu, a shortened and, in their day, more fashionable form of the ancient Hebrew name Yeshua. Yeshu may have been their firstborn; in time, there were at least seven children in the family. Yeshu's brothers were James, Joses, Simon, and Judas. We don't know the names of the sisters, although there were at least two.

Yeshu was born and raised in the Galilean village of Nazareth, a small, distinctly Jewish place, but one that was only four miles away from the cosmopolitan Roman-controlled capital of Sepphoris, a fast-growing city of forty thousand people, with an acropolis, a bank, and an import-export trade to major regions of the Mediterranean world. Here, literally within sight of Nazareth, Greek was the language of commerce.

Yeshu's father, who was probably a day-laborer, may have helped to build some of the Roman baths and porticoes that were being constructed in Sepphoris at this time. It would have been natural for Yeshu, as he grew and followed his father in his trade, to make the two-hour hike to the city, in which case his early years would have been spent among some very un-Jewish sights and sounds: Greek plays, Greek philosophy, the lively mix of cultures that characterized a Roman metropolis. It would have been a youth rooted in local tradition but also opening out to the wider world.

Yeshu, of course, is Jesus. This rough sketch of the beginning of a life has little in common with the picture of Jesus' early years that the gospels give. There is no virginal conception, no manger, no frankincense and myrrh. In place of such mythic elements, it has something else: the ring of historical reality. In it we begin to see a person emerging: a Jew, living in a Roman world, surrounded by Greek culture. The details of this sketch are part of the combined work of hundreds of experts from all over the world who are toiling away in the greatest concentration of effort ever amassed on a single historical question: "Who was Jesus?" Over the past two decades or so, biblical scholars have become excited by recent archaeological discoveries and new ways of applying scientific and social-scientific tools to the data they have about Jesus' life and times, and their work has blossomed into a full-fledged movement. The historical Jesus movement has not only taken over New Testament studies but has swept into the popular consciousness. It has raised the ire of religious conservatives and resulted in an enormous amount of data and interpretation, and a nearly equal amount of confusion.

In the following pages I will attempt to sort through the claims, winnow out at least some of the hyperbole, and present what I take to be a core consensus of material, a kind of collective portrait of the most influential life in Western history. Beyond that I will report on what is possibly an even more remarkable phenomenon: how this figure born of scholarly reconstruction is beginning to make an impact on Christian faith.

I am not a biblical scholar but a writer who grew up Catholic, attended Catholic school until the fourth grade, and did a stint as an altar boy before leaving the church in my teens. Although I never returned to organized religion, my early religious experience has stayed with me, whether I like it or not. Historical Jesus work first caught my attention because of its coolly rational perspective. Here, I thought, was a group of intelligent people taking a hard, critical look at a story that is usually approached with pie-eyed piety. Maybe they would cut through the cant and locate the "real" story: maybe they would finally kill Jesus for me.

Of course, they didn't. As I immersed myself in the subject, I realized that many of these people were ministers or priests as well as authorities in ancient history. Far from trying to undo Christianity, many of them were working toward a new definition of it. They were hoping to make a set of very ancient beliefs digestible to a modern mind so that the seeds of wisdom locked within them could take root. To their way of thinking, they were attempting to save Christianity from the choking clutch of literalness.

This aspect of the work is what seems to account for the remarkable popular interest in the topic. Dense, jargon-packed scholarly books on the subject make bestseller lists. When experts appear on radio call-in shows the phones light up. There are ministers of all denominations who say they have felt a burden lifted from their shoulders by this approach to the gospels, and they are suddenly offering their congregations an entirely new Jesus.

But not everyone likes this new image of Jesus, or thinks it has merit. Christians of a more traditional bent maintain that these scholars miss the point. "It's a curious thing about the contemporary historical Jesus scholar," says evangelical scholar Craig Blomberg. "He can't believe in the miraculous, and he comes up with a Jesus that doesn't do supernatural healings." If one starts from a critical, suspicious bent, the thinking goes, one is closed off from the mystic pull of the Christian saga and left with no choice but to try to unravel the whole thing.

This is a devastating criticism—devastating because it is accurate. Historical Jesus work, taken alone, is both deeply engrossing and amazingly limited. It strips a god down to mortal dimensions—a terribly ambivalent enterprise, which, however, is exactly what it is designed to do, for by definition there can be no such thing as a scientific proof of the supernatural. Science works on the natural world; the field of history is concerned not with myth but with real events.

But while the bulk of this book is devoted to a close-up look at this fascinating, interdisciplinary search for Jesus of Nazareth, I hope that as one proceeds through it another perspective will begin to take shape. It has to do with the realization that scientific truth—test-tube truth, literal truth—occupies only one slender band of the spectrum of human reality. There is such a thing as truth that is beyond verbal expression. Spirituality is concerned with *that* kind of truth. The vital question in all of this is whether there is a connection between these two types of truth, these two ways of knowing. If the phrase "gospel truth" still has meaning today, how closely does it have to be tied to the literal, historical level?

That is a question we each have to answer. A historical meditation on the New Testament can't replace a spiritual meditation, but it is possibly, for some, a necessary accompaniment to it. While millions of Christians will continue to live quite well in complete ignorance of the subject, many people—including many bishops, ministers, and biblical authorities—believe that it can help make the Christian experience more meaningful. Of course, Jesus research can also provide evidence for dismissing the New Testament as the fairy tale of a more primitive era. It is only a tool, and how we use our tools is up to us.

CHAPTER ONE

JESUS RULES

It is an ideal setting for detective work. The Flamingo Hotel in Santa Rosa, California, with its 1950s modernist architecture, pink neon sign and pink flamingoes patterned into the paving stones in front, is a Raymond Chandler kind of place. It doesn't take much effort to imagine a gumshoe in trenchcoat and fedora lurking among the palm trees, sniffing out a corpse or a killer.

Once inside, you might be forgiven for thinking the people gathered here are something other than detectives. In the banquet hall, around a rectangle of conference tables, flanked by an American flag and the flag of the State of California, beneath an enormous disco ball, thirty-two men and women sit, some poring through printed material, some in whispered conversation, others squinting as a speaker leans into a microphone to make a point. Flashbulbs go off. A camera crew is adjusting lights. Reporters scribble notes.

It might be a government hearing. It could be a chess match, to judge from the lively interest of the hundred-odd onlookers, the way they observe points and counterpoints being fired across the tables, the way they nod or screw up their eyes to grasp the significance of a claim. But the subject matter has nothing to do with government or games. One of the presiders calls for order:

"Very well, are we ready to vote? The first proposition, then, is this: *'Jesus was crucified.'*"

These are indeed detectives, and the person they are searching for, whom they believe has been hidden by two thousand years of myth, is Jesus of Nazareth. Collectively, this group of biblical scholars is known as the Jesus Seminar. From the time it was founded in 1985, the Jesus Seminar was derided by conservative Christians as a kind of secular-humanist version of the McCarthy hearings. Only instead of hunting Communists with mad-dog frenzy, these liberal scholars, according to their detractors, are out to destroy none other than Jesus Christ, Second Person of the Holy Trinity, to slice him to pieces with the vicious blade of scientific reasoning, leaving in his stead a withered human corpse and the pagan god they worship: a cold, amoral universe governed only by the laws of physics.

The Jesus Seminar is the most visible manifestation of the remarkable wave of biblical scholarship that has become known as the historical Jesus movement. It has incited such wrath partly because it has been so very public in its deliberations: not just welcoming visitors but aggressively courting media attention. (How many scholarly groups have their own full-time publicity director?) While mainly comprised of authorities on ancient history, paleography, and like subjects, it is freewheeling enough to have admitted into its deliberations Hollywood director Paul Verhoeven—the sex-and-violence maestro who brought you *Basic Instinct* and *Showgirls*—who, unlikely as it may seem, has been preparing to make a movie about the historical Jesus.

It is the seminar's conceit of debating the authenticity of the words and deeds of Jesus as recorded in the gospels and then *voting* on them that has ensured both media coverage and academic ridicule. Far from shying away from controversy or explaining away its tactics, the seminar ups the ante, sticks a finger in the face of the academy with its showy method of voting. After the first proposition, whether Jesus was crucified, has been stated and debated, a red plastic tray is passed around. It contains plastic beads of four different colors—red, pink, gray, black. The scholars take turns dropping beads into a container. Red means "I believe this piece of the gospel story is authentic." Pink means "Maybe." Gray is "Probably not," and black is "Definitely not." Deciding the fate of Jesus of Nazareth by vote would seem to be bad enough, but color-coding their results in the editions of the gospels that they publish is a deliberate play on the sacred Bible tradition of printing the words of Jesus in red ink.

The subject of this meeting is the crucifixion, and the results of the first vote do not support the worst fears of detractors: the beads are counted, and the outcome is a definite red. There *was* a crucifixion, the scriptural minimalists have decided. Ensuing votes reveal that the seminar fellows are nearly unanimous on a few other core items as well: that Jesus died in Jerusalem, and under the authority of Pontius Pilate.

But other traditions don't fare so well. At an earlier meeting the scholars voted that the Last Supper never happened. And did Jesus really say, "I am the way, the truth and the life"? The Jesus Seminar, drawing on textual and historical studies, thought not. In all, they have voted only eighteen percent of the words of Jesus as recorded in the gospels to be authentic.

Subjecting one of the most hallowed of human texts to the base principle of democracy: it's easy to make fun of the idea—indeed, it's hard not to. "Forgive me, but I think that's one of the funniest things on earth," says James Strange, arguably the world's foremost archaeologist of the Galilee and a man whose work informs much Jesus research. "This business of taking a vote on truth: there isn't any other academic discipline that would take votes. It's got to be because of the Christian background of these people. They're modeling themselves on the great church councils of the fifth century, which took votes on truth." To Christian leaders of the far right, as well as many ordinary Christians, the scholars of the seminar are nothing short of Antichrists. Recently a cottage industry of anti–Jesus Seminar books and publications, some of them quite virulent, has sprung up.

There are legitimate complaints to be made against the Jesus Seminar, especially that it gives the impression it is doing objective scholarship, free of presuppositions, which is an impossibility. But most of this criticism applies equally well to virtually all New Testament scholarship today. In fact, colored beads and press releases aside, the Jesus Seminar is not far in its perspective from the mainstream of biblical scholarship.

That mainstream can be found at another gathering, the annual meeting of the American Academy of Religion and the Society of Biblical Literature, at which seven thousand scholars of religion, biblical studies, and archaeology—old men with Einstein hair, Buddhist monks in saffron robes, business-suited feminists, black-habited Orthodox nuns—conduct what amounts to the world's largest conversation on things spiritual. The hottest topic under discussion here, so compelling that panel discussions devoted to it pack hundreds of scholars, as well as journalists and members of the public, into standing-room-only auditoriums, is the historical Jesus. This much larger gathering of authorities is more traditionally sober in style and represents a broader range of backgrounds than the Jesus Seminar, but listening to them talk and read from their books and papers makes it clear that they too are intent on prying the Jesus of history apart from the figure of faith and lore. Whether it is historian Helmut Koester of Harvard University lecturing on the layers of development in the passion narratives or Israeli archaeologist Hanan Eshel analyzing recent discoveries from Roman Palestine, it is apparent that virtually all researchers in the field believe that they are onto something new—that now, after two millennia, they have fresh insights into the life and times of Jesus of Nazareth.

The search for the historical Jesus, however, is not a recent phenomenon. It began two centuries ago in Germany, among a collection of Enlightenment intellectuals—not unlike those in America who decided at almost exactly the same time to put bold new thinking about democratic rule to the test. These men who brought a similarly open intellect to the pages of the New Testament often suffered for it. Hermann Samuel Reimarus, professor of Oriental languages at Hamburg University, generally considered the founder of the field, wrote the first major book that challenged the historical truth of the gospels in the 1760s but, fearing reprisals, arranged to have it published after his death.

When his countryman David Friedrich Strauss published a massively detailed *Life of Jesus Critically Examined* in 1835, in which he used critical methods to determine that the gospels were written not by followers of Jesus but by later Christians who wove fact, legend, and fantasy together, he was barred from teaching theology for the rest of his life. (In fine modernist fashion, Strauss went on to propose replacing Christianity with a new "religion" based on science.)

The field might have languished in the back rooms of academia were it not for several turns of events in this century. Discoveries of caches of ancient manuscripts in the deserts of the Middle East gave investigators an enormous amount of new material to compare against the gospels, and brought the idea of confronting biblical truth with hard evidence into the public's imagination. The rapid development of high technology has assisted this work, helping with the dating and sorting of parchment fragments and analysis of other archaeological finds. Perhaps most significantly of all, as churches began to lose members in the 1960s, divinity schools in the United States downsized, and scholars who had worked all their lives in Christian-run institutions moved over to public universities, where they found a much broader concept of academic freedom. This in turn encouraged young intellectuals who might not have cared for the more cloistered air of the seminary to come into the field, resulting in a still more vigorous historical approach to the New Testament. Today, with the historical Jesus a regular on the covers of the national news weeklies and jargon-ridden academic books on the subject making bestseller lists, an enterprise that began with closed-door timidity has become a part of popular culture.

Those at the forefront of this work today are not necessarily anarchists or revolutionaries. One of the leaders in the field is John Meier, a priest and professor at Catholic University, a soft-spoken man with a thin alabaster face, pink lips, and slicked-back hair. Father Meier is so determinedly staid in both his appearance and his prose that he could be a figure out of the 1940s, a parish priest along the lines of Bing Crosby in *The Bells of St. Mary's.* He has thus far published two volumes of a massive trilogy on the historical Jesus, and he is generally considered to be the most exhaustive of commentators, and one of the most restrained in his conclusions.

But for a conservative, and one writing under the Vatican's authority, Meier can be shockingly dispassionate. He discusses evidence that the historical Jesus was illegitimate, that he was married, and various other topics that might raise eyebrows in a parish house. More importantly, he shares the view of all mainstream scholars that the gospels, as the product of human hands, underwent stages of reworking, and that therefore the picture they present to us today is not historical. Meier agrees with his colleagues that the historical figure can only be got at by pulling apart the layers of theology, by deconstructing the gospels. Being a good critical historian, he dismisses the historical truth of the supernatural elements—walking on water, changing water into wine—and manages to avoid confrontation with Rome by refusing to draw conclusions at sensitive places, such as the raising of Lazarus from the dead: "As in other stories of raising the dead, the question of what actually happened cannot be resolved by us today. It is possible that a story about Jesus healing a mortally-ill Lazarus grew into a story of raising the dead."[1] This may seem like soft-pedaling, but when you consider that Meier is a Catholic priest, working at a major Catholic institution, writing with the Vatican's approval, who questions some of the most revered supernaturalism of the traditional Jesus story, and, more importantly, insists that the notion of gospel truth can and should be subjected to critical analysis, you begin to get a picture of how sweeping this approach has become.

Still, officially sanctioned Catholic scholars are relative latecomers to the field.* They have been forced into the fray by the intensity with which historical Jesus work has taken over biblical studies: it simply can no longer be ignored. One of those most responsible for that intensity, someone who contrasts in every way with John Meier's reserve, is Robert Funk, the founder of the Jesus

*There is a long history of unsanctioned Catholic scholarship, or scholarship that, upon later review, was censured by the church.

Seminar. Former professor of New Testament at Harvard and Vanderbilt, a past president of the Society of Biblical Literature, and one of the world's premier authorities on the parables of Jesus, Funk is one of those figures found in any discipline, who by devoting himself to questioning its very validity winds up being viewed in strident terms: trailblazer or loon, depending on your point of view. A white-haired, red-faced Buddha of a man who presides over the seminar's deliberations with collar open and quips at the ready, Funk is personally responsible for much of the outcry against the Jesus Seminar and the field in general. Some Funkisms:

"Christianity, as we have known it in the West, is anemic and wasting away."

". . . [T]he authority of the Bible is gone forever. It cannot be restored."

"Jesus himself is not the proper object of faith."

We must "give Jesus a demotion."[2]

Whereas scholars like John Meier—and the majority of those attending the AAR/SBL convention—are content to continue speaking and writing largely to and for other scholars, Funk and others like him insist that there is a broader cultural significance to what they are doing. The work of the Jesus Seminar, and of all contemporary Jesus researchers, in Funk's view, represents a shift on the part of biblical scholars away from the tyranny of the church and toward cultural honesty. As far as Funk is concerned, scholars have known the truth—that Jesus was nothing more than a man with a vision—for decades; they have taught it to generations of priests and ministers, who do not pass it along to their flocks because they fear a backlash of anger. So the only ones left in the dark are ordinary Christians. "The enterprise in which we are engaged has taken on some of the earmarks of a new movement," Funk declared in a speech to several hundred scholars and members of the public during the course of the Santa Rosa meeting. "It has attracted steady media attention; it has garnered growing support and members; and it has generated an organized opposition. Those features indicate that we have succeeded in mounting a campaign against religious ignorance, arrogance, and pettiness."[3]

This is manifesto talk. In the mind of firebrands like Funk, historical Jesus work is not just of academic or private, soulful interest; it is a direct challenge to the Christian Right, an attempt to wrest religious discourse from the control of the Pat Robertsons and Ralph Reeds, to allow doubters, dissenters, and honest questers to explore a new path to Christianity—a "post-Christianity"—without feeling the tyranny of orthodoxy. It is also the first volley in a war to redefine the basic tenets of Christian faith: to demote Jesus from Christ to prophet, from *the* bringer of truth to *a* bringer of truth. If Funk had his way, Jesus would be knocked off his divine pedestal and take his place alongside Lao-tzu, Socrates, and Nietzsche.

Funk goes much farther than most scholars. Most do not have a far-reaching agenda, or they have a different sort of agenda. One thing that emerges from studying the various experts is the realization that scholarly objectivity is a myth: everyone has his or her bias, which results in a different Jesus. Paula Fredriksen of Boston University, herself a convert to Judaism, believes that the importance of the work is in revealing the Jesus of history as a Jew speaking to Jews about Judaism, and in putting to rest the notion that he was out to form a new religion. Marcus Borg of Oregon State University, a devout Episcopalian, finds Jesus to be a mystic, a "spirit person" with a direct link to the divine. Consequently, Borg believes that Jesus is still uniquely important to us today, even if he is not the preexistent deity of traditional faith.

The tendency to conceive of Jesus after one's own image has gone on as long as this work has. Over the past few decades, we have had a nonsexist Jesus for feminists, a liberal Jesus for liberals, an existential Jesus for existentialists, even, for one prominent scholar of a generation ago, a gay Jesus. One might think of this tendency to project as an occupational hazard of New Testament scholars. That said, however, the most impressive thing about the wide variety of work being done today is not the different spin each scholar gives to it but the *extent of consensus.* The one thing nearly all have in common is a desire to find a human being at the end of their search—as real, as physical, as bound by the laws of time and space as the rest of us.

The same can be said for the millions of nonspecialists who are drawn to the work. For those who want to know more, whether because they would like to see Jesus demoted or validated, the experience is both stimulating and disorienting. It is a bit like entering a dream world in which things seem familiar and yet somehow totally different. But the researchers would argue that it is their undertaking that amounts to a wake-up to historical reality, while the dream—holy or not—is what we have been experiencing for two thousand years.

CHAPTER TWO

IN THE BEGINNING

Nazareth is generally described as a town in the hills. Approaching it by car from the broad, fertile plain to the south, this seems like an absurd understatement. The engine whines as you switch back up the sheer side of a mountain. Date palms give way to firs, cedars, and scattered olive groves. Your ears pop. When you finally crest the ridge, the city rises higher yet. There are houses on stilts, slotted into the slopes, wide windows to take in sweeping views of the patchworked valley four hundred meters below. With its steep, winding downtown streets, Nazareth comes across as a kind of San Francisco of the Middle East. The onetime village of a few hundred residents is now a clanging, pulsating city of more than forty thousand, with department stores, gas stations, and factories. Pilgrims who arrive hoping to drink in some of the ancient bliss that sustained the baby Jesus two millennia ago have their work cut out for them.

Their best hope is to cruise past the Astoria Restaurant at the intersection of the two main streets, Casa Nova and Paul VI, cut left at the Place de la Femme clothing shop, head up the hill through a thicket of souvenir hawkers, and pull up alongside the monolithic modern building that dominates the skyline, the Basilica of the Annunciation. It may look like a grain silo from the street, but once inside you see that this mammoth and zealously modern structure is built around a small grotto, now dramatically lit—the exact location that tradition has ascribed to the event known as the annunciation:

> . . . the angel Gabriel was sent from God unto a city of Galilee, named Nazareth, to a virgin espoused to a man whose name was Joseph, of the house of David; and the virgin's name was Mary. And the angel came in unto her, and said, "Hail, thou that art highly favored, the Lord is with thee: blessed art thou among women."[1]

Thus, according to the Gospel of Luke, began the earthly life of Jesus of Nazareth. We recognize Luke's language as theological, fabulous, mythic; to a modern ear the tone is closer to Aesop than to historical reporting. This is both the strength and the weakness of the gospels for us: we want to give in to their voluptuous caresses, but our hard-nosed rationality finds that very voluptuousness suspect. We have a two-bit detective inside us who demands just the facts. And so we dig.

Less spiritually uplifting than the grotto, but more edifying to archaeologists, is the area beneath the courtyard of the basilica, where excavations of ancient Nazareth were begun in 1955. This work has been analyzed recently by archaeologists Jack Finegan, Eric Meyers, and James Strange. By following their findings, we can begin to work our way back to Jesus' time.

The Nazareth of the first century was a small and insignificant village high in the hills, fed by a single spring, which guaranteed that it would remain small and insignificant, at least until modern irrigation arrived. The traditional slotlike tombs that ringed the outskirts indicate a distinctly and devoutly Jewish population. Olive presses and millstones speak of a humble, workaday existence. This was a place where villagers met at synagogue on the Sabbath to study the Torah, where the faithful woke at dawn and, with the sun slanting over the savagely beautiful shoulders of mountain, chanted the Shema—"Hear O Israel: The Lord is our God, the Lord alone. You shall love the Lord your God with all your heart, and with all your soul, and with all your might"[2]—and recited it again before going to bed. It was a place where the Laws of the Hebrew Bible were imprinted on the mind, and where the promises of the prophets flowed like blood through veins.

Here, according to modern scholarly reckoning, sometime in or before 4 B.C.E., presumably without angelic fanfare, a woman named Miryam gave birth to a son. The name she chose for him—Yeshu, a form of Yeshua, or Joshua—would become Iesous in Greek, in Latin Iesus. We infer the date of birth from the fact that both Matthew and Luke place it in the reign of Herod the Great, who died in 4 B.C.E., and that both suggest that it occurred near the end of that reign. (The idea that Jesus was born four years "Before Christ" is just one of many anomalies in this new portrait. When scribes of the sixth century initiated the Christian-era calendar and the tradition of reckoning years as "Before Christ" and "Anno Domini," it seems they miscalculated by about four years.)

As far as we know, Yeshu spent his childhood and early adulthood in Galilee. But life would not necessarily have been entirely bucolic. The vibrant and distinctly hellenized capital city of Sepphoris, with its Roman mosaics, banks, and law courts, occupied the next hilltop, less than four miles away. John Dominic Crossan, professor emeritus from DePaul University and one of the major figures in the field, considers that the closeness of such a huge and recently rebuilt city would have been a strong source of tension to the peasants of Nazareth. "The new cities encroached on the peasants' land and dislocated their lives," he says. He surmises that the proximity of Sepphoris may have planted the seeds of unrest in the mind of the young Jesus. But James Strange believes that, tension or no, such a major city, with its multicultural marketplace, would have been a constant draw for a peasant boy living less than two hours away by foot.

And what kinds of stimuli would he have found there? As Marcus Borg says, "It is rather intriguing to imagine Jesus going to the theater as a young man."[3] While there is no direct evidence for this, it was entirely possible. So many aspects of a kind of lifestyle that we do not associate with Jesus were within easy reach, and this, combined with the view of many scholars that Jesus' teaching comprised a mixture of Greek and Jewish philosophy, means that a radical reevaluation of Jesus' background is in order.

But first, what about the traditional picture? Why begin in Nazareth at all? What happened to Bethlehem and the manger, the shepherds and the Wise Men? What happened to Christmas? Why do scholars consider all of it fantasy? When did Christmas really begin, if not with the birth of Jesus?

According to one view it began sometime between 64 and 67 C.E., when Peter, leader of the disciples of Jesus, was executed by Nero's soldiers. Throughout antiquity, the story went that Peter's martyrdom took the form of an upside-down crucifixion, in mock acknowledgment of his discipleship, but this tradition is spurious. What is fairly credible is that in the roughly thirty-five years from the time of Jesus' death, Peter had contributed to the vigorous spread of the new Christian movement. His travels had taken him to Joppa, Caesarea, Antioch, Samaria, and finally to Rome. In all those places he had spoken about the deeds and sayings of his dead master. He didn't lecture from notes, of course; it was all inside him, a precious reservoir of memory and anecdote. When he died, it all died with him.

Or at least, according to this theory, that was the fear of some of his followers. But an ancient source claimed that Peter had an interpreter, a fellow believer who, apparently, had traveled the Mediterranean world with him and translated his backwoods Aramaic speech into the Greek spoken in the wider world. This interpreter would have to have been a conscientious man, a Jew of the Diaspora as opposed to one who, like Peter, came from Palestine itself, and a man of rather homespun education. He himself surely knew many of the stories of Jesus: he had heard Peter recount them. And he knew stories from other sources as well: incidents, sayings, bits of gossip passed on as Jesus' fame spread. In a seemingly small act that would eventually become one of the more significant in world history, he decided to pull all of this material together and write it down.

If Papias, a church leader of the early second century, can be believed, this was how the first gospel came into being. Papias claims that the author of the Gospel of Mark was a follower of Peter. Whether this is true is a matter of conjecture; most scholars prefer to think of the writer of the first gospel as anonymous, and use "Mark" purely for convenience. But the most important aspect of this theory—the date of the composition of the first gospel—is acknowledged by most authorities. Scholars generally believe that Mark was written around 70 C.E., just after the great Jewish War, when, after a three-year siege, Roman troops invaded Jerusalem and destroyed the Temple. As will be seen later, this destruction came to have enormous importance for the development of both Christianity and Judaism.

If Mark did follow Peter on his synagogue-by-synagogue lecture tour of the Empire, he saw firsthand how the story of Jesus was being received. There was some interest among Jews, but they began to distance themselves from it as the idea developed that this teaching was not simply a new interpretation of the Torah but a replacement of it. It was probably surprising, and possibly troubling, to people like Mark that Jesus' own people were turning away from his teaching, while Gentiles were drawn to it.

And then came the war, and the destruction of the Temple, the center of Judaism. This terrible act must have seemed prophetic to the early Christian movement. For they believed that the kingdom of God that Jesus spoke of was literally at hand, that the destruction of the evil rulers and the institution of a new rule by God's elect was imminent. "Truly I tell you, this generation will not pass away until all these things have taken place,"[4] Mark wrote. And now the Temple was gone: "the clearest signal imaginable that the Christian interpretation of Scripture was right and the Jewish one wrong," as Paula Fredriksen puts it.[5]

So here was Mark, witnessing the passing of one age and the beginning of another, just as was predicted. Someone had to make a record, and more than that, a document that believers could point to as the basis of their faith. And so Mark wrote. His prose wasn't pretty, though the King James translation makes it seem so. It was a rushed, homespun, storyteller's kind of Greek, with liberal use of the present tense ("And Jesus says to them . . .", "And he takes Peter and James and John along with him . . ."[6]), and constant repetition of the Greek *euthus,* "immediately": "But immediately he spoke to them . . .",[7] ". . . immediately they left their nets and followed him,"[8] "Immediately the leprosy left him . . ."[9]

This is a rough, breathy telling, with a Jesus in constant motion, as if in a hurry to get his work done before the End comes. And, hugely significant to most scholars, Mark's gospel does not end with a resurrection but with the women coming to the tomb and finding the stone rolled away from the door. A figure dressed in white tells them Jesus has gone. "So they went out and fled from the tomb, for terror and amazement had seized them . . ."[10] And we are left, as perhaps Mark and his first readers were left, waiting, expectant, ready for the End to arrive.

But the End *didn't* come. Mark was wrong about that. And he makes other errors as well: in Palestinian geography, in facts about the practice of Judaism in Palestine. So the question arises: If Mark could be wrong on these matters, what else might he be wrong about?

This brings us to the main problem in historical Jesus work: the reliability of the texts. The name of the person who wrote the first gospel doesn't matter. What does matter is how we should read his work. How did this author intend to be read? Mark was not writing history. History as we understand it is a modern creation, involving the application of critical analysis to various kinds of data and formulating a hypothesis to account for the data. Mark did not work this way. He assembled treasured stories—isolated incidents and utterances, devoid of context—and lined them up like jewels within a necklace of his own devising. As Papias himself says: "Mark, who was Peter's interpreter, wrote down accurately, though not in order, what he remembered that the Lord said and did."[11]

Mark was not writing for a modern audience, one that expects sources to be acknowledged and facts to be hard. He and his readers had a different understanding of truth. After gathering his materials, Mark would have assembled them into a narrative, adding (sometimes inaccurate) color details to it, but adding something else as well, something that is hard for modern readers to appreciate. Following the established practice, he would have examined the events in the life of his spiritual leader through the lens of Jewish history. He would amplify his hero's accomplishments by creatively associating them with events from the lives of Abraham, Moses, and the other larger-than-life figures of the Hebrew Bible. The Hebrew Bible is filled with examples of this technique at work: Moses parts the Red Sea; later, when the tradition wants to assert that Elijah was a great prophet like Moses, he parts the waters of the Jordan. When Elijah dies, Elisha literally inherits his mantle, and, as a sign that the Force is now with him, he too parts the waves.[12] Is this a coincidence? Of course not. The writers of the Hebrew Bible use this storyteller's device to associate today's prophet with those of the past—in effect, to give him credentials.

This was such a common device in ancient Judaism that it is one of the great creative forces behind the Hebrew Bible. It has no single name, though the Hebrew terms *midrash* and *pesher* refer to different literary techniques for bringing the past to bear on the present. It was important, because for the Jews truth didn't come from scientific experiment but from their own history, which they believed was woven with divine threads. Jews of the first century particularly seemed to think of their own time as wickedly modern, and of past generations as closer to God. So by creating parallels with stories from the Hebrew Bible, Mark would reach a fuller understanding of Jesus' nature and message, and spell out to his audience an important point: that Jesus was connected to Jewish history, was in fact the summation of Jewish history.

Examples of Mark's reliance on Old Testament models for Jesus' career are scattered throughout his gospel. Raymond Brown and David Aune have pointed out the similarity between the miracles Jesus performs in Mark and the miracles of the prophet Elisha in the books of Kings. Just like his illustrious predecessor, Mark's Jesus heals a leper, raises a young man from the dead, and multiplies loaves to feed a crowd. To the pious, these parallels are an indication of divine logic. To critical scholars such as Geza Vermes of Oxford University, they betray an "obvious dependence" of Mark and the other evangelists on the Old Testament.[13] In the later gospels, this reliance on older models is even more pronounced. In fact, Matthew and Luke, by creatively reworking Mark, are actually using Mark in the same way Mark uses sources from the Hebrew Scriptures.

Many Christians today, when first confronted with the notion that the gospel accounts of Jesus are built upon reworked pieces of the Hebrew Bible, react strongly. "You mean that maybe these things did not actually happen?" an incredulous woman asked Bishop John Shelby Spong, the Episcopal bishop of Newark and a popularizer of Jesus research, during a lecture on the Gospel of Luke. "This means that you are saying that Luke was lying. He told these things as if they were true when he knew they were not!"[14] Bishop Spong couldn't make her see his point that to someone of Luke's time borrowing a piece of ancient Scripture and affixing it to your story was not meant to *deceive* but to help *perceive.* This is one of the major hurdles necessary to jump in order to get closer to the historical Jesus. There are layers that must be peeled away, layers that the original writers may never have intended to be taken as literal, here-and-now truth in the first place.

One of the most unusual and momentous uses of this device in the whole New Testament is the virgin birth story. But there was no virgin birth story in Mark's gospel, for the simple reason that, according to scholarly consensus, it hadn't been invented yet. Mark was written thirty-five years after the death of Jesus—thirty-five years in which stories spread by word of mouth. Inevitably, different batches of stories took different paths around the Empire. In Ephesus, they may have told of Jesus healing the blind and crippled, while in Rome they told stories of the crucifixion and the empty tomb, and in Syria they honored the sayings of the dead teacher. There was no official canon, no ecumenical council to affix its seal of approval to certain of these bits of hearsay. They were rumors, traveling on the wind, exciting interest or scorn, coalescing here and there into a body of belief to support a particular community of followers but still passing by word of mouth, still changing. They were stories of an extraordinary teacher and healer, and his extraordinary message.

Exactly what that message consisted of has been almost totally obscured by twenty centuries of institutionalization, but it, along with the life of Jesus, is now being excavated by scholars. One of the notable results of this work has been a renewed interest in the teaching of Jesus, which traditional Christianity neglected in emphasizing his redemptive death. One might say that teaching had to do with a new way of envisioning the emotion of love, an impossibly idealistic way, a way that, if taken seriously, would affect the entire political and social order. The message caught fire among the oppressed masses of the Roman Empire: slaves and beggars, farmers and tentmakers, soldiers and whores. They were real people, with names like Tertius, Jason, Apelles, Tryphaena, Phoebe, Priscilla and Aquila. By chance, these particular individuals, while remaining featureless, have been preserved for all time by virtue of the fact that Paul, roaming the Empire in about 50 C.E., sent greetings from them in a letter to the newly founded church at Rome. Paul's epistles have become ossified, hardened into the official canon known as the New Testament. But read them simply as letters written from one human being to another and what emerges more powerfully than the onslaught of oratory about sin and redemption are the glimpses of simple humanity: people communicating, people caught up in the new love fad. "Timothy, my co-worker, greets you; so do Lucius and Jason and

Sosipater, my compatriots . . . Gaius, who is host to me and to the whole church, greets you." This was what Paul evidently dictated, but his scribe became swept up in the stream of good will, and so, in the midst of those greetings, is this: "I Tertius, the writer of this letter, greet you in the Lord."[15] And so for all time Tertius, about whom exactly nothing else is known, is preserved. Just one slight example that reveals the humanness of the documents that have become known as the New Testament. And what is human is made by human hand, subject to human whim and fancy.

There was also no virgin birth story in Paul's letters, the earliest written records of Christianity, dating from just fifteen or so years after the crucifixion. While the letters are filled with passionate devotion to the figure of Jesus Christ and point quite distinctly to his death and resurrection as the centerpiece of faith—indicating that in little more than a decade people in farflung corners of the Mediterranean world had begun to reorient their lives around this new center—they are utterly silent on the subject of divine birth. This part of the story had not yet become necessary.

Nor was it necessary in Mark's day, twenty years later. Inventing it became important only as Jesus expanded into a whole new role: God of the Gentiles. To the hellenized Gentiles of the Empire—people who were used to their gods' having miraculous beginnings to show that, right from the start, they were different from ordinary mortals—this Jesus, this Son of God, if he were worthy of worship, ought to have a divine birth.

This is where we see a variation on the Jewish practice of creative borrowing from ancient writings, for virgin birth was not a tradition in Jewish history. No Jewish story or legend spoke of the coming Messiah being born of a virgin. But there were dozens of precedents for divine-mortal coupling and virgin birth in Greek culture. Many Greek heroes were sired by gods, either through old-fashioned penetration or something more grandiose, such as

Jupiter's visiting himself upon Danae in a golden shower in order to beget Perseus. Mithras, a Persian god whose mystery cult swept the Roman world at about the same time as Christianity and whose worship has several striking parallels with Christianity (his birthday, December 25, was eventually appropriated by Christians), was supposed to have been conceived of a god and born of a rock. The decidedly historical Alexander the Great was posthumously given a virgin birth to indicate that he was divine, despite stories of his mother's healthy sexual appetite. Plato was said by later devotees to have been virginally conceived, and so was Augustus.

Helmut Koester of Harvard University believes that all of these divine-birth stories, including that of Jesus, have one common ancestry: ancient Egyptian myth. In the hellenistic Mediterranean world, Egyptian religion was something like New Age belief is today. People looked to the then ancient tales of the strange gods of Egypt as a grab bag of mystery. The divine birth of Horus from his mother Isis had particular appeal; statues of the two gods were popular throughout the Mediterranean region.[16] Of course, no historian can prove that early Christians formed the myth of the virgin birth of Jesus under the influence of these stories, but the model of a god conjoining with a mortal to produce an extraordinary offspring was well established in the Greek world of the first century.

It is not until the next gospel, Matthew, possibly written in Antioch, around 90 C.E., that we see the results of this Greek influence. Clues in his gospel convince scholars that "Matthew" (as with Mark, all of the gospels are referred to by their traditional names for convenience, though no one knows the names of the actual authors) was a learned Jew who had determined that Mark's gospel was out of date. There were two problems with it. First, it did not address the current crisis that Christianity faced. The movement had initially spread through the Empire via synagogues, and Jews were the first followers. But in the aftermath of the Jewish War, Jews throughout the Empire had been busy swearing off innovation. They were now rallying around their oldest and most hallowed texts—the Laws and the Prophets—and blamed upstart sects, particularly the followers of Jesus, for their problems. Sometime around the seventh decade of the common era they began tossing Christians out of the synagogues.

This resulted in an angry clash between the two groups over which one embodied the true nature of Judaism. Matthew needed to update Mark by making Jesus prefigure this conflict: he needed to have Jesus come down squarely on the side of the Christians. His Jesus takes on the Pharisees—the dominant force in Judaism in Matthew's day, but only one of many sects during Jesus' time. His Jesus becomes the fulfillment of the Hebrew Scriptures—which in one swipe makes Judaism an incomplete religion. According to most scholars, the historical clash between the two groups accounts for Matthew's distinctly anti-Jewish language. His Jesus calls the Jews "vipers," "snakes," "hypocrites," "blind fools," and "descendants of those who murdered the prophets."[17] Thus in Matthew we see Christianity pulling away from Judaism and becoming a distinctly Gentile movement.

The second problem that Matthew found with Mark's gospel had to do with the Gentile sense of the divine. The Greek-educated Gentiles expected certain things of a god. So, while Matthew still found much of value in Mark (for ninety percent of Mark is repeated, almost word-for-word, in Matthew), he made some important additions to it. For one thing, he attached a new beginning. Although Matthew had to satisfy the expectations of an audience who had Greek notions of divinity, he was also still a Jew, concerned to present Jesus as fully within the Jewish tradition. And so he pored through the ancient Hebrew texts in search of a story to associate with Jesus' birth, one that would at the same time impress the growing community of Gentile believers. It had to be something that fit with Gentile ideas about a divine figure's birth. He decided, finally, on a passage in the book of Isaiah: "Therefore the Lord himself shall give you a sign; Behold, a virgin shall conceive, and bear a son, and shall call his name Immanuel."[18]

And that, according to this theory, was all the Gentile would-be believers needed. They had a god, one with truly miraculous beginnings. The story pushed one of the buttons that, to them, signified divinity: virgin birth. So was born a tradition that would echo for twenty centuries: Jesus Christ, Messiah, born of a virgin, in fulfillment of the Scriptures. An entire epoch of mankind—European civilization—would build itself up around this powerful notion.

But, seen from a strictly rational perspective, the virgin birth account is full of holes. As Matthew tells it, the angel appears to a distraught Joseph and informs him that his betrothed has not been unfaithful but is pregnant by the Holy Spirit, and that she will bear a son:

> All this took place to fulfill what had been spoken by the Lord through the prophet:
>
> "Look, the virgin shall conceive
> and bear a son,
> and they shall name him
> Emmanuel,"
>
> which means, "God is with us."[19]

The first problem with this passage is one of translation. What Matthew read as "virgin" simply didn't mean that in the original Hebrew. The original word was *almah,* which meant "young woman," referring specifically to a girl who had reached puberty and was marriageable. "It was certainly not confined to denoting men and women without experience of sexual intercourse," writes Geza Vermes, the world-renowned scholar of ancient Judaism.[20] In fact, it was commonly used of women until they gave birth.[21]

The translation error is not necessarily Matthew's, but in fact goes back more than two hundred years before him. When, in the third century B.C.E., the Septuagint, the first Greek translation of the Hebrew Bible, was created—for the benefit of the growing masses of Jews who had spread across the Empire, and who no longer spoke Hebrew but the common language of the Empire—*almah* was translated with the Greek word *parthenos,* which at the time may have carried several meanings. But by Matthew's time, the Greek word evidently only referred to one who has not had sexual intercourse. And so Matthew came across the passage in the Septuagint and apparently thought he had found a miraculous prophecy, one suitable for his hero's beginnings.

A second major problem scholars have with the virgin birth story is quite obvious to anyone who reads the relevant passages carefully. The passage from Matthew leads one to believe that Isaiah was talking about the coming of a great leader, a Messiah, who would guide the chosen people to heaven, or at least to a better place. In fact, Isaiah is talking about nothing of the kind. In the passage, King Ahaz of Judah is facing attack from two enemies. His prophet, Isaiah, declares that the attackers will be vanquished and their own lands deserted. When will this occur? Isaiah points to a certain pregnant woman—an *almah*—and prophesies that "before the child knows how to refuse the evil and choose the good," the two foreign kingdoms will be laid waste.[22] As Paula Fredriksen says: "Isaiah 7:14 is not a messianic prophecy. In its original context, it represents God through the prophet assuring King Ahaz that evil days are fast approaching for his enemies."[23] So then, Matthew took a sentence that said in effect, "Before that young woman's child is very old, your enemies will be done for," and made it seem to mean, "A virgin shall give birth, and this child will become the Messiah, the Lord-Made-Flesh." Clearly, Matthew was wrong in thinking that Isaiah was referring to a virgin, and he was bending scriptural interpretation to the breaking point in trying to relate the Isaiah situation to Jesus' birth.

Of course, Matthew is not the only gospel writer who tells the story of the virgin birth. An account is also found in Luke's gospel, which is generally dated at somewhere between 80 C.E. and 100 C.E. But scholars find that playing the story in stereo leads to more difficulty, not less. The fact that Luke and Matthew both tell virgin birth stories is not in itself proof of a historical fact. It only indicates that a virgin birth legend may have begun to circulate sometime before they each wrote, and each took a stab at making it work. The real difficulties begin when the two birth sagas are compared to one another.

Matthew has Mary and Joseph living in Bethlehem when Jesus is born. They then take him to Egypt to avoid persecution by Herod, before finally settling in Nazareth. In Luke, the couple's home is in Nazareth, not Bethlehem; they only travel to Bethlehem because of a decree of Caesar that a census be taken and taxes be collected. Why the discrepancy? Scholars say the differences between the two versions actually give away the game. They indicate that both Luke and Matthew were driven not by a desire to record historical fact but a desire to present Jesus as fulfilling another Old Testament prophecy: that a Messiah would come from Bethlehem, the city of David. Their problem was that the historical Jesus was born in Nazareth. So how do you fulfill the prophecy and still allow for the fact that Jesus was known to be associated with Nazareth? Two different scenarios were invented. Both were awkward. Matthew's required inventing a whole messy episode, a creative borrowing of the Passover story of Pharaoh ordering the death of all first-born Jewish males. In Matthew, King Herod, fearful of the birth of a new king, orders the death of all children under two years of age living in Bethlehem. As Raymond Brown has indicated, such an occasion of mass infanticide, if it actually took place, would surely have been noted in the writings of the Jewish historian Josephus, who painstakingly recorded the brutalities of Herod.[24] As for Luke's story, it required fudging dates so that the Messiah would be born during a census that took place in the governorship of Quirinius, when the historical Jesus would have been ten years old. Beyond that, the census story is itself a problem: there are no historical records of a census in which subjects of the Empire were ordered to return to the city of their birth to be taxed, as Luke suggests.

Those intent on a rationalistic study of the virgin birth story have uncovered numerous other problems. The German theologian Uta Ranke-Heinemann has dissected the notion on physiological grounds. It is, she points out, a concept that could only be meaningful to a prescientific culture. "The making of Jesus was to be exclusively God's creative work," she writes, "comparable to the creation of Adam from a lump of clay. A woman, however, is not a lump of clay. The whole miraculous narrative of the virgin birth was composed at a time when nothing was known of the female ovum."[25] The ancient idea of God making a woman pregnant, Ranke-Heinemann says, is tied to the presupposition that children sprang from the male seed, while the woman merely provided the soil. The third-century Christian writer Tertullian made this point plainly when he wrote that "the whole fruit is already present in the semen."

If Jesus' divine birth is to be taken literally today, it would seem to necessitate either ignoring the knowledge of how sperm interacts with ovum to produce a new cell with genetic material from both, or positing a scenario in which God and Mary had sex. And the latter is certainly not what Matthew had in mind. He was a Jew, after all, and the God of Israel, the almighty YHWH, who was so far above mankind that his very name could not be spoken, did not work that way. Zeus might cavort around the Greek countryside siring demi-mortals as the whim took him. It was precisely because the Jewish God was so far beyond that kind of meddling that he had become increasingly attractive to the Gentiles; in the first century, pagans all over the Empire took to visiting synagogues to share in the exotic experience of monotheism. (It was possibly thanks to this trend that Christianity took root, for it was the Gentiles in the synagogues who ultimately embraced the new teaching about Jesus.)

But the physiological argument, interesting though it is, is unnecessary for most scholars. A cold reading of Matthew and Luke shows their theological designs. The realization that they appropriated the entire virgin birth notion from Isaiah cancels out the need to explore the numerous other difficulties.

It should be noted that this historicist reading of the origins of the virgin birth story is not based on hazy speculation or the work of one or two renegade scholars. So total is the scholarly consensus regarding the "translation error" at its heart that in the New Revised Standard Version of the Bible the "virgin" passage in Isaiah is now rendered as "Look, the *young woman* is with child and shall bear a son . . ."[26] And where the Catholic church once furiously defended the virgin birth as a real, historical event, John Meier, a Catholic scholar writing under the Vatican's imprimatur (which assures the faithful that the work "is free of doctrinal or moral error"), can only conclude wanly that "taken by itself, historical-critical research simply does not have the sources and tools available to reach a final decision on the historicity of the virginal conception as narrated by Matthew and Luke."[27] Meier's Catholic colleague Raymond Brown, also writing under the imprimatur, goes further, acknowledging that "the infancy narratives are primarily vehicles of the evangelist's theology and Christology."[28]

What this shows, then, is that critical scholars can demonstrate forcefully that the virgin birth story is more mythic than historical. One can take one's pick of arguments. But where does this get us? Surely these highly educated people have better things to do than prove that a fairy tale can't have historical reality—especially since the millions upon millions for whom it does have both historical and transcendent reality will certainly never read or be swayed by their arguments. Cults of the Virgin Mary are alive and well; as recently as 1995, a statue of the Virgin "weeping tears of blood" drew thousands to a village in Italy, despite DNA analysis that proved the blood to be from a man. Clearly, historical analysis is not being done to convince these people.

Possibly the most salient feature of contemporary historical Jesus research is its split personality. On the one hand, it functions as a sharklike trial lawyer with a particularly soft witness on the stand, a hardheaded rationalist who needs everything reduced to historical fact. But its other self—which is on the rise in the most recent work—is a religio-aesthete who is capable of meditatively sucking nourishment from the bosom of myth. The whole Western world has this split, and has had it since the Enlightenment; the reason this work is happening at all is that the rationalist has gained the upper hand in so many of us: we can't simply let the myth live and breathe in us. We smell a rat. So we pull up the floorboards, searching for duplicity, a hidden agenda. Even the Vatican can't stop from joining in the criticism game—tearing apart the gospels with a bit more decorousness than others, but just as thoroughly.

Some scholars find the hidden agenda to be political. Christian scholar and former nun Karen Armstrong, in her book *The Gospel According to Woman,* sees the Virgin as a tool used by the church to keep women off balance: "As a role model, the Virgin Mary is impossible. With the best will in the world, no woman can imitate the Virgin Mary. She cannot be a virgin and a mother at the same time."[29]

But is that the total function of this story: to keep women subordinate? Or is there a deeper function of myth: not to cloud reason but to help us perceive a truth that is inexpressible through rational means? In discussing the divine birth of a revered figure, are we not talking about truth of another order? Edward Beutner, a Catholic priest and member of the Jesus Seminar, someone who proves that it is possible to be both a passionate Christian believer and a critical New Testament scholar, put it as follows: "Are the infancy narratives true? Is Mozart's Twentieth Piano Concerto true? They are both true transformatively, in my experience."

It would be pointless to deny that these first-century men and women had a real, transcendent experience associated with Jesus of Nazareth. We will never know what it was, but we can at least recognize that it was so profound that they came to feel that this human being had been touched by the Divine. And they communicated this by embedding the story of his birth in the satiny folds of myth. While we are busy separating myth from history, we ought not to lose sight of the history within the myth: if it doesn't express the literal truth of the birth of Jesus, surely it expresses the literal truth of his impact on his followers.

One other aspect of the virgin birth is worth noting because it may give us a piece of evidence about the historical Jesus. A number of scholars suspect that what underlies the story—indeed, what may have given rise to it—is an issue that, in the ancient world, would have meant nothing short of scandal. From the early second century, Jewish writers observing the rapidly spreading

Christian religion noted with a sneer that the supposed divinely inspired figure at its center was in fact a bastard. Swirling around the gospel stories, according to some scholars, are whispered cries of "illegitimate."

Technically, even by the traditional reading, this charge is true, for according to the accepted interpretation, Joseph, Mary's betrothed, is not the actual father of the child. But a careful reading of Matthew's account may suggest a more mundane kind of illegitimacy. Jane Schaberg, in her 1987 book *The Illegitimacy of Jesus,* argues that Mary was most likely raped, and that Matthew constructed an elaborate theological architecture to try to transform that nasty reality into a myth he could build a tradition on. The first suggestions of this come from the wording in Matthew's first chapter. Mary, betrothed to Joseph, is found to be pregnant. Joseph, "being a righteous man and unwilling to expose her to public disgrace, planned to dismiss her quietly." But then an angel appears and tells Joseph that the child is "from the Holy Spirit." So instead of dismissing Mary, Joseph marries her, "but he had no marital relations with her until she had borne a son; and he named him Jesus."[30]

There is a lot of between-the-lines information packed into these few verses. First, the fact that Matthew has Joseph believing his betrothed has had sexual relations with another man is revealing. Why would a devout Christian writer bring up such an impious notion if it were not already a topic of discussion in the early church? So Matthew tries to tackle the issue that critics have already been snickering about by having Joseph himself wonder who conceived the child, only to have a messenger from the Lord himself set him straight.

The next verse reveals, among other things, that the gospels are not final, frozen images of the life of Jesus but part of a developing tendency to remove Jesus and his mother from the human realm.

For even while Matthew is busy giving Jesus a divine birth, he lets drop a very human detail: that Joseph "had no marital relations with her *until* she had borne a son." Implying, of course, that afterward they did have marital relations. This will not come as a shock to liberal or casual Christians; but to those who hold to the idea that Mary was utterly pure (a notion that developed into an obsession in later centuries, culminating in 1854, when Pope Pius IX declared the Virgin Mother herself to have been immaculately conceived, i.e., untainted by original sin), this reference to sexual intercourse is a continual thorn in the side.

The last item of telling information in the passage is the seemingly innocuous note that Joseph named the boy Jesus. What Matthew is saying here, however, was clear to an ancient audience. For by naming a child, a Jewish husband officially declared his paternity. Matthew does this in order to satisfy another point. He opens his gospel with a genealogy listing the kings of Israel, in an attempt to show that Jesus was in the direct line of King David. He gives a name-by-name toll of the descent, culminating with "Jacob the father of Joseph the husband of Mary, of whom Jesus was born . . ."[31] Matthew gives the blood descent down to Joseph, but Joseph is not the blood father of Jesus. Therefore, it is only by having Joseph name Jesus, claiming him legally as his son, that Jesus is heir to David's throne.

Matthew's genealogy affects the virgin birth story in another way as well. One thing about the genealogy that has bothered theologians for centuries is the mention of several women among the men who, in the ancient view, carry the bloodline. Why are we told that "Abraham was the father of Isaac, and Isaac the father of Jacob," and so on, with no mention of the women involved, but then learn that Judah was the father of Perez and Zerah "by Tamar," and Salmon the father of Boaz "by Rahab," and Boaz the father of Obed "by Ruth," and that David was the father of Solomon "by the wife of Uriah . . ."?[32]

A solution to the puzzle has been worked up over the past two decades by a group of scholars who realized that all of the women mentioned are associated with scandalous sexual behavior. In other words, Matthew is softening the blow of Jesus' questionable legitimacy by indicating that in several previous instances it was necessary for the royal bloodline of Israel to be passed on via less-than-ordinary means. Bastardy, it may even be suggested, was a badge of honor, the way hemophilia was for the inbred royalty of Europe.

This line of argument certainly doesn't prove that Jesus was illegitimate, but it may indicate that the charge of illegitimacy was an issue for the early church. And it has some major backers. Raymond Brown, in his towering work *The Birth of the Messiah,* concludes that "it is the combination of the scandalous or irregular union and of divine intervention through the woman that explains best Matthew's choice in the genealogy."[33]

Another argument cited by the proponents of illegitimacy has to do with the presence of Joseph in the gospels. Why does he drop from sight once Jesus attains adulthood? One theory is that Joseph died sometime during Jesus' childhood, but this doesn't explain why the adult Jesus, on entering Nazareth to preach, is identified not with reference to his father but, against all convention, as "the son of Mary."

Of course, the illegitimacy question can never be proved or disproved, but, approaching the New Testament from a psychological perspective, it could be seen as meshing with certain aspects of the teaching that Jesus would eventually develop. To the Jews of the time, the startling—even scandalous—thing about Jesus' teaching was what Crossan calls its "radical egalitarianism." All people are equal in God's eyes: even the leper, even the prostitute, even the outcasts of society. In fact, everything is upside down in Jesus' teaching. The poor are wealthier than the rich. The sinners are first in line to enter heaven. And the fatherless, far from being unloved, are among the luckiest of all: for God is their father. If this is a philosophy for weaklings, it is even more a philosophy for bastards.

If the birth narratives were pious invention, it follows that all of their constituent elements have nothing to do with the historical Jesus. Luke's saga, with its trip from Nazareth to Bethlehem, its shepherds and manger, is all fancy. It may be fancy that is fixed in the Western psyche, and perhaps not many of us—including the scholars—would have it otherwise. But according to core scholarship, these things no more occurred than did the very un-Jesus-like extracanonical infancy stories, which circulated in the century after his death. Of these, the Infancy Gospel of Thomas is an amusing one that has come down to us. Its young Jesus strikes quarrelsome playmates dead with a look, and when villagers complain to Joseph, the terrible young Lord makes them all blind. In another of its stories, the boy Jesus is playing on a roof with a friend. The friend slips, falls, and dies, and his parents accuse Jesus of pushing him. Indignant, the young Lord brings the playmate back to life—but only so the boy will prove him innocent.

But the birth narratives and the other infancy "gospels," fictional though they may be, reinforce an important fact about the historical Jesus. To have inspired such passionate inventiveness he must have been an absolutely remarkable man. Whatever the scholars strip away from the traditional story, the Jesus that they end up with must somehow jive with that indisputable fact: he has to be a figure of astonishing originality.

So much, then, for what we *don't* know about Jesus' beginnings.

Having sliced away all that may be seen as nonhistorical from the gospel accounts of his birth, what can be reasonably asserted about Jesus' early years? He was a Jew born in Nazareth, in or just before 4 B.C.E. He had a mother, Miryam, and a father, Yosef. He was one of at least seven siblings. His father may have been a laborer. Aramaic was his mother tongue, he probably had at least a working knowledge of Greek, and may have been taught to read the Bible in Hebrew at the synagogue in Nazareth, though it is also quite possible that he was illiterate.

One of the tools scholars apply to the New Testament texts is known as the criterion of embarrassment. Since the gospel writers' purpose was to provide a fixed image of Jesus that could serve their churches, it is argued that any information in the gospels that doesn't fit this image—any information that could embarrass the church—certainly wasn't invented, and so must date to the historical Jesus; it must have been so well known, in other words, that the church didn't dare tinker with it. In the matter of his family, Mark, the earliest of the gospel writers, has Jesus preaching in his hometown, where he is received skeptically: "Is not this the carpenter, the son of Mary and brother of James and Joses and Judas and Simon, and are not his sisters here with us?"[34] The idea that Jesus had brothers and sisters was to be a source of acute discomfort to the church for a very long time, leading to reams of theological arguments attempting to make it fit with the virginity of Mary (they were actually cousins, or, no, they were step-siblings by another wife Joseph must have had). Since inventing the story could serve no purpose for Mark, and since the information could only embarrass the early church, working as it does against the notion of Mary's virginity, scholars reason that the information is a strand of the "real" story. Jesus really must have had four brothers and two or more sisters. More evidence for this is the fact that Luke, who like Matthew had a copy of Mark's gospel in front of him when he wrote his, conspicuously chose to leave out this reference to the siblings of Jesus. But even in the later writings the issue cannot be completely expunged, for James goes on to become a significant player in the early Christian movement. He appears repeatedly in Acts, where he is continually referred to as "James, the brother of the Lord."

What's more, there are numerous references in early Christian literature to members of "the family of the Lord" living in Palestine, possibly in Nazareth, well into the second century. One authority mentions an uncle, Cleopas, a cousin, Simeon, and two grandsons of Jesus' brother Judas. So it seems likely that Jesus had a sizable extended family.

The consensus that Jesus was born in Nazareth comes as a result of recognizing scriptural interpretation at work. Of the two choices of birthplace we are given in the gospels—Nazareth and Bethlehem—Bethlehem is suspect because it was where the evangelists believed Jesus *had* to come from if he were to fulfill prophecy. Add to that the fact that while Bethlehem is only mentioned in the infancy narratives, which are thought to be wholly invented, Nazareth appears throughout the New Testament as the home of Jesus. On this point, the consensus is even more general than for the virgin birth. John Meier acknowledges that the "somewhat contorted" means by which Matthew and Luke try to work Bethlehem into the story indicates that the Bethlehem birth "is not to be taken as historical fact but as a *theologoumenon,* i.e., as a theological affirmation . . . put into the form of an apparently historical narrative."[35]

But what kind of place was Nazareth? How did it affect the man who was to change the world so profoundly? The traditional telling is scanty when it comes to psycho-social influences. We are to believe that a peasant boy from an insignificant Galilean village, a boy humble in every respect, suddenly burst onto the Mediterranean scene at the age of thirty and, for a period of one to three years, spouted ideas that changed the world. How could it happen? Where could his ideas have come from? Why, from God. His divine birth and wondrous resurrection are evidence that this was a man apart from all others, a being from heaven implanted in a human female to live, for a time, as a man among men. He didn't need to learn and to absorb influences.

Such purely theological thinking may be enough for some, but many people living in a late-twentieth-century world, a world shaped by Freud and Einstein, have a need to know more. The presumption that Jesus was human presupposes that the environment he grew up in helped to form his adult self and his message.

What, then, can be inferred from an examination of the place where he grew up?

Attempting to answer that question takes us back to Nazareth today, where local tradition is more hopeful than scholars are about the historical accuracy of the gospels' references to Jesus' early life. There are churches built on the supposed site of nearly every incident in the gospels associated with Nazareth, from Mensa Christi, which was constructed around a stone tabletop upon which the risen Christ purportedly dined with his disciples, to the Chapel of Fright, near the precipice from which, according to Luke 4:29, the locals, irritated by Jesus' teachings, tried to toss him. Scholars give credence to none of these sites, and they are doubtful of the historical truth of the incidents.

But a number of statements can be made. First, although Galilee overall was something of a crossroads, where people of different nationalities and religions mixed, Nazareth was a deeply Jewish village. This is inferred from both the traditional Jewish tombs excavated and from the fact that Nazareth was chosen as one of the twenty-four new centers from which the chief rabbis hoped to rebuild Judaism following the destruction of the Temple in Jerusalem in 70 C.E. To qualify for this, it would have to have been untainted by other religions.[36]

Second, excavations from the region indicate the typical layout of the kind of house Jesus may have grown up in: a few rooms grouped around a central courtyard. "Ovens and other domestic installations stood in the courtyards," write James Strange and Eric Meyers. "Outside staircases led to flat roofs, for these were ideal working areas and doubled as sleeping places in the hot summer months. . . . Windows were small and located high up for letting light in, not for seeing out."[37]

One of the most treasured pieces of the gospel saga is the tradition that Jesus was a carpenter who learned his trade from his father. This depends on one slender reference in Mark's gospel: "Is not this the carpenter, the son of Mary . . . ?"[38] But the Greek *tekton* and the underlying Aramaic word *naggara* do not mean carpenter so much as laborer; they could be applied to a stonemason, woodworker, or builder. Matthew changes Mark's text to "Is not this the carpenter's *son*?"[39] Some scholars speculate that he did this because by Matthew's time Christians had begun to bristle at the idea that their divine figure was once a mere laborer, and so Matthew used this means to distance Jesus from "carpenter."[40] In any case, many scholars see no reason for Mark to have invented the *tekton* reference, and so conclude that it is true. But they would make the historical Jesus not a skilled carpenter, but a humble laborer. Needless to say, however, the claim that St. Joseph's Church on Casa Nova Street in downtown Nazareth is built on the site of "Joseph's workshop" is pure fancy.

So then, let's assume that the historical Jesus was a *tekton*, a laborer. When combined with recent insights from archaeology, this commonplace assumption gives us a new lead on Jesus' early life. We know that Sepphoris, only four miles away, was totally rebuilt in the years 4 B.C.E. to 26 C.E., or throughout virtually the whole of Jesus' life. Wouldn't it be logical for workers from a nearby village to be engaged in this massive undertaking? It was common for Jewish laborers to travel from place to place in search of work, and Eric Meyers suggests that the boy and his father could also have traveled to other nearby cities engaged in rebuilding projects, such as Tiberias on the Sea of Galilee.[41]

John Meier speculates, "If Jesus had been employed in Sepphoris during the period of its magnificent reconstruction, he would have been brought into contact with urban culture in a strongly hellenistic city. The experience might have helped loosen the natural provincialism adhering to conservative Jewish peasants from the countryside."[42] Meier hastens to add that there is no direct evidence that Jesus spent time in Sepphoris. But the idea is supported by simple topography. Standing at the site of ancient Sepphoris, which today is a sweep of ruins across a hilltop, silent stones among trees and cacti, your eyes are drawn to the urban sprawl of Nazareth on the next hill. Two thousand years ago the situation was exactly reversed: a peasant boy in the sleepy hamlet of Nazareth couldn't have helped but look north across the valley to see the shimmering and exotic Roman capital, a city of precisely the same population that Nazareth has today.

Strange and Meyers also emphasize the importance of topography in appreciating outside influence on the historical Jesus. Nazareth, they point out, looks down upon the Via Maris—the Way of the Sea—the principal trade route through lower Galilee, which linked Sepphoris to other major cities. As Sepphoris grew in importance—which it did throughout Jesus' life—the increased traffic along this route would have meant a steady stream of outside influences. "The real question," the archaeologists write, "is whether anyone in Lower Galilee who lived in so busy an area could have escaped the dominant cultural tendencies of that region."[43]

So old notions about the remote Jewishness of Jesus' hometown are being dramatically revised: Nazareth may have been a Jewish village in the hills, but it was within gazing and strolling distance of the might of Rome and the glory of Greece. And this fact fits with a growing consensus regarding Jesus' teaching. A sizable number of scholars today believe that his teaching contained a mixture of Jewish thought and ideas from Greek philosophy, and that these two major streams flowed together in one man to produce a new perspective on the human condition. In the traditional picture of Jesus—a humble Galilean peasant whose pool of knowledge was strictly rural—there is no way to account for this mixture; one can only pull out the divinity trump card. At the other end of the spectrum are the various creative accounts dreamed up over the years that have Jesus journeying to India or elsewhere in order to absorb foreign strains of thought—all of which require impressive leaps of imagination. In between these two extremes is the center of current scholarship, which keeps the young Jesus in Galilee but acknowledges the three centuries of Greek influence in that area.

So then, perhaps the teenager from the traditional Jewish village watched the parade of travelers heading to the big city, and in time made regular treks there for work, and once there found himself staring at Greek mosaics, watching races and wrestling matches in the gymnasium, possibly even taking in theatrical revivals of Aristophanes and Euripides or encountering Greek philosophers. This might account not only for outside influence in his teaching but also for his later shunning of the Roman world. The Jesus of the gospels never visits Sepphoris, Tiberias, or Caesarea, the Roman strongholds of Galilee; his rejection of these centers of foreign power may make better sense if we imagine him, earlier in life, falling under their spell.

This is a radically different view of the young Jesus from that taught in Sunday schools, where teachers gloss over the formative years because that's what the gospels do. In the standard telling, Jesus is born miraculously and at age twelve is seen discussing theology with the rabbis in the Temple. And that's all. Nothing more is taught about him until about the age of thirty, when he encounters the Baptist.

But while the new wave of critical scholarship rejects even these few gospel details about his early life, it is rapidly coloring in the picture of the overall milieu in which he lived. This is leading to a whole new perspective on Jesus the man and the movement he spawned. And the highest of high-tech tools are being used to pierce the most basic layer of the historical Jesus' reality: his Jewishness.

CHAPTER THREE

A MOTHER RELIGION GIVES BIRTH TO TWINS

The drab cinder-block building sits baking under a Middle Eastern sun. Inside, walking through linoleum hallways beneath buzzing florescent lights, with vague chemical smells wafting through open doorways, you might be in any university science building anywhere in the world.

In an upstairs lab, a man and woman bend over what looks like a piece of ancient bone. A small test tube on the table beside them holds a tiny brown chip. Other tubes contain clear liquid. On a nearby table are notebooks filled with columns of numbers, and large film strips with rows of dashes—the telltale indication that DNA analysis is going on.

Here at Hebrew University, on the outskirts

of Jerusalem, history and science are converging in a very concrete way, for the material inside the test tubes has nothing to do with tracking a criminal or perfecting a new strain of wheat. It is the parentage of Christianity and modern Judaism that is under analysis.

The man leading the work—who is indeed bent over a piece of ancient animal bone at this moment, attempting to locate the home range of a herd of ancient goats—is Dr. Scott Woodward, a molecular biologist from Brigham Young University. In the early 1990s, while working on genetic diseases, Woodward realized that in order to understand how genetic mutations perpetuate he would have to examine them in human populations over time. Really old human DNA, however, is hard to come by. You may find ancient remains, but the DNA is almost always fragmented and unrecoverable. To complete his work, Woodward would have to find some exquisitely preserved bodies. But where?

Woodward met Professor Wilfred Griggs, an archaeologist at Brigham Young who had been excavating a burial site in Egypt that contained upwards of 1.2 million individuals, many of them mummified. This proved to be a gold mine of ancient genotypes; it opened up previously undreamed-of possible uses for genetic information-gathering techniques. Woodward was soon involved in tracing the modern ancestors of ancient Egyptians, as well as in trying to explain the wide prevalence of random DNA sequences in human genetic material—mutations that exist in most of us, which seemingly serve no purpose but which are dutifully passed on from generation to generation.

In 1993, Woodward was in Egypt giving a lecture about his DNA sampling of mummies. Dr. Joseph Zias, an anthropologist at Rockefeller University, happened to be in the audience. After the lecture, he asked Woodward if the same technique could be applied to parchment: specifically, to the Dead Sea Scrolls. Yet another unimagined use for the technology was born.

Today Woodward leads a high-tech team that is trying to pull meaning out of a very low-tech form of communication—a kind of meaning the writers of the Dead Sea Scrolls never imagined they were imparting. After the scrolls were discovered in the late 1940s and early 1950s, and as the intact and nearly intact scrolls were translated and made public, there was an initial rush of pronouncements about the beliefs of the sect that produced and gathered them between the years 152 B.C.E. and 68 C.E. But soon the breakthroughs stopped coming, as experts were left with thousands of fragments, some the size of pencil shavings, their ends frayed so that puzzlelike fittings were impossible to make. The scholars knew there were several hundred different manuscripts in this mess, but how to sort them out?

Enter Scott Woodward. Most of the scrolls are composed of parchment—animal tissue—which has a discernible genetic code. If some of the thousands of scroll scraps could be found to have come from a particular ancient goat or sheep, it would be a fair bet that those scraps were all part of the same manuscript. DNA analysis has proved to be an ingenious method for dramatically reducing the complexity of the task. In effect, Woodward and his team have before them a gigantic pile of jumbled pieces from a thousand different puzzles, which they are now able to sort into distinct piles. With this head start, scholars will resume the work of actually assembling the individual puzzles.

There are numerous other ways in which this work may assist the scholars as well. If the geneticists can match some of the parchment with a particular herd of ancient goats—say, one from Syria or Egypt—it might alter theories about who wrote the scrolls. If certain key scrolls were found to come from different regions, that might indicate that the community who wrote them was in fact widely dispersed, and not, as some have argued, a single, close-knit society. Even some of the already assembled scrolls—those whose meaning has perplexed scholars—may be shown to have incorrect pieces in them, which would be an advance of a sort.

This next phase of deciphering these ancient texts is excruciatingly difficult work, but even after fifty years it is being conducted with amazing intensity, and the steady stream of popular books on the topic testifies to the enduring fascination with the scrolls on the part of ordinary people. Geza Vermes, one of the translators of the scrolls and the author of *The Dead Sea Scrolls in English,* has spent a long time trying to understand the ongoing fascination with them. "The outstanding characteristic of our age appears to be a desire to reach back to the greatest attainable purity, to the basic truth," he concludes. Somehow, we aren't satisfied with the words on the page anymore, yet at the same time we feel angst—maybe even jealousy—at the idea that these same words *were* enough to inspire and transport our ancestors. Our solution is to dig beneath them, to try to discover the simple truth that we surmise lies buried there.

The Dead Sea Scrolls are seemingly tailor-made to fit this desire. And their importance is genuine. They are so potentially revelatory because they breach an ancient barrier that for two millennia has closed us off from the world in which Jesus lived. If you were a Jew of Palestine whose life spanned the first century C.E., you would not have considered the career of Jesus of Nazareth the most significant event of your era; in all likelihood you would not even have noticed it. The one massively important event that would have overshadowed all others for you occurred forty years after Jesus died. In 70 C.E., after four years of rebellion from their unruly Jewish subjects, Roman legions swept into Palestine and all but annihilated the Jews: destroyed their capital city, their Temple, their way of life. The Jewish historian Flavius Josephus, who served as a general during the war, records the Roman onslaught with near cinematic vividness:

> They poured into the streets sword in hand, cut down without mercy all who came within reach, and burnt the houses of any who took refuge indoors, occupants and all. . . . They ran every man through whom they met and blocked the narrow streets with corpses, deluging the whole city with gore so that many of the fires were quenched by the blood of the slain. At dusk the slaughter ceased, but in the night the fire gained the mastery, and on the eighth of Gorpiaios the sun rose over Jerusalem in flames.[1]

Josephus's claim that 1.1 million people died in the war is an exaggeration, but the devastation was so profound that even today archaeologists at sites throughout Judea find their excavations punctuated by a layer of black soot at precisely the same level. The black line visible in the Western Wall in Jerusalem is matched by blackened ruins at the aerie fortress of Masada, where militant Jews of the Zealot movement were the last to succumb to the Roman armies, and at the Essene settlement at Qumran, where Roman arrowheads still stuck into the outer walls bear witness to the fact that the war brought an end to the Dead Sea Scrolls community along with much of the rest of the Jewish world.

So the year 70 C.E. marked a kind of holocaust in ancient Jewish life. And although few people realize it, it also marked the beginning of a new age of mankind. That is because the Roman destruction of Jerusalem brought an end to what is called Second Temple Judaism. The Judaism that Jesus thrived in was, along with the Egypt of the Pharaohs, the last of the so-called temple cultures of the ancient Near East: a civilization in which religion and politics were blended into one entity, in which life was centered around a great temple and its rulers.[2] Jesus and his family would likely have made occasional pilgrimages south from Nazareth to Jerusalem, where they would have taken part in that most evocative of primitive rituals, the slaughter of animals: paying homage to the terrible majesty of one's God with a bleating, shrieking, and blood-spouting venture across the line that separated life from death.

But if one great religion vanished under the leather-soled feet of Roman soldiers, two new ones sprang into being as a result of it: Christianity and modern Judaism. Both religions are fantastically removed from the Judaism that existed before; they are not so much parent and child but, as the historian Alan Segal puts it in his book *Rebecca's Children,* twins born of the same mother.

Until the middle of this century, no one even realized the vast extent of the difference between the Judaism that existed during Jesus' lifetime and the Judaism of just half a century later. That is thanks to the terribly efficient job the Romans did. They so utterly effaced the Jewish presence that the Jews who survived were forced to huddle together and reassess their entire self-understanding. They emerged from the huddle with a new, stripped-down, unified front. Since the Temple was no more, there would be no focal point of worship. Animal sacrifice became a thing of the past. Odd dissident sects would no longer be tolerated. The hereditary line of priests was snuffed out. In place of these, one sect, the Pharisees, became dominant. And the doctrines of the Pharisees—a commitment to the Torah and a legalistic tradition of interpreting it to fit everyday life—would redefine the religion for the next two millennia.

Meanwhile, another huddle was taking place. This one involved Jews and Gentiles who had become attached to the teachings of Jesus of Nazareth. These iconoclasts were forced out of the synagogues. They responded by forming communities of their own, based on the Jewish model, relying on the Hebrew Bible as the backbone of their belief, but incorporating the new teachings about Jesus as well.

No one in modern times appreciated the gulf that existed between these two late-first-century sects and the Jews of the prewar period. No one had a clear idea of what the Judaism of Jesus was. At least not until 1947, when a Bedouin shepherd boy searching for his stray goat encountered what later became known as 1Q: a cave in the Judean desert that contained the bulk of an ancient library that was to become known as the Dead Sea Scrolls.

From the very beginning, the scrolls aroused expectation and anxiety. These emotions were largely driven by Edmund Wilson's article on the topic in *The New Yorker*, published in 1955 as a book, *The Scrolls from the Dead Sea*. Wilson claimed that there was a direct link between the Essenes—the community that produced the scrolls—and the early Christian movement, and declared that "it would seem an immense advantage for cultural and social intercourse—that is, for civilization—that the rise of Christianity should, at last, be generally understood as simply an episode of human history rather than propagated as dogma and divine revelation."[3]

Wilson further maintained that the members of the small, secretive team of Christian scholars working with the scrolls were pulling their punches, deliberately downplaying what an objective observer would clearly see as parallels between the Qumran community and early Christianity. These parallels, Wilson argued, frightened the scholars because they challenged Christianity's uniqueness; they indicated that Christianity did not spring Athena-like from the head and heart of Jesus but rather grew out of the fertile soil of early Judaism. Jewish authorities too, Wilson maintained, were equally concerned that the material would radically alter the view of Jewish origins, and maybe threaten the canon of the Hebrew Bible.

Those on the official scrolls team today consider themselves above such unscholarly biases, and many observers believe that Wilson significantly overstated the case for ulterior motives. But the plodding forty-year pace of the original team, in which translations were made public drip by drip, kept conspiracy theories percolating. One recent book has argued that the Vatican was suppressing the scrolls because they contain information about the historical Jesus that belies the Catholic image of the Messiah, information with the potential to topple the Vatican's entire edifice of dogma. It is more likely, however, that the slow pace of output was due to professional jealousy and entrenchment on the part of a group of scholars who each viewed their own portion of scroll fragments as a project-for-life. This find was, after all, the most remarkable in the history of biblical archaeology, and the scholars knew they weren't likely to get another such chance to commune directly and privately with actual writings penned by human beings who were alive during the most vibrant period of Jewish history and the very birth of Christianity.

The private party ended in 1991, when two outside scholars secretly got hold of a concordance to the scrolls: a list of every word that appeared in all the analyzed fragments, together with the words that occurred on either side of it. They wrote a computer program that pieced these disjointed bits together; the result was a complete transcript of all the Dead Sea Scrolls that had been deciphered to date. The lock had been picked.

The scholars published their results at nearly the same time that the Huntington Library in California, which possessed a set of negatives of the scrolls, announced that it would make them public. The Israel Antiquities Authority and the scrolls team issued complaints and threats, but the genie was out of the bottle, and nearly everyone was happy about it. As the *New York Times* put it, ". . . the scrolls and what they say about the common roots of Christianity and Rabbinic Judaism belong to civilization, not to a few sequestered professors."[4]

Until the scrolls came to light, the most important source of information on first-century Judaism was Josephus, who was born around the time of the crucifixion. Josephus was both an ardent Jew and a practical man who, following the destruction of Jerusalem, devoted his life to explaining and interpreting the Jewish world for the Romans. He wrote books about the war with Rome and the history of the Jewish people, and in these he left to posterity information about the various Jewish sects and how they interrelated.

But his information, important though it is, is brief, and in places corrupted by later Christian copyists who felt no compunction about inserting their own material. Here is the most famous instance—his one mention of Jesus—with the material believed to be inserted by a later copyist set in italics:

> About this time there lived Jesus, a wise man, *if indeed one ought to call him a man.* For he was one who wrought surprising feats and was a teacher of such people as accept the truth gladly. He won over many Jews and many of the Greeks. *He was the Messiah.* When Pilate, upon hearing him accused by men of the highest standing amongst us, had condemned him to be crucified, those who had in the first place come to love him did not give up their affection for him. *On the third day he appeared to them restored to life, for the prophets of God had prophesied these and countless other marvellous things about him.* And the tribe of the

> Christians, so called after him, has still to this day not disappeared.[5]

So then, what we have from Josephus is only a few pages on several of the Jewish sects that existed at the time of Jesus, and we can't be sure how much of this information is trustworthy. It's no surprise, then, that scholars have tended to envision the Jewish landscape through which Jesus walked as being pretty much like what it was later, when it was controlled by the Pharisees. In this, they are following the gospel writers. When the Jews expelled Christians from the synagogues, the Christians retaliated by creating their own written documents to explain and buttress their beliefs. In these gospels, Jesus is seen squaring off against the Pharisees in order to show that he is superseding Judaism. The Pharisees are depicted as petty, neurotically concerned with ritual, legalistic; Jesus is expansive, forgiving, wise. The evangelists set up the Pharisees as a foil for Jesus, and for them "Pharisee" is virtually a synonym for "Jew."

For many years, scholars were content with this representation. It was a neat and tidy way to account for the split between Christians and Jews: it showed the split going all the way back to Jesus. But it wasn't historically accurate. It is highly doubtful that the historical Jesus would have had such run-ins with the Pharisees, for the simple reason that the Pharisees weren't in the leadership in Jesus' day. Beyond this, as Paula Fredriksen has noted, many of the situations over which Jesus and the Pharisees clash in the gospels would not have presented religious problems for the Pharisees of Jesus' time. "It is blasphemy! Who can forgive sins but God alone?" is what Mark has the appalled Pharisees cry after Jesus cures a man and announces that his sins are forgiven.[6] But in Jesus' day, a time of free-form seeking among Jews in which magicians and prophets roamed the countryside and gained large followings (Crossan calls the original followers of the historical Jesus "Jewish hippies"), disease was commonly associated with sin, and it was acknowledged that any healer was in effect wiping away sins.[7] The shift in attitude from Jesus' time to that of the gospel writers must have been a bit like the change from the free experimentation and revolt against the existing order of the 1960s to the social and political conservatism of the 1980s. Things that were tolerated in the earlier decade had now become sacrilege. Declaring oneself a forgiver of sins was no longer politically correct.

So now that scholars all over the world have ready access to the fragments from the caves in the Dead Sea, what secrets are the fragments yielding? What do the Dead Sea Scrolls tell us about Judaism before the destruction of the Temple? What do they reveal about the birth of Christianity?

In a nutshell, this new wave of analysis is confirming Edmund Wilson's basic claim: Christianity grew out of first-century Judaism. When we read the scrolls and the gospels side by side, the historical Jesus comes into focus as a product of his time. "Blessed are the poor in spirit," Jesus declares in the Sermon on the Mount. That phrase has long puzzled historians and theologians; who exactly are the poor in spirit? The phrase appears in no other early Jewish writings. But it shows up in the Essene scroll called "The War of the Sons of Light Against the Sons of Darkness." In fact, "the poor," and "the poor in spirit" seem to be names the Essenes used to refer to themselves. Similarly, Jesus' admonition to "turn the other cheek," unknown in the Hebrew Bible and until recently thought to be pure Jesus, appears in the Essenes' Manual of Discipline.[8] At the least, such "matches" seem to indicate that elements of Jesus' teaching were in the air.

Beyond this, Essene rituals included a kind of baptism as well as a ritual meal presided over by a "Messiah":

> Fo[r he shall] bless the first (portion) of the bread and the wi[ne and shall extend] his hand to the bread first. Afterwa[rds,] the messiah of Israel [shall exten]d his hands to the bread. [Afterwards,] all of the congregation of the community [shall ble]ss, ea[ch according to] his importance.[9]

This is obviously reminiscent of the Last Supper. As James VanderKam, professor of Old Testament Studies at Notre Dame puts it, these parallels suggest that "a larger number of the early Church's beliefs and practices than previously suspected were not unique to it."[10] Here, in writings dating from Jesus' time and just prior to it, are words and practices strikingly similar to ones found in the gospels.

But the most important parallel between the scrolls and the New Testament has to do not so much with rituals but a state of mind. The big debate among New Testament scholars today concerns whether Jesus was an apocalyptic prophet, as he is portrayed in the gospels, or whether that is later overlay. Apocalyptic thought appears in the Hebrew Scriptures, and it was important *after* Jesus. But what about during his lifetime?

To answer that question, consider an event that comes near the end of the gospels:

> Then they came to Jerusalem. And he entered the Temple and began to drive out those who were selling and those who were buying in the Temple, and he overturned the tables of the moneychangers and the seats of those who sold doves . . .[11]

This action, recounted with such matter-of-factness in all the gospels, is, for E. P. Sanders, one of the dominant figures in New

Testament scholarship today, the very key to the riddle of the historical Jesus. Sanders constructs his entire opus, *Jesus and Judaism*, around this passage.[12] Every Sunday school child knows that Jesus entered the Temple and drove out the money changers, and nearly every New Testament scholar asserts that it did indeed happen. But the question is *why?* Why did he do it? What was he up to? Christians have long held that he was "purifying" the Temple, enforcing a separation of church and bank. The Temple, in this reading, had become defiled by moneygrubbers, and he decided to clean it up. But this answer doesn't wash. It reveals a total lack of understanding of first-century Judaism. The Temple was the heart of life for first-century Jews; animal sacrifice was its chief function, and money-changing was a normal and necessary part of this, as pilgrims arriving from all parts of the Empire exchanged their impure money for the Temple's own coinage, the Tyrian shekel.[13] No, the old "purifying" argument doesn't fit with these basic facts; behind it is the notion that Jesus was "cleansing" Judaism, preparing to replace it with Christianity. It is not history but Christian propaganda.

So what was he doing? One line of thinking—dominant since Albert Schweitzer inaugurated modern Jesus research with his 1906 book *The Quest of the Historical Jesus*—holds that he was enacting the apocalyptic scenario spoken of throughout the Hebrew Bible. At some future time, prophetic passages promise, the current age will come to an end. At this time, the righteous of Israel will be rewarded and everyone else in the world will be punished. Apparent indicators of the End Time are scattered throughout the Hebrew Bible but appear most frequently in Isaiah. God will gather the twelve tribes of Israel together once again, the Gentiles will submit to God, and the Temple will be rebuilt.

Fair enough, but these prophecies were hundreds of years old in Jesus' time. What evidence is there that they held sway in his time, that people actually felt themselves to be living in the last days?

Outside the New Testament, the evidence was scanty—until that day in 1947. The Essene documents, which date from more than a century before Jesus' birth until a few decades after his death, portray a sect that was positively inflamed with end-of-the-world passion. Josephus, in his account of the Essenes, gives the idea of a wan philosophical community. In the scrolls, however, they come across as full-blooded religious fanatics, living in a stark desert wilderness and staring red-eyed across the rim of creation, waiting for something big to happen. These were Jesus' contemporaries, and they were drugged on apocalypse.

Where did this rabid commitment to closure come from? Jews had always believed history was a steady march of moral progress. They had always seen themselves as being in a covenant with God. Alan Segal says that the Hebrew word for covenant, *brith,* translates better as "contract," and that most Jews of the ancient period believed that God's agreement with Abraham amounted to an almost literal legal document, whereby the party of the first part, God, would lead the party of the second part, the Israelites, to the promised land provided that they obeyed his moral laws.[14]

But in later centuries it seemed that things weren't working out according to the plan. As time went by, foreign invasion—first by the Assyrians and Babylonians, then the Persians, the Greeks, and finally the Romans—became more frequent and more cruel. If history was a progressive climb up the ladder to heaven, it seemed clear that the Jews were actually slipping downward. What was to be done?

According to psycho-historical speculation, the oppressed Jewish mind was forced to abandon the whole history-as-a-steady-march-to-heaven theme and invent a new paradigm. A new crop of visionaries sprang up who looked through the gray misery and saw a light shining in the distance. The promised land wouldn't be reached by the steady march of history, they decided: it would come in a rush, with a dramatic and violent ending of the present world. God would keep his covenant—the people of Israel would still lead the nations into the new world of righteousness. But it would come not as a result of the gradual accumulation of goodness but as a result of the massing of wickedness into a foul load so heavy that it would collapse history itself.

This cultural neurosis is what distinguishes late Second Temple Judaism—the Judaism of Jesus—from its more ancient form. Not everyone of the time subscribed to it, but, according to Sanders, Jesus' action in the Temple—the action that led to his arrest and crucifixion—was apocalyptic plain and simple. Jesus believed he was igniting the End Time scenario that Isaiah seems to prophesy:

> "I am the Lord . . . who says of Jerusalem, 'It shall be rebuilt,' and of the Temple, 'Your foundation shall be laid.' "[15]

Another indication Sanders finds that Jesus was clearly and consciously of the apocalyptic mindset is the calling of twelve disciples: they represented the twelve tribes of Israel, who, according to the prophets, would reunite at the end of history.

If Sanders is correct, we have a tidy theory to account for who and what Jesus was. He was a Jew of his time, an apocalyptic prophet who believed that the end of the world was approaching, and who was wrong.

But there is more to the picture than this. Many scholars today believe that Sanders ignores another major force—a force that we take for granted as shaping world history, but which, until recently, was never applied to Jesus.

CHAPTER FOUR

GREEKNESS

Beneath a taut blue tent of Aegean sky, cut only by the rude projection of the Pnyx hill to the south and the more dignified rise of the Acropolis to the east, a group of men stand facing one another in lively discussion. Even without the landscape, you would know where we are. Everything from the drape of the tunics to the lavishly inflected Greek tells you this is Athens, and this is the fifth century B.C.E., the golden age, the fountainhead of Western civilization.

"Does he who desires the honorable also desire the good?" The older man at the center of the group poses the question.

"Certainly," answers the self-confident young man who initiated the discussion by wondering aloud about the nature of virtue.

"Then are there some who desire evil and others who desire good?"

"Yes."

The older man looks surprised. "Do you really imagine, Meno, that a man knows evil to be evil and desires it anyway?"

"Certainly, I do."

"And does he think that evil will do good to him who possesses it, or does he know it will do him harm?"

The young man frowns; he is beginning to lose some of his self-assurance. "There are some who think that evil will do them good, and others who know that it will do them harm," he replies.

"Well, and do those who desire evil and think that evil is hurtful to the possessor know that they will be hurt by it?"

The young man is scratching his head now. "They must know it," he answers.

"And does anyone desire to be miserable?"

"I should say not."

"But if there is no one who desires to be miserable, there is no one who desires evil, for what is misery but the desire and possession of evil?"

The young man is by now tied in knots, undone by the wizardry of his elder. The others in the group are beaming, sighing, relaxing with sheer intellectual pleasure.[1]

This is Socrates, more or less as depicted by his pupil, Plato, dazzling the young gentlemen of Athens. Plato's *Dialogues* became bestsellers in antiquity in large part because they revealed something strange and exciting, something no one had ever experienced before. It was a new way of approaching the metaphysical. Over many centuries, the societies of the Near East had developed complex systems for thinking about the Big Questions. These systems are called religions; some would call them primitive religions. The Assyrians and Canaanites and Egyptians all conceived of such notions as good and evil concretely. God was good incarnate. Evil was personified as Rahab or Lotan, the sea god or dragon god. Re, the sun god and bringer of light, was the father of mankind. Osiris, a god who died, ruled the underworld, and became the deity of death. This was an efficient way to deal with the ungraspable.

The Greeks of the fifth century B.C.E. introduced abstraction into the world, and promptly became drunk on it. Heraclitus, Parmenides, and Socrates dealt not so much in gods as in *concepts.* So was born philosophy.

But philosophy was the domain of the elite. Throughout the Greek world the common folk still trafficked in gods: Poseidon controlled the seas; Aphrodite personified the philosophers' concept of love. According to Nietzsche, the reason all masks worn by actors in early Greek tragedies featured the same stern face was that all the actors were representing one or another facet of Dionysus, the god of fertility, art, intoxication, and madness: these seemingly very different areas were all seen as connected through the force of nature as it penetrates man in varying degrees. The first tragedies paid homage to Dionysus' hold over man, as did the mystery cults in which people threw off the restraints of civilized life and gave themselves back to nature: roaming the hills in an orgiastic frenzy of sex and bloodshed, tearing apart live animals with their bare hands, and devouring the dripping pieces in celebration of the wildness within us all, the wildness that must be honored.[2]

Philosophy and pagan worship: these two Greek ways of dealing with good and evil, different as they are, both contrast profoundly with the Jewish way. God, to the ancient Israelites, was impossibly grand, unswervingly righteous, and utterly distant. God's image could not be captured in art. God was both the personification of Good and yet an abstraction: the remote YHWH, whose very name could not be spoken.

Socrates taught Plato. Plato taught Aristotle. Aristotle tutored the young Alexander, who went on to conquer the world and brought Greekness with him like a glorious influenza. He founded cities everywhere from Persia to Egypt, and the infection called hellenism took hold in every place he went. In the centuries after Alexander's conquest of Palestine, hellenism gathered strength among the Jews. Cities on the Greek style sprang up. This is evident today at archaeological sites from Dan to Beersheba: Greek theaters for watching Greek plays, Greek columns for holding up Greek buildings.

So, yes, even many Jews—the fiercely independent Jews—succumbed to Greekness. You wouldn't realize this from reading traditional biblical scholarship, which erected a wall between Palestine and the wider Mediterranean world. As Burton Mack writes, "Hellenistic influence has been downplayed by scholars in the interest of buttressing the picture of Jesus appearing in the midst of a thoroughly Jewish culture. Unfortunately for this view, archaeological evidence of hellenization in Galilee continues to increase."[3] And not only in Galilee but in Judea, Samaria, and the Decapolis as well. The Jewish world in which Jesus lived was awash in hellenism, and contemporary biblical scholars are finding its influence everywhere—including, ultimately, in the historical Jesus.

One of the avenues by which Greek thinking penetrated Judaism was, of all things, the Hebrew Bible. Shift the scene forward two centuries from Socrates, to the third century B.C.E. and the hellenized world Alexander wrought. Another meeting of wise men is taking place. The participants are all Jews of the Diaspora, Jews whose forebears left the homeland and forged new identities in the major cities of the Greek world. They have kept some ties to Jerusalem, but the most basic one, the Hebrew language, they have all but lost. So a decision is made—a momentous decision, an unprecedented one—to commission a translation of the Hebrew

Bible into Greek, the common tongue. Exactly how the translation was achieved has been swallowed up by legend. The story went that the king of Egypt set seventy-two different Jewish scholars to work simultaneously and independently on a translation, and—wonder of wonders—when they were finished all seventy-two works were identical. Anyone who has ever tried to translate a gum wrapper into another language will tell you how likely this feat is. It is a fable meant to assuage the Jewish masses on a sensitive point. It had long been believed that Hebrew, the language in which Yahweh himself dictated the Ten Commandments, was itself holy. Tradition held that every word of the Bible was perfect and immutable. (This view was maintained in spite of the hundreds of discrepancies—some of them quite significant—between different ancient versions of biblical books found at Qumran.) If the Bible was perfect, then, how could anyone think of translating it? Wouldn't it mean mangling the very word of God? The farfetched story of the creation of the Septuagint ("seventy," after the number of translators in one variant of the story) was intended to show that God was directing the work, that one should think of the authors "not as translators but as prophets and priests of the mysteries," according to the first-century writer Philo. And so the faithful could rest assured that Hebrew wisdom, Hebrew concepts, survived the journey to a foreign tongue intact.[4]

But, in fact, they didn't. The conservatives who fought against a translation were right. It would have been deeply shocking to Jewish curmudgeons such as the Essenes—who had retreated into the desert to keep the faith pure—to learn that the Hebrew Bible itself would become an instrument for the infusion of Platonism, Stoicism, even Aristotelian logic, into the Jewish consciousness. For the Septuagint, created in the third and second centuries B.C.E., became a cross-pollenizer of the two great Mediterranean cultures.

There is no better example of what happened in the translation than Exodus 3:14. God appears in a burning bush before Moses to tell him he will lead the Israelites out of Egypt. Moses wants to know by what authority he will speak to the people: "If I come to the Israelites and say to them, 'The God of your ancestors has sent me to you,' and they ask me, 'What is his name?' what shall I say to them?" God replies not with an ordinary name, but with the first-person singular of the Hebrew verb "to be." *Ehyeh.* "Thus you shall say to the Israelites, 'I AM has sent me to you.' "[5]

In the Septuagint, *ehyeh* becomes *ho on*—Being. The two seem nearly the same—merely different forms of the same verb—but they are worlds apart. "I AM" is The Creator; "Being" is a concept. When it makes the transition from Semitic it registers with the Greek-speaking world in an already familiar way. The thundering, roiling God of the Israelites, a God of anger and mercy, a feeling God, becomes the divine, immutable, supremely cool One of Greek Stoic philosophy. One stroke of the stylus, and the Hebrew Bible has found Plato. As Paula Fredriksen says, "Greek concepts, in brief, did not need to be read into Scripture. They were already there, by virtue of the new language of the text."[6]

This leads directly to a new wave of Jewish thought and writing, such as that found in 4 Maccabees, which from its opening sounds like it could have been written by one of those eager young students of Socrates: "The subject that I am about to discuss is most philosophical, that is, whether devout reason is sovereign over the emotions. So it is right for me to advise you to pay earnest attention to philosophy. For the subject is essential to everyone who is seeking knowledge, and in addition it includes the praise of the highest virtue—I mean, of course, rational judgment."[7]

The Septuagint would go on to have an even greater role in shaping primitive Christianity. It would become the "Old Testament," the means by which the first Christians would enter the world of the Hebrew Scriptures. "In it the first Christians sought the prophecies which justified their interpretation of the life and death of Jesus," wrote C. K. Barrett forty years ago, "and sometimes the Greek text was more accommodating than the Hebrew." The prime example of this, as we have seen, was the "virgin" translation of Isaiah 7:14.[8]

The infiltration of Greekness into Judaism wasn't confined to the intellectual realm. Cushions, mattresses, and bed linens made in Greece were features of Jewish homes in Palestine, as were Egyptian vases, glasses, and textiles. Aristocratic Jews and foreign residents of Palestine preferred Greek wine and olive oil to the local stuff, and had it imported from Rhodes. There was a lively slave trade. Greek businessmen owned and managed large vineyards and farms in Palestine; there was a highly developed network of inspectors, import and export officials, and tax collectors. The thousands of Greek buildings and mosaics found throughout the area meant a steady stream of Greek architects and craftsmen.

One result of this continual contact with the Gentiles was that in the century after Alexander more and more Jews took Greek names. Beginning with the books of the Maccabees, we encounter Jews with such un-Hebrew names as Antipater, Theodotus, Sosipater, and even Alexander.[9]

Greek names suggest Greek language. The traditional line of scholars has been that the city-dwelling sophisticates of Jewish Palestine knew Greek, while the peasants spoke only Aramaic, but this view is rapidly changing. The German scholar Martin Hengel estimates that one-third of the epitaphs on ancient tombstones found in the Jerusalem area are in Greek. After the discovery of the Dead Sea Scrolls, excavators of other canyons in the Judean desert found artifacts that belonged to Jews who had holed up during the second war with Rome (132–135 C.E.). These included letters, deeds, and contracts, many of which are written in Greek; some of the legal documents are then paraphrased in Aramaic "for the benefit of those who did not feel comfortable with the Greek original," according to Irish scholar Sean Freyne.[10] One letter states plainly, "This letter is written in Greek as we have no one who knows Hebrew."[11] All of this suggests that the Greek language was much more commonplace in Palestine than previously thought. Burton Mack goes so far as to argue that "southern Galilee was largely Greek-speaking in the first century, though of course bilingual."[12]

The hellenization of Palestine came to a climax in 175 B.C.E., when the grecophile high priest Jason formally declared Jerusalem a Greek city, which he called Antioch-at-Jerusalem, and founded a gymnasium there. Now, a gymnasium of the hellenistic age was not merely a sports center but a place for indoctrinating young men of the Empire into Greek culture. At the gymnasium, would-be gentlemen of the important cities studied philosophy, rhetoric, and of course the Greek language, focusing on Homer. Establishing a gymnasium was the first step toward "civilization" for cities on the fringes of the Greek world. It invariably meant that the well-born young men would throw off much of their native culture in their zeal to become fashionable.

One might expect a violent reaction from the Jews, and eventually there was one, but, tellingly, it didn't come for a while, and then only after truly outrageous changes were asked of them. In the meantime, the cream of Jerusalem's young manhood flocked to the gymnasium, where they took turns arguing à la Plato, then stripped naked and headed for that focal point of the gymnasium, the *palaestra* or wrestling arena, to show off their moves and their bodies. The zeal for hellenism among these bronzed young Jews came to a head, so to speak, in the hot fashion trend of the time: epispasm, an operation to stretch the penis skin, undoing circumcision. What more pronounced indication could there be that Greek was cool?[13]

A revolt against all this foreignness did finally come, and it set in motion the political and religious forces that helped to form both the historical Jesus and Christianity as we know it. Antiochus IV Epiphanes, the Seleucid ruler of Syria and Palestine, decided in 169 B.C.E. to speed up the hellenization of the Jews. Not understanding his subjects in the least, he had it in mind to make Judaism just one more tribal exponent of Greek culture: he would turn Yahweh into yet another manifestation of Zeus. Jewish law forbade any foreigner from entering the inner court of the Temple, under pain of death, but Antiochus "arrogantly entered the sanctuary and took the golden altar, the lampstand for the light, and all its utensils," according to 1 Maccabees, which provides a kind of newspaper account of the desecration and ensuing war.[14] Antiochus then erected a statue of Zeus in the Temple. He blithely declared to the people of Palestine—Jews as well as Gentiles—his intention "that all should be one people, and that all should give up their particular customs."[15] He outlawed Sabbath observance and circumcision. As if to cap all of this fine work, almost as if his intention was to drive the Jews to madness, he had pigs sacrificed at the Temple.

Surprisingly, according to 1 Maccabees, "many even from Israel gladly adopted his religion; they sacrificed to idols and profaned the sabbath"[16]—which is a measure of how far the Jews had strayed from their roots. But enough Jews resisted the attempt to wipe out their religion to throw Antiochus into a murderous fury. He sent his troops to butcher all those who defied him: "They put to death the women who had their children circumcised, and their families and those who circumcised them; and they hung the infants from their mothers' necks."[17] Josephus records the savagery inflicted on the rebels in even more graphic detail: "They were whipped, their bodies were mutilated, and while they were still alive and breathing, they were crucified, while their wives and the sons whom they had circumcised despite the king's wishes were strangled, the children being made to hang from the necks of their crucified parents."[18]

At last, a hero emerged. When the king's soldiers confronted an elderly Jewish priest called Mattathias and tried to force him, in front of the people of his town, to make a sacrifice to Zeus, he pulled what can only be called a Hollywood stunt: shaking free of the soldiers, he killed a Jew who was approaching the pagan altar to make the sacrifice, spun and killed the soldier, then tore down the altar. Then, before he and his sons ran into the hills to escape, he let out a Spartacus-like cry: "Let every one who is zealous for the law and supports the covenant come out with me!"[19]

Soon other Jews joined the father and sons in their resistance, and a scrappy guerrilla force sprang into being. Under Mattathias's sons Judas (called Maccabeus—"the hammer"), Jonathan, and Simon, the rebels finally captured Jerusalem in 165 B.C.E., ushering in an era of Jewish self-rule. The Maccabean victory, still commemorated in the festival of Hanukkah, would become the stuff of legend for the Jews of a later era, living under the even more onerous Roman domination. It would be proof that a holy war, led by a strong and righteous man, could release the Jews from oppression. The Maccabees, in other words, would later inspire thoughts of a coming Messiah.

This inspiration would show up in the most basic ways. By the time of the Roman presence in Palestine, it had become common for Jews to name their children after the great heroes of the Bible. Thus, Jesus is named after Joshua; his brothers James, Joses, Simon, and Judas are named after the Israelite patriarchs Jacob, Joseph, Simeon, and Judah. This expression of nationalistic pride can be traced to the Maccabean victory, and indicates the extent to which this event helped to politicize the Jews of Jesus' time.[20]

The war also had a remarkable theological consequence. According to many scholars, it seems to have brought about a fundamental change in Jewish belief. For the ancient Jews of the Bible, there was no afterlife. Sheol, the realm of the dead in the Hebrew Bible, is "the Pit," a land of eternal darkness, "the land of forgetfulness." Ecclesiastes, written about eighty years before the war, expresses this with almost gleeful bleakness: "The living know that they will die, but the dead know nothing; they have no more reward, and even the memory of them is lost."[21]

But in the midst of the Maccabees' struggle against Antiochus, the Book of Daniel was written, evidently as propaganda to inspire the troops. What will those valiant rebels who die for Israel have to look forward to? "Many of those who will sleep in the dust of the earth shall awake, some to everlasting life,"[22] the author of Daniel informs his readers. Similar references soon become more and more prevalent in Jewish writings ("the righteous live forever, and their reward is with the Lord"[23]), until by the time of Jesus only one sect, the Sadducees, still clings to the old belief that with death comes only dust.

Sometime in the mid–second century B.C.E., it appears, the Jews found heaven. But where did they find it? Uta Ranke-Heinemann notes that the Greeks believed in an immortality of the soul long before the Jews did. She points out that Josephus was quite certain where the Essene belief in immortality came from: "Sharing the belief of the sons of Greece," Josephus writes of the Essenes, "they maintain that for virtuous souls there is reserved an abode beyond the ocean, a place which is not oppressed by rain or snow or heat, but is refreshed by the ever-gentle breath of the west wind coming in from the ocean; while they relegate base souls to a murky and tempestuous dungeon, big with never-ending punishments."[24]

So here, suddenly, and probably as a result of Greek influence on Judaism, we have heaven and hell. Ranke-Heinemann makes an interesting aside: the two characteristics of this new hell are "first, fire, and second, darkness, two things that don't go together." The reason for this, she argues, is that this new Judeo-Christian hell is actually a conflation of two older places: Sheol, the dark pit of nothingness, and Gehinnom, the "valley of fire," which was an actual valley south of Jerusalem where human sacrifices were supposed to have been made, and which was appropriated by rabbis in the second century B.C.E. as an afterlife place of punishment for the wicked. In the Greek of the New Testament, this fiery pit of torment becomes "Gehenna," as in Matthew 18:9: "And if your eye causes you to stumble, tear it out and throw it away; it is better for you to enter life with one eye than to have two eyes and to be thrown into the Gehenna of fire." As different traditions about the afterlife merge in the remarkably fertile period around the time of Jesus, then, we end up with the paradoxical place we know today: a dark and fiery hell.[25]

But back to the Maccabees. Following their momentous victory against the Greek-Syrian tyranny, the family of Mattathias became hereditary rulers of Palestine. Instead of leading a renaissance of Jewish tradition, as one might expect, the Hasmoneans, as they became known, soon adopted many of the very hellenistic ways they had bravely fought against; they too became intoxicated by Greekness. They strengthened ties with Rome, and even with Antiochus' son.[26] They employed Greek mercenaries and issued coins with both Hebrew and Greek writing.

Most ominously, in 152 B.C.E. Jonathan Maccabeus appointed himself high priest of the Temple. To appreciate the significance of this requires some explanation. The Temple in Jerusalem was the center of the Jewish faith, the holiest spot on earth. This belief went all the way back to the founding of Jerusalem in 996 B.C.E., the establishment of a monarchy, and the gathering of various desert tribes into one people, the Israelites, all of which is attributed to David. David's son, Solomon, erected a temple to Yahweh, the god whose worship was the main source of unity to the tribes. David's chief priest, a man named Zadok, became the high priest of this first temple. So revered was this official that it was decreed only members of his bloodline could carry on the office. From roughly 1000 B.C.E. onward, then, the high priests were chosen from the Zadok family—a priestly equivalent of royal succession—and the members of this priestly family became known after their ancestor: Sadducees.

With the title came enormous power. Its holder controlled the vast Temple treasury, into which Jews all over the Mediterranean world contributed funds. And by controlling the system of animal sacrifice, the high priest effectively oversaw the devotion of every pious Jew. After the division of the monarchy following Solomon's reign, the high priest became the most powerful Jew in the world.

One of the many outrages committed by Antiochus was his breaking of the Zadokite succession when, in 175 B.C.E., he installed one of his henchmen as high priest. The devout Jews who had fought under the Maccabean brothers clearly did so with the expectation that should they be victorious they would reinstitute the sacred family. But as the Maccabees consolidated their power, they found that the office of high priest was so potent they couldn't afford to give it away. They decided instead to institute a new priestly bloodline: their own.

The founding of the Essene sect likely dates to this time. When some Jews of a traditional bent realized that the Maccabees meant to steal the high priesthood, they rallied around a certain charismatic priest of the Zadokite succession. According to one scholarly theory, this man can be identified with the most prominent figure in the Dead Sea Scrolls, the Teacher of Righteousness. When these supporters of the Zadokite succession lost out to the Maccabees, who were determined to keep control of the Temple, they retired to the desert, where they formed their own community, railed against what they saw as the pretenders in Jerusalem, and waited for justice. According to this theory, the villain of the Dead Sea Scrolls, the so-called Wicked Priest, who persecuted the community and even tried to assassinate its leader, was either Jonathan or Simon Maccabeus. Thus began the Essenes of Qumran.[27]

Remarkably, it turns out that the parallels between Essenism and various earlier Greek societies are just as numerous as those shown earlier between the Essenes and the early Christians. Martin Hengel shows that the Qumran sect was by its very nature infused with Greekness. It was unheard of in the Jewish world, Hengel points out, for men to leave their families and communities in order to form their own society. Jewishness had everything to do with responsibility to family and community. The kind of retreat the Essenes engaged in could not have been possible in the time of the ancient Israelites. Imagine Moses, coming down from Mount Sinai with the Ten Commandments to find his people worshiping a pagan idol, giving up on them and forming his own small society of "true believers." No, this clubbishness was something new to Judaism, something brought from the Greek world. And while there are no other known parallels for it in the Judaism of the time, amazingly enough it shares many traits with the fellowship the Jesus followers would shortly form.

There were many types of special groups and associations in Greek society, but the one that most likely influenced the Essenes—and perhaps the historical Jesus—was the philosophers' school, and in particular the Pythagorean school. Pythagoras, the Greek philosopher of the sixth century B.C.E., founded a community of mystics in which, like the Essenes and the followers of the historical Jesus, common meals were important and all property was shared. This included intellectual property, which was very valuable to the group since they were in essence seekers of divine wisdom as it manifested itself in the physical universe. Mathematics was a holy art to the Pythagoreans; they saw it as proof of the existence of a Creator. The Pythagorean theorem was not a problem-solving device but one of God's fingerprints. The world around us may be transitory, the Pythagoreans believed, but there is another, eternal world, which is accessible by the intellect.

Bertrand Russell calls Pythagoras "intellectually one of the most important men that ever lived," for in basing religion on mathematics he presaged both the scientific method and the systematic theology of the Christian church: these two very different approaches to reality proceed in similar Pythagorean ways, moving from "self-evident" inner truth to grander theorems. But Pythagoras was influential long before Christianity came along. The second-century Jewish writer Aristobulus believed that Pythagoras had received his training under the Law of Moses, indicating that Jewish reverence for the philosopher was already longstanding.[28] Hengel asserts that the Teacher of Righteousness referred to in the Dead Sea Scrolls may have directly or indirectly become familiar with Pythagoras' scientific approach to religion. Certainly the Qumran sect and the Pythagoreans seemed to compete in ritual oddities. Both were extremely rigid and bound their adherents to exceedingly strange-sounding oaths. The Qumran group believed in a hierarchy of angels, and swore its members to commit to memory the secret names of the angels. They believed that oil was evil, and that the skin must always be kept dry. They abstained from sex. They considered it a sin to lift a pebble or to pull an animal out of a pit on the Sabbath. The Pythagoreans' most famous oath was against the eating of beans, but they were also not to sit on a quart measure, not to let swallows share their roof, and, surely the most trying of all, not to pick up what had fallen. Looked at this way, it doesn't seem surprising that both sects died out. As Bertrand Russell says of the Pythagoreans, "The unregenerate hankered after beans, and sooner or later rebelled."

If rigidity condemned both the Pythagoreans and the Essenes, flexibility would help the early Christian movement to flourish. The first century of the common era was one of massive change; finding God in a dead Jew may have seemed odd to many people, but those who did so were plugging themselves into one of the most potent blendings of cultures the world had ever known. What all of this scholarly digging shows is that the two centuries before Jesus' birth were an astonishingly fertile period, in which the coming together of Judaism and Greece—sometimes in angry clashes, sometimes more in the manner of lovers coupling—resulted in the birth of a litter of new ideas, new ways of being and of envisioning human reality: apocalypse, heaven and hell, the belief that history might yield up a Messiah as deliverer, the model of a group setting itself apart from society and dedicating itself to God and deliverance.

As often seems to happen at such times, when an age is turning, it was left to one individual to redirect these various streams, to make them flow together. During the Middle Ages, the English language acquired outside influences—aristocratic French, churchman's Latin—like barnacles. Shakespeare made it all work together, blended it into something wholly new, and so redefined what was sayable. Something similar, but much bigger, was about to happen in first-century Palestine. Not just the sayable, but the thinkable, the believable, was about to change forever.

CHAPTER FIVE

THE BIG DIPPER

This is, perhaps, a good place to pause and reissue a warning. What we have been involved with up to now—what the whole field of New Testament scholarship takes as its coin—is theory. No one can prove that Jesus formed his community of disciples under the influence of the Greek philosopher's school, just as no one can prove that he was or was not virginally conceived. Faith has it all over historical analysis here: if by faith one knows something to be true, then it is true. Faith doesn't rest on data. If one is compelled to venture out into the land of historical reconstruction, the best one can hope for is honest inquiry and educated guesswork. If the picture that results makes sense, that's good. And if this in turn puts one's Christian faith on more solid footing, that's even better.

But because it attempts to work with both the bland methodologies of history and the hot coals of spirituality, New Testament studies is a queer field, and the New Testament scholar is a conflicted creature. His prodigious training has taught him to proceed carefully, on all fours, sifting for every clue, and to report results meticulously and conservatively. On the other hand, he is a bird with a song in his heart. He knows he is working with kernels of gold, shiny nubs that are alive with meaning. Lurking in the back of his mind is the suspicion that if tended in just the right way, a way no other scholar has discovered before, these grains might just let the Divine loose in the world.

When you start to have such thoughts, it's time to put away the books and take a sabbatical. Delusions of grandeur are an occupational hazard, akin to the power trips of state troopers and Hollywood super agents. Most scholars recognize this and back off when they feel the trill start to rise in their throats.

But some do not. John Allegro is the example par excellence. Allegro was a renowned biblical exegete from Manchester University and an original member of the Dead Sea Scrolls translation team. Then, out of the psychedelic haze of the 1960s, he was visited by the stunning insight that Christianity was the result of a group hallucination on the part of the apostles while they were under the influence of a certain magic mushroom. He published his theory in a book, *The Sacred Mushroom and the Cross,* and was promptly drummed out of the profession in an uncharacteristically public way: fourteen major scholars authored an item in the London *Times* slamming the work.

Another, less flamboyant example of this tendency was Dr. Morton Smith of Columbia University. One of the great powerhouses of biblical criticism in the second half of the twentieth century and a mentor to many of today's top scholars, Dr. Smith was rummaging in the library of Mar Saba Monastery in Israel in 1958 when he found an eighteenth-century scrap of paper containing what purported to be a copy of a "secret" version of the Gospel of Mark. Around the scant twenty lines of text, which feature a certain naked youth whom Jesus raises from the dead and who then "remained with [Jesus] that night, for Jesus taught him the mystery of the Kingdom of God,"[1] Smith wove an elaborate theory: that Jesus' free-love society amounted to a homosexual ecstasy cult. This was too outrageous even to become scandalous, and many scholars dismissed the idea outright, but Smith clung to it and continued to develop it until his death in 1990.

In contrast to Allegro, however, Smith's championing of a highly speculative theory hasn't tarnished his image among authorities, whose books and papers are littered with references to his works. They have to be, for Smith is responsible for some of the most provocative insights of historical Jesus research, including one that helped throw the field wide open in the 1970s. It is an insight with both contemporary and ancient relevance. It has to do with Jesus, but first of all with the man who is always discussed before him, the one known as "the forerunner."

To look at John the Baptist as if his whole point in life had been to introduce Jesus, however, would be bad history. It is only when we look backward through a theological lens that he becomes a role player in a much bigger drama. John is a full-fledged historical personage in his own right, one of the most well-documented figures in the entire first century. He features prominently in all four gospels, in the extracanonical Gospel of Thomas, and in the Acts of the Apostles. Josephus, theologically unconnected with the early church, devotes more space to John than to Jesus, heaping praise on his "eloquence that had so great an effect on mankind." Many Christians today have a hard time crediting what scholars generally acknowledge: that in his time John was considerably more famous than Jesus.

To understand how this could be, consider a couple of modern images:

When Norma McCorvey, the "Jane Roe" of the landmark *Roe v Wade* abortion case, became Born Again in 1995 and renounced her historic role as symbol of the pro-choice movement, the press photo that went around the country showed her waist-deep in a suburban swimming pool, her face a squinting mixture of rapture and embarrassment, next to a grinning preacher. The media handlers in the pro-life movement had chosen what for them was the ultimate image of conversion.

In 1993, a Fundamentalist church in Colorado Springs made news when it lured children to "The World's Largest Water Fight," a carnival promising free candy and a squirt-gun battle. But when the children arrived, they were lectured that without baptism they wouldn't be allowed into heaven; then they were stripped and immersed in a tank. Angry parents threatened to sue. One of the organizers defended his group's zeal on the grounds that the children, some as young as five, were free to make their own decision. "Just as Adam blamed Eve and Eve blamed the serpent, they're blaming us for their own choice," he said.[2]

How can this ancient ritual continue to inspire such fervency? We have long since made do without animal sacrifice. Why does baptism still hold such symbolic power for so many of us?

The simple answer, of course, is found in the New Testament: John did it to Jesus. But that merely leads to other questions. What drove John out into the wilderness in the first place? Why did people from all over Judea travel on foot or by mule across miles of punishing desert to experience his curious ritual? And what brought one young man all the way from Nazareth, eighty miles to the north, into the blinding Dead Sea wasteland?

One way to answer these questions is via politics. While the Jews of the previous century were settling into a love-hate relationship with their Hasmonean rulers, a much larger force was sweeping across the Mediterranean world. By 133 B.C.E., Rome had expanded its empire from the Italian peninsula as far west as Spain and as far east as Asia Minor. Over the ensuing decades, the Empire steadily wrapped itself around virtually the entire perimeter of the Mediterranean, encompassing southern Europe, North Africa, and the Middle East. The sliver of land called Palestine was bypassed for a time as the Romans found it expedient to avoid the odd sect that lived there, with its volatile mix of nationalism and monotheism.

But they couldn't hold themselves back forever. The invasion of Palestine finally occurred in 63 B.C.E., when General Pompey and several thousands of his troops came down from Damascus to Jerusalem. Pompey was preparing to storm the massive walls of the Temple, and the Jews within were steeling themselves for a long battle, when the general came across a curious piece of hearsay and decided to test it. The Jews, he was told, were forbidden to do any labor, including defending a city, on the seventh day of their week. Pompey attacked on the Sabbath; the Jews did not resist, though they did resume their ferocious defense the following day, by which time the Romans had gained the upper hand. In all, twelve thousand Jews died trying to defend their capital.

What odd manner of people was this? Pompey was intrigued. After he had won the day, and while Jews all around him wailed and pleaded, he nonchalantly, in fine Roman fashion, marched straight into their Temple: past the inscriptions warning that non-Jews were forbidden to enter upon pain of death, past the slab of gray rock which according to ancient legend was the very spot where Abraham had been prepared to slay his son Isaac in obedience to his God, and where daily animal sacrifices were now carried out. Then, to the righteous fury of the cowering priests, he proceeded into the innermost chamber, the Holy of Holies, the very heart of the Temple, the place forbidden to all but the high priest himself, and even then only one day per year. Here, the general assumed, he would encounter the marble bird or bronze horse or golden ape that this particular variety of barbarian worshipped. Here he would find some answers.

Instead, to his amazement, Pompey found himself standing in an empty room. He was even more confused than before. These Jews had fought tooth and nail to defend *this*? No one offered to explain to him that God the almighty Creator, whose very name was too holy to speak, was also too terrible in majesty for depiction. That was the secret wisdom at the heart of Judaism: God was not the god of this or that, of fire or rain or the harvest or the seasons; He was All.

Pompey's curiosity was short-lived. He left the Temple and demanded the heads of the Jewish military leaders. Roman rule had begun.[3]

The Romans kept the Hasmoneans nominally in power. Most importantly, the family retained control of the Temple priesthood. Then in 40 B.C.E. a conniving Idumean half-Jew, a commoner who had insinuated himself into the dynasty, befriended the powerful Roman general Marc Antony and traveled with him to Rome, where he prostrated himself before Caesar and the Senate, put forth the case that he was the best man to drag the feral Jewish race into civilized vassaldom, and emerged with as much power as a Jew could expect under Roman rule, and a coveted title: King Herod.

Herod has been given short shrift by history. He was clearly one of the most brilliant leaders of antiquity: a shrewd general, a man with such an understanding of commerce that he turned Judea into one of the major trading nations of the Empire, and the greatest builder in the ancient world. Perhaps the fact that in his increasingly obsessive fear of assassination he murdered three of his sons, his wife, his wife's grandfather, and his brother-in-law accounts for the unsavory reputation history has left him with. (Augustus is reported to have remarked that it was better to be Herod's pig than Herod's son.)

The reign of Herod the Great transformed Judea. Wealth flooded the land—though it was overwhelmingly concentrated among the aristocracy. These powerful families became even more hellenized, their palaces outfitted with colonnaded courts and Roman-style baths and decorated with mosaics and frescoes. The landscape of the country changed as Herod built magnificent cities on the Greek model, added temples, baths, fountains, and marketplaces to existing ones, and a system of aqueducts to ensure the most technologically advanced water supply that money could buy.

In Jerusalem, he constructed a theater and ampitheater, and an elaborate palace for himself overlooking the city. But the centerpiece of Herod's passion for architecture was the rebuilt Temple. Eternally torn between his own hellenistic tastes and a desire to appease his subjects, he apparently calculated that by reimagining the center of Jewish worship on a mammoth scale he would win the hearts of the people. The work took nearly sixty years, and in splendor and sheer grandiosity the completed project ranked alongside the wonders of the ancient world. The complex was so vast it redefined the topography of the city, extending the hillside well into the Kidron Valley. Such a colossally difficult engineering project required massive new supporting walls, which remain one of the most distinctive features of Jerusalem to this day. The upper portions of the Western Wall (the "Wailing Wall" in older nomenclature) and its extension were added on by the Crusader kings of Jerusalem; Herod's lower portion is clearly defined by the enormous stones he used to manage the stress. The largest of these has been estimated to weigh 415 tons; to put that in perspective, the largest stone in the Pyramids is estimated at about fifteen tons. If historians debate how the Egyptians moved the stones used in building the Pyramids, they are utterly at a loss to figure out how Herod transported such weights, weights that even today would tax the heaviest of heavy-duty equipment.[4]

Israeli archaeologists are now in the midst of excavations around the base of the Temple that give real glimpses of this monumental structure and its surroundings as John and Jesus would have seen them. On the southwest side, they have dug thirty feet below the present ground level to lay bare the paving stones of one of two Herodian streets that ran along the Temple wall; to one side are the foundations and stone beams and lintels of shops that lined the street. Yaakov Billig of the Israel Antiquities Authority, who with Ronnie Reich is excavating the area, envisions the first-century city clearly: "This was downtown Jerusalem. There would have been thousands of people going back and forth along here. You can just imagine that here they sold the sesame bagels and postcards and whatever by-products were necessary for changing money and giving sacrifices at the Temple."

And if the massive wall rising above this ancient shopping mall isn't enough to impress one with the magnitude of Herod's achievement, Billig and his colleagues have also unearthed an ancient tunnel, which runs twenty feet below street level. "The Western Wall went beyond the natural valley," he said, "so after it would rain, the water was going to come down along here. You have to have a good drainage system, and this is it." The archaeologists have followed the drainage tunnel hundreds of feet in each direction from the southwest corner and still haven't reached the end, and all that way it is roofed by an exquisitely laid arch of bricks: the work of hundreds of toiling laborers and skilled masons, all hidden from view for two thousand years.

The Temple was as much a monument to Herod as anything else, and he evidently couldn't resist the impulse to make it reflect his cosmopolitan proclivities. He tricked it out with Corinthian columns and gold friezes, and over the main gate he installed a massive golden eagle. The Jews were as scandalized by the impiety—"graven images" in the Temple!—as they were puffed with pride by the grandeur of the place. In fact, to the common people—the people who were left out of Herod's "economic miracle"—these ungodly ornamentations spoke as clearly as anything of the increasing wickedness and contamination of the nation under Herod.

And there's the rub: according to one prominent view, the prosperity that Herod brought about, part of an economic upturn throughout the Empire, actually made life worse for Judean and Galilean peasants. Over the past decade or so, New Testament scholars have expanded their bag of tools for exploring Jesus' time and place, and one of the most prominent of these is anthropological modeling. The thinking goes that studies of peasant societies around the world—from contemporary Latin America to nineteenth-century Russia to the ancient Near East—can shed light on one another. This is a controversial approach, but for scholars who follow it, it puts the railing oratory of the biblical prophets—from the Old Testament to John and Jesus—in a new perspective.

In all of these peasant societies, according to the model, the rulers and property owners generally comprise about eight percent of the population; the ninety-odd percent who work the land end up paying a full two-thirds of their crops to these elites, in the form of taxes or rent.[5] In Palestine, this would surely have been onerous, but it was a system that endured for centuries—until the Romans arrived. In Judea and Galilee, peasant farmers had always paid taxes, but there were built-in reprieves, such as an exemption every seventh year. What's more, according to Leviticus 25:23, "The land shall not be sold in perpetuity, for the land is mine . . ." The ancient Jewish idea of real estate would thus have been far removed from Roman legalism, and considerably closer to the notion of

American Indians such as the Shawnee chief Tecumseh: "Sell a country? Why not sell the air, the great sea, as well as the earth?"

Rome rolled over this quaintly traditional system like a tank through a wheat field. The Romans added their own tax to that of the Jewish authorities; Herod enforced Rome's decrees with grim efficiency. The burden for the peasants became excruciating, and anyone not able to pay up lost his land. Subsistence-level farmers became the homeless people of the Empire.[6]

This, according to some scholars, is what underlies the rise of first-century Jewish prophets. But not everyone agrees with the scenario. "Modern New Testament scholars often imagine that Palestinian Jewish farmers were taxed more viciously than any other people," writes E. P. Sanders. "On the contrary, they were almost certainly better off than Egyptian peasants, and they were probably better off than Syrian peasants."[7] Paula Fredriksen takes issue with the whole idea of applying data about Nicaraguan peasants to Jesus' time. "There is a kind of methodological chutzpah to it," she said in an interview, "a conviction that the evidence is imperfect but you can take a method and superimpose it over what we have and rely on it to fill in the holes. I think this is incautious and unwarranted as a procedure."

These criticisms may be valid, but, as far as scholar Marcus Borg is concerned, the value is in the results. The cross-cultural model actually offers a decent explanation for what made prophets like John and Jesus so attractive: people were in agony, and these men offered a way out. Beyond this, this approach clarifies another point. The old thinking was that John and Jesus were railing against Israel, as if the nation itself and its religion had become corrupt. This fed the prevailing idea in Christianity that it had superseded Judaism. "Then," writes Borg, "some ten to fifteen years ago, as models of peasant societies began to have an effect on biblical scholarship, the awareness that ancient Israel was a two-class society divided between oppressive urban elites and exploited rural peasants generated a very different perception of the prophetic message. Their indictments were directed not at *Israel,* but at the elites in particular."[8]

What such work is trying to do is pull back from the tight focus on the text of the Bible and see Jesus in a larger context. Burton Mack gives an even wider angle. This entire period in history, Mack argues, is governed by one major force: the devastation of ancient societies, first by Alexander the Great and then by the Romans. When the armies of these great conquerers engulfed Egypt, Syria, Palestine, and other regions, resulting in mass dislocation and enslavement, ancient cultures fell apart. These cultures had tied together religion and economics: people paid both taxes and homage to their ruler. Now, without their time-honored support systems, people all over the Mediterranean were floundering, searching for meaning. Mystery cults, in which displaced people gathered to worship a god of their ancestors and hoped to extract answers from him or her, flourished at this time. According to Mack, Jesus' career, and its later startling success, can be attributed to this cross-cultural hunger for meaning, a need to find truth in the old ways.[9]

At any rate, when Herod died in 4 B.C.E., five days after murdering his heir, the dispossessed saw the chaos in leadership as an opportunity. As the shriveled body of the monarch was placed on a solid gold bier, draped with purple cloth and sprinkled with gems, minor rebellions went off like celebratory firecrackers throughout Palestine. Archelaus, one of Herod's sons who managed to avoid his father's deadly embrace, ascended to the throne and, having apparently first asked himself what his father would do, decided that the most prudent way to deal with an unruly mob in Jerusalem was to send his entire army out to slaughter them. Three thousand were killed.[10] Archelaus has gone down in history as an impressive footnote: he was so tyrannical that the Jews actually begged Rome to take direct charge of them, rather than leave them in his hands. Augustus eventually decided to bring Judea under direct Roman rule, to be carried out through a Senate-appointed prefect. In 26 C.E., Pontius Pilate would become the fifth man to hold this increasingly difficult post.

Augustus also split Galilee off from Judea and gave charge of it to one of Herod's other sons, Herod Antipas, who would last much longer as a leader. He would not be king, however, but would hold the title of tetrarch, again reflecting Rome's tighter rein.

So the Roman presence became more pronounced in Palestine beginning right about the time of Jesus' birth. And Roman justice, and Roman punishment, held sway, as the excavation of a cemetery in northern Jerusalem indicates. A team from Hadassah Medical School performed belated autopsies on thirty-five Roman-era bodies, presumably of Jews who had fallen afoul of the authorities. One had had her skull shattered; a young man had been slowly roasted to death; a four-year-old died of an arrow shot to the skull. We will look more carefully at the most famous find, the body of a man in his twenties who was crucified right around the time of Jesus' crucifixion, in a later chapter.[11]

So then, as Judea became more prominent as a Roman client state, two internal forces grew. A small but increasingly ferocious nationalistic resistance movement developed, which looked to the days of the Maccabees' victory for inspiration. And a new crop of homegrown prophets and magicians sprang up throughout the land, warning of evil times ahead. Several names, each with a few stories attached, come down to us. Honi the Circle Drawer, Bannus, Hanina ben Dosa: men with no ties to Temple authority but with a personal channel to God, which enabled them to predict coming disaster and to perform miracles. The commoners regarded these individuals as folk heroes who proved that God's grace came not necessarily through the corrupt establishment channels—the ruler or the priests of the Temple—but with a kind of mysterious democracy. As oppressive conditions grew, stories of these heroes' pious forbearance from the everyday world took on more resonance. Typical is one in which Hanina ben Dosa was once seen deep in prayer as a poisonous snake coiled around his ankle. The holy man did not interrupt his prayer, and the snake bit him. Onlookers were amazed when the snake promptly died. "It is not the snake that kills," said the unruffled holy man, "but sin."[12]

All of these prophets attracted followings. But John the Baptist was different. And so we come back to the question: Why him? What made him stand out from the crowd of other magicians and sages who populated the increasingly angst-ridden landscape of Herod's Palestine? His message was a brand of apocalyptic eschatology: the certainty that the world, so clogged with corruption, was about to come to an end, and only those who followed the correct path—*his* path—would end up on the right side of things. He was, by all accounts, a hell-and-brimstone kind of guy. But so, anciently, was Elijah; so was Jeremiah. Prophets of doom, castigating Israel for straying from the way of the Lord, for succumbing to the customs of the Gentiles, had been around for centuries. What was different about John? Was it that with the coming of the Romans and their newer, state-of-the-art kind of repression, the people were all the more ready for a scorching visionary?

That no doubt played a part. But there was something more, something that shoots a ray of insight straight to the historical Jesus, his career, and his execution. Morton Smith put his finger on it: "By John's time," Smith wrote, "the only place in the country where Jews could legally offer sacrifices was Jerusalem, and its services were expensive. To introduce into this situation a new, inexpensive, generally available, divinely authorized rite, effective for the remission of all sins, was John's great invention."[13]

In other words, John's baptism was a total package: besides offering spiritual succor, it packed a political and economic punch. Jews were supposed to make a pilgrimage to the Temple in Jerusalem three times a year, for the festivals of Booths, Weeks, and Passover, where they mollified the Lord and demonstrated their gratitude to Him by making sacrifice. The animal one sacrificed was directly related to one's financial status, and in turn reflected how much respect one got from one's neighbors. A well-to-do family purchased a calf; two pigeons was a poor man's sacrifice. It was all perfectly legitimate: a part of the purity system that had been in existence for centuries. But geopolitics had changed, and that meant change in the local economy. Control of the Temple had evolved into a kind of dictatorship; like the popes of the Middle Ages selling indulgences, the priests of the Temple exploited their monopoly. What was happening, in this reading, seems fairly clear: as religion is used as a form of political and economic control, a pious but poor people's blood pressure begins to rise.

If this theory is anywhere near correct, then John's genius, John's audacity, was to attempt to short-circuit this system. In doing so, and doing so with considerable popular success, he would have raised the immediate attention of the Sanhedrin, the politburo of ruling priests and leaders of Judea. Any follower of John's who went on to success in his own right would also warrant automatic monitoring. Here then were the roots of the political suspicion of Jesus. John was a direct threat to the Temple, the center of power in Palestine. Merely by associating with John one became a dangerous character.

Where did John come from? Needless to say, the stories that link his miraculous birth to a woman past menopause with

Jesus' divine birth to a virgin are not considered historical. But a growing minority of scholarship is coalescing around another conclusion regarding John's origins. Consider that, like the Essenes at Qumran, John believed the End was at hand. Like the Essenes, John declared that he had been sent into the wilderness to prepare the way of the Lord. Both John and the Essenes of Qumran saw the world as sharply divided. There was Good and there was Evil. Nothing lay in between. The sectarian scrolls found at Qumran make this dualism very plain: "[God] has created man to govern the world, and has appointed for him two spirits in which to walk until the time of His visitation: the spirits of truth and falsehood. Those born of truth spring from a fountain of light, but those born of falsehood spring from a source of darkness."[14] The Essenes called themselves "the Sons of Light." Both the fourth gospel and Paul's writings, possibly reflecting language inherited from the Baptist, see the followers of Jesus as "the sons of the light."[15] Nowhere else in Jewish literature is this phrase used.

Most strikingly, the Essenes, obsessed as they were with purity and cleansing as they atoned for the moral filth all around them and prepared for the coming End, practiced a ritual baptism, a modified form of the ritual bath common in ancient Judaism.

For the German New Testament authority Otto Betz, the French scholar Jean Steinmann, famed Israeli archaeologist Yigael Yadin and others, this evidence points to one conclusion: "I believe that John grew up as an Essene," writes Betz, "probably in the desert settlement at Qumran. Then he heard a special call of God; he became independent of the community—perhaps even more than the Essene prophets described by Josephus. With his baptism of repentance, John addressed all Israel directly; he wanted to serve his people and to save as many of them as possible."[16]

Geography also inclines one to link John and the Essenes. Both located themselves in the same punishing, forbidding wilderness:

the Dead Sea desert east of Jerusalem and south of Jericho, a landscape nearly devoid of life, human or otherwise. Luke says that John was born to a priest named Zechariah and that "the child grew and gained strength and spirit, and he was in the desert places until the day of his manifestation to Israel."[17] While it is generally believed that the account of John's birth is more theologically driven than anything else, Luke seems to have had no particular reason for inventing the statement that John grew up "in the desert places." And add to that the fact that Josephus tells us the Essenes, who were celibate, increased their numbers by adopting young boys and training them in their ways. And note also the interesting point that the Essenes were known to have kept bees and eaten locusts, which coincides rather neatly with John's famous diet of "locusts and wild honey."

This speculative scenario, then, has the son of a priest—perhaps the old man had died—being adopted by the pious ascetics of the desert. Now imagine the boy grown. He has soaked in much of the Essene doctrine: he has the holy fire in the belly, the certainty that wickedness had fallen like a hammer on Israel, that among the most defiled were those in control of the Temple, the belief that only the "Sons of Light" would remain once God has done his terrible cleansing.

Skeptical scholars point out the many differences between John and the Qumran sect. For one, the Essene literature is simply mad with ritual observances: holy days, angel names, purity rites, orders of rank. There are rules for how and what to eat, how and when to relieve oneself. John, however, is the ultimate iconoclast. He has only one rule—"repent"—and only one ritual. The Qumran baptism, skeptics note, was a routine washing, and each priest washed himself. John's baptism, of course, was a single, life-altering event, and John himself administered it.

But these differences between John and the Essenes hardly

seem to distance John from the community. In fact, they could easily be seen as linking him to Qumran: Who but a disillusioned follower would adhere to the program so closely, yet change it where he thought it went astray? Steinmann argues that John became "a dissident of Essenism."[18]

One might imagine John struggling with the elitist nature of the Qumran rites: they were for none but the elect. The end of the world was coming, and this small group in the wilderness knew how to prepare for it *but would not share the saving knowledge.* In this scenario, John would have to have been something of a man of the people. *Why,* he might have asked the leaders of the sect, *do we keep this wisdom to ourselves? If Israel is at risk, why can't we warn her?* To the morally intractable priests, nearly two centuries of isolation in the desert—two centuries of perfecting their purity in order to set themselves apart from those who had usurped the Temple in the time of the Maccabees, and from the rest of the Jews, who had continued to do obesience at the defiled Temple—to the Essenes, these long decades of separation had reinforced their belief in their own spiritual superiority. Those outside their walls were so unclean they were beyond salvation.

And so, in a moment lost to history but a moment of supreme historical import, John walked away, and into the desert. What did he feel upon leaving the confines of the fortress-like compound? A sudden giddiness, a loss of bearings? Did he look heavenward, half-expecting the End to come at that moment in a sudden rending of earth and sky? Or had his belief undergone a change? Had he worked out that the apocalypse would require a catalyst, someone to start a flood of holiness that would engulf the wicked? Had God by now communicated to him that it was his special role to enlist volunteers for this cause?

For, as some see it, in John's mind the sword of righteousness that would smite the wicked would be held in a human hand. The apocalypse wouldn't rain down from the sky; it would come as a holy war. The model, it seems, was none other than the foundational story of the Jews: the story of the Exodus and the conquest of the Promised Land. Joshua had led the wandering Israelites in the holy attack on Jericho that had delivered them into Canaan in fulfillment of Yahweh's promise to Abraham. Several other first-century apocalyptic prophets had tried to reenact this most revered of events by leading bandit assaults on Roman-occupied Jerusalem, believing they were empowered by God. Their attacks failed. John apparently did not fancy himself a general. He heard the Voice, but it didn't order him to attack, only to prepare the way.

As Crossan has it, John's program was thus far more threatening to the Roman authorities than that of any ragtag band of peasants. Those could be simply dealt with. But John was something different. "John plants ticking time bombs of apocalyptic expectation all over the Jewish homeland," Crossan writes. "That left Antipas no crowd to strike at, so he struck at John himself."[19]

This is something we tend to gloss over in considering the New Testament period. We think of apocalyptic oratory as a kind of fad, a sign of the times. But it was more than a sign; to people like John, *God was really coming to smite the wicked.* And it would happen soon.

So then, if something like this was in John's mind, if he was about to begin warning the Jews and initiating them into a holy cause, what was the most likely context? Where should he base himself?

Did it even require a moment's thought? After the Exodus, after the forty years in the wilderness, Joshua had led the Israelites across it and into the Promised Land. Elijah had ascended to heaven from its banks. Elisha had cured a leper by having him wash in its holy waters.[20] *The River Jordan.* All Israel recognized the sacred role the

Jordan had played in their history. It was God's river. Really, there was no other choice for a would-be baptizer.

And so John began preaching. No one knows where along the river was the exact spot of his baptizing, though tour guides today will be glad to show it to you. But the main geographical fact is clear: John located himself miles from the nearest town and twenty-five miles from the main population center of Jerusalem—an excruciating twenty-five miles across a deadly desert. Even today, driving the stretch, one gazes out across dunes that are the very definition of barrenness, one's hand fiddling with the air-conditioning vent, and stray thoughts of panic rising up: What if we break down here? There is nothing, *nothing* out there but a sledgehammer sun. And despite this fantastically out-of-the-way location, or perhaps because of it, the people came. A trickle at first, then more, and finally "the people of Jerusalem and all Judea were going out to him, and all the region along the Jordan, and they were baptized by him in the river Jordan, confessing their sins."[21] Clearly, it was a time of such turmoil, such yearning, that one who hasn't lived through war or famine or political repression can scarcely imagine it. And John pressed the right buttons, said just what the people longed to hear: that there was a way out. They came to him in droves.

And one day, in one of the many groups arriving from the west, there was a young man from Galilee. A laborer, the son of a laborer, whose life to this point had mostly been spent in his hometown of Nazareth, with perhaps regular trips to the nearby Roman city. A sharply intelligent young man who had grown to adulthood within the bosom of his community, experiencing Roman rule and Greek culture but remaining true to Jewish life. A man who until now evinced no special interest in apocalyptic fire, for Mark says that when he returned home to Nazareth it was as if no one knew him: "They said, 'Where did this man get all this?

What is this wisdom that has been given to him? . . . Is this not the carpenter, the son of Mary . . . ?' "[22]

What made him come out into the desert? Was he merely going to see what all the fuss was about? No doubt John was the talk of the streets in Jerusalem, where Jesus may have traveled for the festival. On the other hand, if Matthew is correct—"Then Jesus came from Galilee to John at the Jordan . . ."[23]—then the Baptist's fame had spread all the way to Galilee, and Jesus had made the eighty-odd-mile trek just to see this new prophet. What would cause him to undertake such a journey? Had something happened that awakened a sudden yearning inside Jesus, something that drove him to seek out the fire-breathing prophet on the shores of the Jordan?

We will never know, but Stevan Davies suggests one possibility. It is, Davies asserts, "historical nonsense to think that it was only *after* his baptism for the repentance of his sins that Jesus *began* to be the sort of person who might be accused of being 'a glutton and a drunkard and a friend of tax collectors and sinners.' "[24] In other words, since the gospels make clear that the post-baptism Jesus was no ascetic like the prophets of old—he went to feasts, drank wine, associated with prostitutes and lowlifes—why should we assume that his pre-baptism lifestyle was any different? Might it not, then, have been disgust with a dissolute lifestyle that led him to a search for meaning? This is pure speculation, but speculation that has occurred to scholars for decades, for it fits with several other traditions: that, against the overwhelming cultural pressure, Jesus seems never to have married; that, as the gospels indicate, there was tension between him and the rest of his family ("not even his brothers believed in him,"[25] says the fourth gospel); that his father may have died when Jesus was a child or that, in a somewhat more tenuous argument, the boy was born illegitimate.

This sort of reading-between-the-lines will never be verifiable;

at the very least, though, it reminds us of the vast psychological depths that were surely a part of the historical Jesus' makeup. That is, we will never know why Jesus went in search of John, but there *was* a reason, one that had to do with the kind of person he had been up to that time.

If John had been raised in the desert, if he did indeed wear the garb of the wilderness ("clothing of camel's hair with a leather belt around his waist"[26]), if he was infused with the spirit of God, a spirit that shone in his eyes with such intensity that people readily acknowledged his special connection to holiness, then he must have presented quite a sight to this young man from the north. "Repent!" was his cry, which sounded across the empty sweeps of desert. "Repent, for the kingdom of heaven has come near!" So filled was he with the Other, so removed was he from the day-to-day world, that he lashed out not just at the rich priests sitting comfortably in their lavish houses in Jerusalem, but at his own "audience," those who had ventured all this way to see him. "You brood of vipers!" he called them. "Who warned you to flee from the wrath to come?" No one would escape that wrath—and being one of the Chosen would not matter: "Do not presume to say to yourselves, 'We have Abraham as our ancestor'; for I tell you, God is able from these stones to raise up children to Abraham." His voice bore a tone of absolute certainty about what was imminent: "Even now the ax is lying at the root of the trees; every tree therefore that does not bear good fruit is cut down and thrown into the fire."[27]

All of this, most scholars agree, is most likely authentic dialogue, as is what immediately follows—scorching words, words that have seared their way through history:

> I baptize you with water for repentance, but one who is more powerful than I is coming after me; I am not

> worthy to carry his sandals. He will baptize you with the Holy Spirit and fire. His winnowing fork is in his hand, and he will clear his threshing floor and will gather his wheat into the granary; but the chaff he will burn with unquenchable fire.[28]

The major point to note about this ringing passage is that it would make perfect sense even if Jesus of Nazareth had never existed. Today we read "one who is more powerful than I is coming" and think "Jesus." But that is only because of the redactional work of the evangelists; it is only because of material that scholars are in agreement is of considerably later vintage. Who else could John have had in mind? Obviously, any apocalyptic prophet believed that *God* was coming to wreak holy havoc.[29]

Scholars feel certain John's message as recorded above is reasonably authentic because these passages are preserved in *all* of the early traditions—in all four gospels, the sayings collection known as Q, and in the Acts of the Apostles—and they are so preserved *despite the fact that they present early Christianity with a huge headache.*

The nature of that headache becomes clear from what follows in the Synoptics. "Then Jesus came from Galilee to John at the Jordan, to be baptized by him," says Matthew. And there is the difficulty. "Right at the beginning of the ministry of Jesus stands the independent ministry of the independent Baptist," writes John Meier, "a Jewish prophet who started his ministry before and apart from Jesus, who won great popularity and reverence apart from Jesus, *who also won the reverence and submission of Jesus* . . ."[30] That last clause, which I have italicized, points to what made the early church leaders writhe. One could not have one's divine figure bowing down before a mere prophet. The fact that this scene is depicted in the gospels argues strongly in favor of its authenticity under the criterion of embarrassment: it certainly wasn't invented by the evangelists, so it must be there because it was too well established to leave it out altogether.

So they put a spin on it—or, rather, various spins. In Mark, the earliest, there is the simple statement, "In those days Jesus came from Nazareth of Galilee and was baptized by John in the Jordan."[31] By Matthew's time this had evidently begun to cause problems, so Matthew invented a reluctance for John, implicitly acknowledging his inferiority: "I need to be baptized by you, and do you come to me?"[32] Luke raises the ante on Matthew by declaring in his gospel that the fetal Baptist "leaped for joy" in his mother's womb when he learned of the conception of the supremely superior Jesus.[33] By the time of the fourth gospel, even this was not a sufficient degrading of the status of the Baptist: the Gospel of John omits Jesus' baptism altogether.

So the texts come 180 degrees around: from simple declaration of an event to an apology for it to extravagant apology for it to suppression of it. What underlies these texts, aside from simple embarrassment, is the need to make a kind of political point, a point that few Christians today realize the need for, though the evidence for it is clear enough in the Bible. The historical John was a figure of so much greater renown than the New Testament makes him out to be that for much of the first century his followers rivaled Jesus'. Because of this, the evangelists go out of their way to elevate Jesus and lower John, when the likelihood was that for a time Jesus was the disciple and John the master.

It is the fourth gospel, the one many scholars in the past disregarded as largely unhistorical, that gives us insights into this. While the Synoptics present an order of events that has become well known—Jesus is baptized, then immediately leaves John and spends forty days in the wilderness, then John is arrested by Herod Antipas, then Jesus begins his ministry—the fourth gospel gives a totally different scenario, one that two thousand years of tradition have conveniently ignored but that scholars are beginning to line up behind.

First, that gospel puts Jesus on the scene of John's baptizing at the Jordan (without mentioning Jesus being baptized) for at least several days. At one point during this time several of John's disciples—one of them is none other than Simon Peter—decide to follow Jesus. Later, when Jesus decides to go to Galilee to begin his own ministry, these men go with him.

In contrast to the Synoptic picture, this Jesus is clearly a part of John's group for a time. And where the Synoptics have him gathering disciples as he goes about his teaching in Galilee, here it seems they were all originally followers of John.

Later, the gospel reports that Jesus and his disciples go from Galilee back into Judea, and "he spent some time there with them and baptized."[34] The interesting item here is that *Jesus is baptizing*: in other words, this Jesus does not simply go to John for a ritual cleansing and then begin his own very different ministry of healing and teaching. This Jesus is a baptizing prophet, just like John.

Not only that, but while he is in Judea we learn that "John was also baptizing" nearby. In fact, some of John's disciples come to him and complain about the competition: "Rabbi, the one who was with you across the Jordan, to whom you testified, here he is baptizing, and all are going to him."[35] Later, Jesus himself overhears a rumor that "Jesus is making and baptizing more disciples than John."[36]

So here we have a very different scenario from the traditional one, a scenario in which Jesus is first a disciple of John, then leaves his master in order to do his own baptizing while John is continuing his work. In this scenario, Jesus, like John, is an apocalyptic prophet offering an unofficial service—an unauthorized brush of holiness—that competes with the establishment in the Temple. This may seem scandalous to those committed to the traditional version, in which a glassy-eyed, all-knowing Son of God submits to the ritual of baptism, blesses his baptizer for performing the function that the Father in his mystery had ordained, then gets on with his true mission. But to anyone interested in a historical Jesus, this fourth gospel view of events may seem more human. It fits a familiar pattern: all great teachers once learned at the foot of a master before striking out on their own, perhaps eventually to outshine their teacher. In this account, Jesus apprentices himself to John, learns what John has to teach, then reaches a decision to start baptizing others on his own.

What this summary leaves out is that other substance that New Testament scholarship is concerned with: holiness, spirit. Criticism alone can't get at the spirit world, but it seems necessary to note that by not treating the spiritual side of things scholarship does not deny it. The scholars are simply sensitive to the occupational hazard, afraid of getting their work tarred with the epithet *theology*. For this reason, they typically glide past the passage in Mark describing the wondrous effect of Jesus' baptism: "And just as he was coming up out of the water, he saw the heavens torn apart and the Spirit descending like a dove on him. And a voice came from heaven, 'You are my Son, the Beloved; with you I am well pleased.' "[37] If they say anything about this passage, biblical experts merely note that the words of God here seem clearly lifted from Psalm 2, in which God tells a king of Israel: "You are my son; today I have begotten you . . ."[38] Otherwise, it is passed over—it's simply too theological.

But who is to say that this passage isn't a decent attempt to portray in words and images a real experience that transcends reason? It would be foolish to deny that Jesus had a genuine conversion experience that day in the Jordan. How else can one explain what he later became, what he did and said, the effect he had on others?

All of the features of a classic religious awakening—what William James calls a sudden conversion—are here. James notes them in *The Varieties of Religious Experience,* probably the most influential book ever written on religion and psychology: "Voices are often heard, lights seen, or visions witnessed; automatic motor phenomena occur; and it always seems, after the surrender of the personal will, as if an extraneous higher power had flooded in and taken possession. Moreover the sense of renovation, safety, cleanness, rightness can be so marvelous and jubilant as well to warrant one's belief in a radically new substantial nature."[39]

That the historical Jesus found holiness in the Jordan seems an unqualified certainty. Scholars are not afraid to acknowledge this, but they tend to be wary of doing anything with it. Besides that, "holiness" changes as it is defined by an evangelical Christian, a Buddhist, a psychologist. One commentator might say that Jesus underwent a psychological transformation, another that he became possessed by the Holy Spirit; in either reading the historical Jesus becomes in effect the first "born-again" Christian, or pre-Christian.

At any rate, the evidence that is inclining many scholars toward the fourth gospel's version of the events surrounding the relationship between Jesus and John is extremely complicated, but it has to do with a posited "final redactor" of various early versions of the fourth gospel, an editor who tried to smooth over embarrassing patches. The key is a phrase that this redactor evidently added at John 4:2: ". . . although it was not Jesus himself but his disciples who baptized . . ."[40] This is so at odds with the previous verses that many authorities have become convinced this editor was trying to whitewash the record.

The reason the redactor felt the need to do this, scholars hold, is that the early community served by the fourth gospel—possibly in Ephesus—found itself faced with a competing community: a group who had remained loyal to the Baptist. Non-Christian and even anti-Christian groups of Baptist followers continued to exist well into the second century. In Acts (19:1–7) Paul, traveling in Ephesus, meets a group whom he first thinks are Christians. "He said to them, 'Did you receive the Holy Spirit when you became believers?' They replied, 'No, we have not even heard that there is a Holy Spirit.' Then he said, 'Into what then were you baptized?' They answered, 'Into John's baptism.' "

As Meier puts it, the editor of the fourth gospel "is negating a tradition that could play into the hands of the Baptist sectarians," a tradition that "puts Jesus too much in the permanent shadow of the Baptist," so that "Jesus begins to look like the Baptist's disciple, imitator, and (ungrateful) rival."[41] According to many scholars, this tradition, so fearful to the early Christians, just happens to have been true.

So then, some time after Jesus has left his mentor and is performing his own baptism, the political nature of John's ritual catches up with him. John has by now moved north to Galilee and has brought his considerable fame with him. Antipas has heard of him, may even have had a run-in with him, for Mark reports the reason Antipas finally takes John prisoner is that John has chastised him for taking his brother's wife as his own. It is more likely that Antipas feared John's ability to organize discontent into revolution. As Josephus tells us, Antipas worried that John's movement "might lead to some form of sedition, for it looked as if [the people] would be guided by John in everything that they did. Herod decided therefore that it would be much better to strike first and be rid of him before his work led to an uprising . . ."[42]

And so the Baptist was captured, led away in chains, and finally put to death. But not before he had made his impact. The fact that he stirred Antipas to move against him, the attention Josephus gives him in his history of the Jews, the existence of sects devoted to him long after his death all indicate that he was a figure of far greater renown than the gospels give him credit for—that he was, in fact, a celebrity in ancient Palestine. The historical John was subservient to no one but his God, whom he waited for but who never came, at least not in the way he expected.

One measure of the fame he gained throughout Palestine and beyond is the fact that he was one of the few people in antiquity to be nicknamed. He wasn't merely "the prophet John"; in his own lifetime he received an epithet all his own: *baptistes.* From the Greek verb *baptein,* akin to the Latin *immergere,* immerse. Or, as Meier translates it, "the dipper." He achieved immortality of a kind, both through and alongside his chief follower. His desert ritual—so simple and yet so evocative in its symbolism of cleansing and rebirth—would become the principal ceremony of initiation into a global church, though he would surely have been bewildered by the post-Constantine spin it received: ". . . in the name of the Father and of the Son and of the Holy Spirit." Nevertheless, two thousand years after his death, a baby born in Santiago or Oslo or Manila or Gdansk or Tallahassee probably won't get too far along in life before it feels John's mellifluous caress and is welcomed into one of the world's largest clubs.

Meanwhile, as he broke free of John's orbit, Jesus began his own teaching, which, while based on John's, quickly developed into something far grander, far more elegant and ornate and puzzling than the straightforward "repent or die" of his mentor. Looked at one way, it was a message so simple that for some of his followers it was like a light switch turning on. But others, including those closest to him, seemed to find it endlessly confusing—for when they asked him when the kingdom of God, the kingdom John had foretold, would come, he said it was already here.

CHAPTER SIX

"SOME FABULOUS YONDER"

And so Jesus went north to Galilee. He chose not to base himself in his hometown, however, but twenty miles away in the village of Capernaum. Today Capernaum is a small, ghostly paradise: palm trees, flowering bushes, a serene stretch of water the color of sapphire. A good strong sun shines down. A gentle breeze blows and the palm fronds shudder. No one lives here now—square plots of stones where houses once stood are all that remains of a fishing village that thrived for a thousand years before becoming abandoned in the seventh century. The ruins cover a small peninsula jutting out into the lake—for the Sea of Galilee is not a sea at all but the largest freshwater lake in Israel, and the country's chief water supply.

Israelis call it the Kinneret. In the Bible it is

known variously as the Sea of Chinnereth, Gennesar, the Lake of Gennesaret, and the Sea of Tiberias. The land hugging its southern and western shores—the province of *ha Galil,* the Galilee—is dark, rich, and fertile, just as it was in the first century. Josephus records that the Galilee of his time was "so rich in soil and pasturage and produces such a variety of trees, that even the most indolent are tempted by these facilities to devote themselves to agriculture." Today a drive through Galilee is a tour of Middle Eastern agriculture at its highest level: the soil is worked by computerized tractors developed from the Merhava battle tank; vineyards, apple orchards, and orange plantations are elaborately irrigated.

Standing at Capernaum you look out across the wide swath of dreamy blue water to the hills rising on the eastern side. Disorientingly enough, these are the Golan Heights. After a lifetime of reading on the one hand about the Holy Land that Jesus trod and on the other about the Six Days' War and the Intifada, it is jarring to take in two such drastically different Israels in one view; somehow one thinks of them as existing on different planes, geographically as well as historically.

According to the best current calculation—that of John Meier, who takes into account everything from the date of Augustus' death to the possibility that the gospel writers used the Syro-Macedonian calendar—Jesus' baptism occurred early in 28 C.E. and he was crucified on April 7, 30 C.E. That kind of specificity gives the appearance of certainty, but Meier himself readily admits it is based on a fair degree of guesswork. Still, it's the best guess we have, and it means that, when he met John, Jesus was about thirty-two years old, and he died at about thirty-four.

This is where Jesus chose to base himself after he had left the Baptist and struck out on his own—on a two-year career that would change the world. He left the Judean desert—filled with a new awareness, a new life, a new sense of purpose—and headed north, homeward. But why to this precise spot? Perhaps because this was where Peter, one of his followers, lived.

Was Peter his closest associate? Every Sunday school child knows that Peter's real name was Simon, that when, in Matthew's gospel, Jesus asks his disciples who they think he is, Simon is the only one to answer: "You are the Messiah, the Son of the living God." Jesus is pleased:

> Blessed are you, Simon son of Jonah! For flesh and blood has not revealed this to you, but my Father in heaven. And I tell you, you are Peter, and on this rock I will build my church, and the gates of Hades will not prevail against it. I will give you the keys of the kingdom of heaven, and whatever you bind on earth will be bound in heaven, and whatever you loose on earth will be loosed in heaven.[1]

Scholars are nearly unanimous in rejecting the historical accuracy of this outpouring of support. The passage, according to the fellows of the Jesus Seminar as expressed in *The Five Gospels,* "undoubtedly reflects Peter's position in Matthew's branch of the emerging Christian movement."[2] Since Matthew's community championed Peter as the inheritor of Jesus' mantle of leadership, in opposition to other groups which followed other disciples, it behooved Matthew to sketch in a bit of dialogue in which Jesus himself appoints Peter as his heir.

But this neat dismissal of a whole chunk of Jesus lore overlooks one point. Until recently, pious scholars seeking to prove the gospels' authenticity had searched in vain for an underlying Aramaic pun to the Greek one in Matthew—*Petros,* Peter, *petra,* rock. But the Dead Sea Scrolls have enriched the known Aramaic vocabulary, and in several scrolls the Aramaic word *kepha* appears, meaning "rock" or "crag." This matches rather dramatically with the fourth gospel's account of this same incident: " 'You are Simon son of John. You are to be called Cephas' (which is translated Peter)."[3] It is curious, then, that if this speech was made up by the gospel writer, who was writing in Greek, the pun also works in Aramaic, the language Jesus spoke, and was even recognized as such in the fourth gospel.

Further, Paul, writing in the 50s, while Peter was still alive, also refers to him repeatedly as Cephas. But if Jesus' language about founding a church is a later invention, and yet he did call Simon Peter or Cephas, what was it meant to signify? That he was solid in his faith? A great and trusted friend? A brawler, the "Rocky" of his time? Or is it a piece of evidence that Jesus expected the kingdom of God to be in some sense an earthly kingdom, to which he was assigning Simon a key position? In any case, we can surmise a close relationship between the two men, which could have accounted for Jesus' decision to come to this particular Galilean village at the beginning of his new life.

Mark (1:29) tells us that Peter and his brother Andrew lived in Capernaum. Jesus visits its synagogue and casts out a demon, and "as soon as they left the synagogue," Mark writes, "they entered the house of Simon and Andrew, with James and John," indicating that the house is very close by. The beautiful remains of a synagogue standing today date from sometime between the third and fifth centuries, but this was built on the ruins of an earlier synagogue, which dates to the time of Jesus. And just a few yards away are the ruins of what many archaeologists believe was the very house of Peter the fisherman.

The finding of fish hooks among its debris might not seem particularly impressive in itself, since the house stands a few feet from the shore of a body of water that even today is positively choked with fish, but an impressive litter of plaster unearthed from inside, dating from the first to the fourth centuries, contains stylized floral crosses, the word *ichthos* ("fish"), and various prayers to Christ. "Fish" was doubly meaningful to the early Christians: first because of the miracle of the loaves and fishes, second because the letters in Greek form an acronym for Jesus Christ Son of God Savior. All of this evidence matches with the report of the fourth-century pilgrim Aetheria, who wrote, "In Capernaum, moreover, out of the house of the first of the apostles a church has been made, the walls of which still stand just as they were."[4]

It's clear that this was one of the earliest sites of Christian pilgrimage, one that has a very high likelihood of dating to Jesus' life. It's too bad that the ruins, which look for all the world as though they long to rest peacefully, are today overpowered by a Catholic church in the shape of a flying saucer which squats four feet above them.

Mark reports that when a crowd in Capernaum asks for Jesus' whereabouts they are told that he is "at home." Joseph Fitzmyer of Catholic University thinks this means that Jesus had his own home in Capernaum.[5] Others think the reference is to Peter's house, but in either case Jesus clearly seems to have set up shop here.

What was his first activity? Did he baptize for a time, as John's gospel suggests? These matters are far less certain. There is widespread agreement among critical scholars that the various chronologies given in the gospels are the work of the gospel writers, each of whom chose an order of events that suited his tale. (This was recognized as early as the second century, when Papias declared that Mark "wrote down accurately, though not in order, what he remembered that the Lord said and did.") So once we come to the career, we can't follow the order of events in any of the gospels. We are left with a collection of random events—comings and goings, miracles performed, stories told, pronouncements made—that we have to make the best of.

One thing that virtually everyone seems to agree on is that whatever else he may have been—prophet, Christ, miracle-worker—Jesus was also a teacher. There were many kinds of teachers in ancient Palestine. The Essenes were elitists, reserving their wisdom for initiates. The Baptist was more democratic. Jesus seems to have followed his mentor in this: whatever fired him, whatever his own spiritual insight was, he clearly felt he had a duty to share it with whoever would listen. When you stand at the shore at Capernaum today, just behind you is a broad, sloping hillside. It takes a good fifteen minutes to hike up to the summit, from which there is a glorious view out across the lake and a constant high lake breeze coming in. Today this is called the Mount of the Beatitudes, and on the summit sits the Church of the Beatitudes, which marks the traditional site of the Sermon on the Mount. Scholars are nearly unanimous in considering at least the first three beatitudes in Luke[6] to be the actual words spoken by the teacher named Yeshu bar Yosef, perhaps on this very hilltop, twenty centuries ago:

Blessed are you who are poor,
for yours is the kingdom of God.

Blessed are you who are hungry now,
for you will be filled.

Blessed are you who weep now,
for you will laugh.

This isn't much to start with, but it gives us several clues into the spiritual and ethical channel the historical Jesus had become tuned in to. First, this world that was in his head was an upside-down version of the ordinary world. The poor get everything, the hungry get food, the weepers laugh. And they get those things precisely because they are poor, hungry, weeping. Second, it indicates that his audience came from the bottom of the social ladder. Beyond this, we know that beatitudes (from the Latin *beatus,* "happy") were a teaching device popular throughout the ancient world; they typically begin with the word "happy" or "blessed" and go on to say that the hearers will be happy if they pursue a certain course. The structure of these teachings would probably have been familiar to his listeners.

But Jesus' favorite way of teaching seems to have been with parables. The Greek *parabolē* is a translation of the Hebrew *mashal.* The Hebrew Bible is filled with *mashals*; indeed, another translation of the word into English is "proverb." So in teaching with little metaphorical stories, Jesus was adopting another technique with an ancient Jewish lineage, and one that the peasants of Galilee would have recognized. But it is generally agreed that the New Testament parables are not exactly like anything in previous Jewish literature, nor is there an exact parallel in the Greek world. They are, arguably, the historical Jesus' contribution to world literature.

The parables have always been a source of discomfort to the church. The awkward fact is that the parables of Jesus, most of them anyway, don't really make much sense. They have been put through a variety of rhetorical grinders: for centuries they were seen as allegories, then more recently as ethical riddles, as encapsulations of the kingdom of God, as psycho-social literary creations. All of these attempts have involved some sort of decoding: crack the shell and find the underlying meaning.

The problem is that one expects the parables to be fables with little morals attached. In fact, most are irreverent, anti-social, downright rude. What's worse, they seem to play off of the audience's very expectation that they will be moral tales. They set up a real-life situation, introduce trouble into it . . . and that's it. The end. No resolution, no moral. They are less like the wise anecdotes of a Solomon, Aesop, or Abe Lincoln than rotten eggs tossed at houses. Defacing houses—wrecking the status quo—seems to be their point. The gospel writers themselves understood this problem very well, and tried to deal with it by putting explanatory words in Jesus' mouth following several of the more awkward parables.

The parables are crucial for anyone interested in the historical Jesus because it was in parables that he attempted to get across what he meant by "the kingdom of God." This phrase, which is virtually nonexistent in earlier Jewish literature, is the heart of his "message." Every Christian denomination has defined it in its own way, and the major debate among New Testament scholars today revolves around its meaning. Did he use it to mean a future post-apocalyptic realm? A post-history, in-the-sky abode where the just would live in the bosom of the Lord? Some sayings seem to indicate this—"Truly I tell you, there are some standing here who will not taste death until they see that the kingdom of God has come with power" (Mark 9:1)—and are considered by most scholars to be the creation of the early church, whose members were starting to worry that the expected kingdom they had envisioned wasn't coming after all. But Sanders points out that even if you set aside all such sayings, there is still the evidence of Paul's writings, which are considerably earlier than the gospels.[7] Paul firmly believed that Jesus had in mind something quite specific, and quite imminent. He wrote to the faithful at Thessalonika:

> For the Lord himself, with a cry of command, with the archangel's call and with the sound of God's trumpet, will descend from heaven, and the dead in Christ will rise first. Then we who are alive, who are

> left, will be caught up in the clouds together with them to meet the Lord in the air; and so we will be with the Lord forever. Therefore encourage one another with these words.[8]

On the other hand, just when his hearers thought that this was his meaning, Jesus seems to have switched gears: "The kingdom of God is not coming with things that can be observed," he tells the Pharisees in Luke's gospel, "nor will they say, 'Look, here it is!' or 'There it is!' For, in fact, the kingdom of God is within you." Similarly, in the Gospel of Thomas, the disciples ask when the kingdom of God will come and Jesus tells them it is already "spread out upon the earth, and people don't see it."[9]

The kingdom of God, whatever it is, is the whole point of the historical Jesus' career. It's what today's scholars continue to dig for. Find it, they seem to feel, and you will find Jesus. The trick is that he seems never to have defined it the same way twice, and every definition he gave seemed to cause as much confusion as insight. One thing most modern scholars agree on is that to Jesus' original audience the parables would have been, if anything, even more strange and irreverent than to us today:

> The kingdom of heaven is like yeast that a woman took and mixed in with three measures of flour until all of it was leavened.[10]

On the face of it there is nothing shocking about this small, well-known parable. We are seemingly being told something about the kingdom being a secret thing hidden within, which causes one to grow in an unexpected way. But a Jewish audience of Jesus' day would not have seen it quite like that, for to them leaven was a symbol of corruption. Leaven was the archetypal unclean food—

leaven or yeast is, after all, a bit of rot that causes a chemical reaction in dough—which is why unleavened bread is featured in the Passover meal, and probably why it became the Christian Eucharist. (Elsewhere in the gospels—in a passage that is probably the invention of the early church but which still shows how leaven was viewed—Jesus tells his disciples to "beware of the leaven of the Pharisees and of the Sadducees,"[11] meaning the corrupted doctrine of those groups.) To the peasants of Galilee, then, Jesus seemed to be comparing the kingdom of heaven to something rotten.

Similarly, there is the parable of the mustard seed:

> He said therefore, "What is the kingdom of God like? And to what should I compare it? It is like a mustard seed that someone took and sowed in the garden; it grew and became a tree, and the birds of the air made nests in its branches."[12]

Again, this short parable would seem to be making a fairly straightforward point, about the kingdom starting from small beginnings and expanding. But scholars have long had problems with it. For one thing, mustard was considered impure by the ancient rabbis. Besides that, mustard does not grow into a tree but into a low shrub, of the sort that spreads, weedlike, through a garden. It is hardly a grand metaphor for the kingdom. Why, commentators have wondered, did Jesus not use the great cedar of Lebanon, which appears in the Old Testament as a symbol of heaven? Some argue that the Gospel of Thomas's version of this parable is earlier than the New Testament versions because in it the mustard has not yet become a tree but is "a large plant." If this is true, then the gospel writers would have found Jesus' choice of seed awkward and began rewriting botany in an effort to improve it.

Another short parable takes a quietly unexpected turn:

> The kingdom of heaven is like treasure hidden in a field, which a man found and covered up; then in his joy he goes and sells all that he has and buys that field.[13]

What surprises here is the man's selfishness. One might expect someone who finds the kingdom of heaven to share it with others, but this man turns secretive, even keeping the knowledge of the treasure from the owner of the field—and Jesus seems to applaud this behavior.

The longer parables are if anything even odder. The Dishonest Steward is the story of a rich man who, when he learns that his steward has been wasting his money, fires him. The steward, despairing what to do with himself, goes to each of his master's debtors and reduces their bills "so that people may receive me into their houses when I am put out of the stewardship." The master then commends the dishonest steward for his shrewdness.[14] And that's it. Luke appends a not very intelligible interpretation to the effect that it's all right to make friends by means of "dishonest wealth"—a total fabrication in the eyes of scholars, which points out all the more how opaque the parable was to the early Christians.

The Good Samaritan, probably the best known and most taught of all the parables, features a priest and a Levite who pass by a man lying beaten and dying by the side of the road, and a Samaritan who finally comes to the man's aid. The good Samaritan has become a simple metaphor for compassion, but, as with the leaven and the mustard seed, it seems calculated to disturb a first-century Jewish audience. The man lying by the road seems dead, and to the priest and the Levite a corpse was ritually impure, hence their passing by. Judea was perennially at war with Samaria in the first century—a state of tribal hatred that extended back at least three hundred years; the idea that a Samaritan would be the hero of a story while a pious priest and a Levite would be the villains would have caused a shock that all but obliterated the message of compassion.

So shock and rudeness, not proverbial wisdom, would seem to be the hallmarks of an authentic parable of Jesus. Take for comparison a parable from the Apocryphon of James, a second-century sayings collection found at Nag Hammadi purported to contain the authentic words of Jesus:

> For the kingdom of heaven is like an ear of grain which sprouted in a field. And when it ripened, it scattered its fruit and, in turn, filled the field with ears of grain for another year.[15]

Here is mundane wisdom about renewal, with none of the shocking reversals or rude imagery: clearly a phony parable.

How are we to understand the authentic parables if their salient feature is lack of sense? *By abandoning sense.* That seems to be the collective insight of a new generation of parable authorities. Robert Funk, in a groundbreaking essay in his 1966 book *Language, Hermeneutics, and the Word of God,* argued that the purpose of the parables was to guide listeners along familiar territory in the everyday world, and then suddenly drop them off into a chasm of nonsense or surprise. Elsewhere, Funk writes that "Jesus, as a maker of parables, invites his hearers, by means of his tales or riddles, to pass over from the attenuated world of jaded sense to some fabulous yonder he sees before him. He calls this fabulous yonder the kingdom of God, and he wonders why others about him cannot see what is so evident to him."[16] The Dutch scholar Edward Schillebeeckx sees it much the same way: "A parable often stands things on their head; the idea behind it is to make you consider your own life, your own goings-on, your own world, from a different angle for once."[17]

Here, then, is a possible key into "the kingdom of God." Jesus saw it, at least some of the time, not necessarily as a place or a time or an event, but as a state. And the way into this alternate state, where alternative wisdom prevailed, was by finding a crack in the wall of common sense and ordinary experience. At least one parable scholar[18] has likened Jesus' language to that of a Zen master, who encourages his disciples to look for wisdom not in words but in the spaces between words, who short-circuits their practical questions about obtaining wisdom by countering with seeming nonsense.

One of the strangest and most alluring of the parables, one in which this anti-sense is strongest, is found in the Gospel of Thomas, one of the so-called gnostic gospels that some scholars think has layers that go back to the time of Jesus:

> Jesus said, "The kingdom of the [Father] is like a certain woman who was carrying a jar full of meal. While she was walking [on] a road, still some distance from home, the handle of the jar broke and the meal emptied out behind her on the road. She did not realize it; she had noticed no accident. When she reached her house, she set the jar down and found it empty."[19]

The Jesus Seminar, which finds this parable to be authentic, notes that the normal expectation would be for the kingdom to be likened to a *full* jar. But normalcy is not the way to glimpse the kingdom of God. According to this current, stop-making-sense reading, Jesus' spiritual epiphany in the Jordan opened him up to a way of seeing reality that cut through ordinary sense; he communicated it, naturally enough, in the terms of a first-century Jew: with reference to God and the prophets, and by way of Jewish storytelling devices. And since it was beyond sense, the words he chose to describe it could only point the way; they could only *suggest.*

"You might think of a parable as like a kite," says Edward Beutner. "What is it about a kite that is so captivating? It isn't the paper and the wood. When you look at a kite flying, you're experiencing the rush of seeing an unseen world. The kite is important because it reveals a whole invisible world that we know is all around us but that we can only see out of the corner of our eye, so to speak."

If this view of the parables has any merit, then it may suggest the ultimate futility of a critical search for the "message" of Jesus. Searching for it with the mind, with conventional wisdom, is probably doomed to failure, for as a Zen master said of an intellectual search for Zen knowledge, "It's much like riding an ox in search of the ox." If this is the case, then maybe we have to look beyond his words to reach some understanding of what the historical Jesus was about. Maybe the kingdom of God was apparent not so much in what he said as in what he did.

CHAPTER SEVEN

MIRACLES

Jesus worked miracles. That was the universal opinion of his early followers, and it is undoubtedly what made him famous in his lifetime.

Actually, what the gospels say he performed were *dynameis,* "mighty deeds," or *semeia,* "signs." Signs of what? Signs of his status: that he was the one spoken of by Isaiah and Daniel, that here was the Son of Man, the eschatological prophet, who would herald the arrival of the new kingdom. However much scholars might dispute the idea that Jesus believed he was the prophet of the Last Days, there is no doubt that he is presented as such in the gospels. Whether or not he saw himself that way, that was certainly how the early church saw him.

And not only that, but these early Christians went one step further in constructing their written gospels. They conflated in the person of Jesus at least *two* figures referred to in various passages of the Hebrew Bible, both of which the Jews of the feverish first century whispered about: the semi-divine eschatological prophet, whom Edras says is "he whom the Most High has been keeping for many ages, who will himself deliver his creation,"[1] and the human Messiah, who in most traditions is a warrior-king who will lead Israel in a great battle.

The miracles are an annoyance for determinedly rationalist Bible critics. The problem seems to stem from forcing a rigid either-or onto the material: either these things really happened and for this one time in history the laws of nature were actually, literally broken, or it's all a lie. This vicious rationalism has resulted in some fairly silly attempts at explaining away: that the walking on water was thanks to an underwater shelf in the Sea of Galilee (of which, presumably, the career fishermen of the lake were unaware); that Jesus had helpers, laden with baskets of loaves and fishes, hidden in caves, ready to create the illusion of a miraculous feeding of the multitude; that when Jesus raised a girl from the dead and said, "The girl is not dead but sleeping," in fact she *was* just sleeping—perhaps in a coma—and the peasants didn't get it.[2]

This sort of thing pleases no one. If one's purpose is to wield a razor-sharp rationalistic cleaver in order to denude the Bible of all its mythic components, it would be better simply to lop off all instances of wonder, starting with the creation of the world in six days. This is what Thomas Jefferson did in his humanist New Testament; he literally scissored away the virgin birth, the miracles, the resurrection, and ended up with a document perfectly suited to his Enlightenment soul: a holey ethical tract devoid of holiness.

But if the purpose is to try genuinely to accommodate two millennia of spiritual wisdom into a modern perspective, a different tool has to be used, one without quite so sharp an edge. These days a new stage seems to have been reached by some scholars, theologians, and thoughtful Christians. Understanding the miracles now means understanding first of all why they are in the gospels in the first place. Surely we aren't meant to emulate Jesus; the gospels don't suggest that all good Christians ought to be able to vinify jugs of water with a wave of the hand. So what's the point?

Isaiah provides the first key. Isaiah was a hot book in the first century: all apocalyptic believers referred to it for details on the approaching End. Never mind that Isaiah was not written with apocalypse in mind; what mattered was that it could be read apocalyptically. Consider this string of prophecies: "[Y]our dead shall live, their corpses shall rise. . . . On that day the deaf shall hear . . . the eyes of the blind shall see. The meek shall obtain fresh joy in the Lord, and the neediest people shall exult in the Holy One of Israel."[3]

Here, it was decided, was the blueprint for what the eschatological prophet would do. Matthew and Luke refer to this list quite explicitly. When some disciples ask Jesus if he is the one who is to come, he replies, "Go and tell John what you hear and see: the blind receive their sight, the lame walk, the lepers are cleansed, the deaf hear, the dead are raised, and the poor have good news brought to them."[4] And again we are told that ". . . the crowd was amazed when they saw the mute speaking, the maimed whole, the lame walking, and the blind seeing. And they praised the God of Israel."[5]

In other words, the Jesus of the gospels performs these miracles—restoring sight to the blind, hearing to the deaf, raising the dead—because it was decided that he was the eschatological prophet, and therefore these precise miracles had to be assigned to him. Reading Mark (the most miracle-packed gospel) in light of this, one can almost see the writer ticking off his list of mighty deeds.

This does not mean that the historical Jesus never performed wondrous acts. In fact, he must have, otherwise no one would have become convinced that he was the eschatological prophet in the first place. So the first stage in trying to process an inherently ancient concept into a modern consciousness is to see how they were made to jive with the ancient writings. But one should resist the either-or temptation; the fact that many of the reported miracles aren't literally true does not negate the tradition. The gospels, the Acts of the Apostles, the letters of Paul and others, and all the extracanonical materials provide overwhelming evidence that the historical Jesus performed acts that astonished those who saw him, that convinced them that here was an extraordinary human being.

So some of the gospel miracles are fleshed-out prophecies. But there are others that seem to have little to do with Jesus or prophecy that are also of dubious historicity. How did these work their way into the tradition?

Posthumously assigning extra accomplishments to a renowned person is a common practice throughout history, so common that it has been given a literary term: epic concentration. Edward Schillebeeckx cites a straightforward example in Matthew, where tax collectors confront Jesus and Peter about paying the Temple tax. They have no money. Jesus tells Peter to cast a line into the lake; the first fish he catches, he says, will have a coin in its mouth. The coin in the mouth of the fish, Schillebeeckx says, was a motif common in ancient folk literature: "Obviously, a fabulous motif is being employed here simply to say that should he need it, Jesus has everything readily available, because the Father is looking after him. No reader at that time would have taken the passage literally."[6]

Another example of a wondrous deed apparently migrating into the Jesus story is the turning of water into wine. When the wine runs out at a wedding party, Jesus orders jars to be filled with water, then instructs the servants to bring them to the chief steward. And lo, the jars are miraculously filled with wine, and of the best quality, too.

As well known and celebrated as this story is, it is decidedly odd, and unlike anything in Jewish lore. Whereas most Jewish miracle-working prophets are stern, ascetic types, here we have one who goes to the trouble of breaking the laws of nature not to relieve suffering or save his people from ruin but to keep a party going. Surely no Old Testament writer prophesied that the eschatological prophet would perform such a sign. So how did this story, which appears only in John's gospel, come about?

Rudolf Bultmann, the great German scholar who towered over the field of biblical studies in the first half of this century, suggested an answer decades ago. The key is a date. The early church liked this miracle, and it eventually became the basis for a festival of celebration, the Feast of the Epiphany. Or did it? For the date still associated with the Epiphany, January 6, was from very ancient times the date of a Greek holiday honoring, among other things, Dionysus, the god of wine. On this day, according to Greek tradition, wine miracles were supposed to occur. "On his feast day, Dionysus made empty jars fill up with wine in his temple in Elis," according to Uta Ranke-Heinemann, "and on the island of Andros, wine flowed instead of water from a spring or in his temple."[7]

We may see an echo here of how the Jesus Christ legend, as it grew and gained momentum, consumed stories associated with older deities, resulting in the pastiche of wondrous deeds found in the New Testament. But this is not a simple dismissal of the significance of this miracle. The more one reads the gospels with critical but searching eyes, the more one becomes convinced of the depth of layers they contain: not just historical layers, but layers of symbolism and fecund devotion. If the John tradition appropriated this miracle from the Dionysus cult, it also wove and rewove it into a fabric rich with shaded meanings. The jars are "for the Jewish rites of purification"—i.e., they are Judaism itself—but thanks to Jesus they contain something new; through Jesus the living water of Judaism becomes rich and intoxicating. Thanks to Jesus, the party can begin all over again. Water and wine—the source of life and the source of intoxication, of organic ecstasy—were vital symbols for the earliest Christians, as evidenced by the fact that they became incorporated into the Christian liturgy, along with other root symbols: bread, blood.

The gospel writers seemed to delight in threading these symbolic essences throughout their work. The fact that their expression of this newfound awareness took such tunneling, stratifying courses is itself a clue to the historical Jesus; to hack it to bits with crude literalism leaves the tradition in shambles and the quester unsatisfied. On the other hand, to view the story as literally true, many commentators suggest, is to turn one of the world's great conduits of spirituality into a dispensary of magic tricks.

Virtually all scholars acknowledge that the so-called nature miracles (water into wine, walking on water, feeding the multitude) are invention—pious invention, meaningful invention, but invention nevertheless. They say more about the early Christian experience of the Divine than about the historical Jesus. If the historical Jesus is to be located among the miracles, experts agree, he is most likely to be found among the healings and exorcisms.

Illness was not a purely physical phenomenon in the ancient world. Disease had as much to do with guilt and sin as with the physical body. In Jewish tradition, this is made quite clear; in particular the rabbis, in their writings, seem to have associated many forms of disease with sexual sin. If a child is born lame, we are told it is because the parents "turn[ed] their table upside down," i.e., had sex with the woman on top. A deaf child results from a man and woman's talking during intercourse. "When a man sleeps with his wife in the days of her menstruation, his children will be struck with epilepsy."[8]

God underlies all of this: God, in this rabbinic tradition, seems to have had a neat chart of punishments to fit various sins. To a politically minded scholar like John Dominic Crossan, this use of God by the priests of the Temple has a specific purpose:

> There is, first and above all, a terrible irony in that conjunction of sickness and sin, especially in first-century Palestine. Excessive taxation could leave poor people physically malnourished or hysterically disabled. But since the religiopolitical ascendancy could not blame excessive taxation, it blamed sick people themselves by claiming that their sins had led to their illnesses. And the cure for sinful sickness was, ultimately, in the Temple. And that meant more fees, in a perfect circle of victimization.[9]

What we have here is a view of the first-century Jewish scene similar to a common view in American politics: that the traditional Republican approach to social programs has the effect of blaming the poor for their poverty. The precursor to Reaganomics, it seems, was Romanomics, and it was a hundred times nastier. But not all historians are in love with this political view. E. P. Sanders thinks Crossan and others of his ilk push the evidence too far:

> Modern scholars often show moral indignation when they discuss ancient peasants. Behind this indignation lies an implicit comparison between the poverty of ancient farmers and laborers and the prosperity of modern Westerners. We can understand the situation only if we look at the ancient Palestinian peasants on their own terms.[10]

Crossan's approach builds on Morton Smith's: like the Baptist, Jesus, in performing healings, was challenging the "religiopolitical ascendancy"—the Temple. He was providing direct access to the kingdom of God. There is certainly some evidence in the gospels to support this view. At one point, Jesus is asked, in a passage that clearly reflects the equating of deformity with sexual sin, "Rabbi, who sinned, this man or his parents, that he was born blind?" In his response we see that Jesus challenged the sickness-equals-sin thinking: "Neither this man nor his parents sinned; he was born blind so that God's works might be revealed in him."[11] This is indeed an affront to the priests, and we see that as Jesus goes about healing the sick he is dogged by suspicious Jewish authorities.

But a political view is one thing; it's quite another to take the step that some scholars take and see the healings as evidence that Jesus was a pure communist/democrat/proto-Christian: he believed that all men and women were created equal, he was against wealth and property and all social divisions, including the division between Jews and Gentiles, and by healing the ritual illnesses of society's outcasts he was welcoming the outcasts back into the human family, telling them it was not they who were sick but the people who erected social barriers.

This approach fuels some of today's scholarship, and while there are some grounds for it in the gospel narratives, it also has an uncomfortably modern sound. With only a little nudging, this Jesus becomes an advocate for "empowerment," "racial healing," and other late-twentieth-century–sounding ideals. Of course, there is nothing wrong with using Jesus to promote such things, but a historian's job is to deal with facts and keep them corralled within their own context.

And the facts—or at least the indications in the gospels—often run counter to this politically correct glaze. "I have not come to bring peace, but a sword."[12] "Go nowhere among the Gentiles . . ."[13] "Whoever comes to me and does not hate his father and mother, wife and children, brothers and sisters, yes, and even life itself, cannot be my disciple."[14] "And you, Capernaum, will you be exalted to heaven? No, you will be brought down to Hades."[15] This is the Jesus of the gospels as much as the "love your enemies" prophet is. He can be angry, partisan, even spiteful. Many of his beliefs—demon possession, the ritual slaughter of animals—are truly primitive. He openly prefers Jews to Gentiles, which is not in the least surprising in a first-century Jew, but doesn't square with the ageless New Age sage that some scholars incline toward. And while experts might discount some such passages as non-historical, if their reasoning is that they couldn't have been said by Jesus because he was more enlightened than that, then their reasoning is circular. (Regarding Jesus' admonition to his disciples to "go nowhere among the Gentiles," for example, the Jesus Seminar has voted against its authenticity on the grounds that "a restricted mission was not characteristic of Jesus"—a conclusion reached by negating the authenticity of exactly such sayings.)

And surely the historical Jesus wasn't a political operative. While rubbing his spittle into the eyelids of the blind man he didn't say, "I heal you so as to empower you, to challenge society to grant full rights of citizenship to even its most unfortunate members." It may be plausible, from a politically conscious twentieth-century perspective, to see this as an effect of Jesus' healings, but it would be anachronistic to suggest that a first-century Jewish peasant had any such thing in mind.

So how can we get beneath this latter-day gloss and catch a glimpse of the "real" Jesus at work? We can't. Getting into the mindset of a pre-Enlightenment, pre-Renaissance, pre-Western civilization, God-soaked Jewish peasant is not an option. But there are other ways to explore the healings. One recent take is that of Stevan Davies, professor of religious studies at College Misericordia and one of the most innovative researchers at work today. In his 1995 book *Jesus the Healer,* Davies suggests that by translating the spiritual terminology of the New Testament into the language of psychology, both Jesus' "miracles" and his own spiritual state take on a whole new aspect. We may not be able to get into the minds of those on-site witnesses to Jesus' work, but by looking at that work in terms that suit our rationalistic, postmodern selves we might find that elements of the gospels that were once dismissed as "supernatural" suddenly become credible.

Jesus' mission begins when the Holy Spirit "descends" on him. He suddenly speaks with a new voice, one in which people recognize authority. While this Holy Spirit has charge of him, he heals various unfortunates who are possessed by demons. The demons often recognize the Spirit in Jesus, and, with ordinary people watching from the sidelines, these two spiritual forces clash like comic-book super heroes. One demon speaks on behalf of both himself and his host: "Let us alone! What have you to do with us, Jesus of Nazareth? Have you come to destroy us? I know who you are, the Holy One of God."[16]

Looked at in modern terms, Davies suggests, we have here two different instances of what psychologists call a dissociative state, in which, in the words of an anthropologist he quotes, "a split-off part of the mind possesses the whole field of consciousness," so that the person's normal, everyday self seems to vanish.[17]

Trance states are common among tribal cultures the world over, from the shamans of Indonesia to the medicine men of Native America. According to Davies, they also account for the Old Testament prophets. When the prophets speak in their altered state, it is with the voice of God. The Book of Isaiah does not say "Isaiah reports that the Lord said . . ." It is simply "The Lord said . . ." When a prophet is filled with the Spirit of God, he speaks *for* God, *as* God. Hence the tradition of believing that the Bible is inerrant, for if God Himself dictated it through these prophets, it cannot contain error.

By laying this modern grid over the ancient texts, Davies suggests, we see Jesus and his contemporaries in something like the way they saw themselves. Jesus may have thought that when the Spirit was upon him he was "the Son of God," and those who heard and saw him may have thought it too. A whole generation of scholars has dismissed the idea that Jesus and his contemporaries believed this of him. But what they were rejecting was the later Christian significance of the phrase. The psychological model may help us to see that in Jesus' day, "Son of God" referred to the same kind of relationship the Old Testament prophets had with God, as mouthpiece, conduit, special spokesman. But not necessarily the prophet's *being* God. That leap came later, when the Jesus cult went Greek.

According to the psychological model, the historical Jesus was in effect seen by his contemporaries as two persons who shared the same body: Jesus of Nazareth and the Holy Spirit. Or, as Davies elliptically puts it, "In the Gospel of Mark, practically everybody but Jesus thinks Jesus isn't Jesus."[18]

Stevan Davies is not maintaining that what early Christians

believed was the Holy Spirit was "really" a dissociative personality state, an alternate persona; he is saying that these are two ways of seeing the same thing. The one just has a more modern cast than the other. They are two different kinds of language; but the underlying reality, whatever it may be, remains unchanged.

But we still haven't determined what miracles Jesus performed. Is it possible to do so? Can we isolate this or that story in the gospels and say, "Yes, here, he really did this one"?

Not really. But, having eliminated the nature miracles from consideration, many scholars show that nearly all the healings and exorcisms could be authentic. And clues from archaeology and history may take us even further, verifying details such as locations.

Every scholar ticks off reasons for and against each of the thirty or so miracle stories having a historical core, and comes up with a tentative list of those that probably derive from Jesus. Comparing the conclusions of the Jesus Seminar with those of John Meier, one finds that, surprisingly, they aren't that far apart in quantity. Where the Jesus Seminar attributes eight miracle stories as authentic to Jesus, Meier finds eleven. In other words, whether you prefer to follow the liberal or the conservative wing of scholarship, you find that roughly two-thirds of the miracle stories in the gospels are thought not to date to Jesus but to be of later origin.

Once again, the consensus among scholars seems more impressive than the disagreements. On the one hand, the group that has been charged with being radically reductionist and anti-Christian declares its belief that Jesus was a healer and exorcist and actually finds several stories that it feels date to him. On the other hand, a Catholic priest writing with the Vatican's approval, whom some scholars have accused of backing away from conclusions that would be at odds with the church, dismisses two-thirds of the miracle stories, including many that centuries of Catholic theology have fervently embraced, as later additions having nothing to do with the historical Jesus.

Meier and the Jesus Seminar agree that Jesus performed exorcisms, though they disagree on which if any of the exorcism stories in the gospels are authentic. And they agree that the three gospel stories of Jesus healing blind people reflect an authentic historical core. Beyond this, these two wings of contemporary scholarship converge on the historicity of one additional miracle story: the Capernaum paralytic.

It is told most fully in Mark. Jesus is "at home" in Capernaum—presumably Peter's house—when a crowd gathers to hear him speak. They fill the house and throng outside the door, and when some people come with a cripple who wants the Master to heal him they are forced to "remove the roof" and lower the man down on his mat. Jesus sees the man's faith and declares, "Son, your sins are forgiven." This causes some Pharisees to be scandalized; they think rather than speak, "Who can forgive sins but God alone?" But Jesus hears their thoughts and responds:

> Which is easier, to say to the paralytic, "Your sins are forgiven," or to say, "Stand up and take your mat and walk?" But so that you may know that the Son of Man has authority on earth to forgive sins—he said to the paralytic—"I say to you, stand up, take your mat and go to your home."[19]

And the paralytic does so, to the amazement of all.

Obviously there is a great deal of later Christian reworking going on here. This mind-reading Jesus is suspiciously all-knowing and god-like, and "a controversy over the authority to forgive sins . . . has been inserted into what was once a straightforward healing tale" according to the Jesus Seminar.[20] But both Meier and the seminar agree that this lakeside incident, with its odd detail of people lowering a sick man down through the roof, "stuck in the corporate memory precisely because of its strange circumstances," in Meier's words.[21] What's more, archaeologists Eric Meyers and James Strange note that typical construction of houses in Capernaum included roofs of "beams, branches, rushes, and mud,"[22] which means that the act of taking apart the roof wouldn't have been as impossible as it might seem.*

But how did Jesus actually do it? What was the secret to his healing powers? How is it possible that the paralytic got up and walked away?

Most critics fall back on that old standby, psychosomatic illness. Most or all of the disorders Jesus heals in the gospels, Davies asserts, come under the heading of "conversion disorders," which the American Psychiatric Association defines as "an alteration or loss of physical functioning that suggests physical disorder, but that instead is apparently an expression of a psychological conflict or need."[23] Typical manifestations include deafness, blindness, paralysis and excessive menstrual bleeding—all of which feature prominently in Jesus' healings.

For this kind of healing to work, the patient must believe in the power of the healer, hence the term "faith healing." Negative evidence that Jesus' healings worked this way is found in the Synoptics, where Jesus, at the high point of his success, goes home to Nazareth and preaches in the synagogue. Where others saw a Spirit-possessed prophet, the Nazarenes see only the boy who used to live there, grown to adulthood and inclined to uppitiness—

*Evidently Matthew found the roof dismantling awkward; he repeats the story but locates it out-of-doors. Luke keeps the roof removal but, interestingly, indicates that the roof is made of "tiles." This detail tells us more about Luke's world than Jesus'; as Edward Beutner puts it, "Luke changes the architecture of the house from Palestinian to Greek."

which prompts Jesus to remark that a prophet is never recognized in his own town. Not surprisingly, Jesus performs no miracles in Nazareth.

If this theory is correct, then it seems to imply that an awfully large number of people in Jesus' time were afflicted with psychosomatic illnesses. But here Stacy Davids, a clinical psychiatrist doing graduate work in New Testament studies who has attempted medical diagnoses of the sufferers Jesus heals, takes this thinking in a new direction.[24] In the ancient view, she argues, illness was not a disordered physiological process but an indication that one's being—spiritual, physical, and social—was out of alignment. There really was, as Crossan suggests, a relation between sin and sickness. And the corollary is that someone who was declared to be a sinner was seen as sick. So healing involved, as Davids says, "restoration of worthiness to participate in the community." Therefore a healer such as Jesus could perfectly legitimately say, "Your sins are forgiven." In healing, he was admitting the sick back into the social family. Believing in Jesus' power meant not only believing in his mysterious medical prowess but believing that he had the authority to readmit these people to society.

Medical science, Davids argues, is only now, and only slowly, coming to realize that the body is not a simple machine to be manipulated with chemicals. Various psychiatrists and medical doctors are exploring the mind-body connection in new ways, ways that sometimes seem close to the ancient understanding. Davids points out one way in which science has long understood the mind's effect on the body: the placebo.

Placebos are dummy treatments: flour capsules instead of drugs, etc. Researchers use them to judge the effects of "real" drugs. But, on average, thirty-five percent of patients in a given study will respond to the placebo, on conditions ranging from arthritis to ulcer to diabetes to shrinking of tumors. This stunning degree of success for a dummy treatment—which is duly acknowledged and figured into scientific studies—points to one conclusion: that, at least in some cases, the forces for healing already exist in the patient. The irony, according to Davids, is that "the placebo effect, once the anchor of treatment in premodern societies, has become a contaminant to be blocked out in the Western, scientific Random Clinical Trial."

What the placebo effect actually means, Davids argues, is that not only "psychosomatic" illnesses can be cured by faith healing but physical illnesses as well. Or, put simply, if belief is strong enough, results are more amazing than smug science will admit.

What this indicates is that there are ways to follow a rationalistic track through the miracle stories and end up with a picture pretty close to that presented in the gospels: people believed, and they were healed. If stating it so baldly makes you uncomfortable, various experts have provided more modern terminology. Whichever language you prefer—religious or scientific—the agreement is overwhelming: Jesus healed.

But healing was only one way the historical Jesus operated, only one way he proclaimed the kingdom of God. The other—more innocuous to us but probably more radical to his contemporaries—had to do with food:

> When you give a luncheon or a dinner, do not invite your friends or your brothers or your relatives or rich neighbors . . . invite the poor, the crippled, the lame, and the blind. And you will be blessed because they cannot repay you . . .[25]

Politically minded scholars think this instruction is authentic Jesus, and believe it represents an important part of his work. If the kingdom of God was in some sense present, and if the parables were a way to break down the walls of ordinary reality to reach this other awareness, and if the social outcasts who reached it were cured of what ailed them, then, according to this reading, another basic way Jesus brought about this new insight was through shared food, or what Crossan calls "open commensality." It is hard for us to appreciate that to a first-century Jew, eating a meal with people who weren't like you was an absolutely scandalous act. Actually, it may not be so hard to appreciate: How often do people today invite the local prostitutes and homeless in to dinner? Or rather, to make the comparison more accurate, how often do people gather a gang of derelicts, knock on a neighbor's door and say, "I've had a great idea: you invite us all to dinner, and in exchange, through the process of letting down your barriers and sharing with your fellow human beings on this most basic level, you'll come to know the kingdom of God." We can only imagine how much more undesirable such a neighbor would be in a small peasant village, where maintaining social boundaries was a matter of religious importance.

Crossan thinks this activity and the healings are related: both were a challenge to the existing order, the healings by offering an alternative to the Temple, shared meals by breaking down divisions between social classes. Thus, by the seemingly innocuous actions of healing the sick and advocating dinner parties in which the dining companions, rather than the dishes, were the surprise, Jesus extended John the Baptist's mission and became, to the Jewish authorities, and probably to a good many upstanding citizens, a troublemaker.

At this point some authorities, notably Marcus Borg, erect a bridge between critical scholarship and theology. Borg agrees with Crossan on the importance of "magic and meals" as two ways Jesus believed he was offering the kingdom of God to ordinary lives. But

Borg goes further, carrying this perspective into church with him, so to speak, relating the politically provocative act of open commensality to the Christian Eucharist:

> Ultimately, the meals of Jesus are the ancestor of the Christian eucharist. The centrality of meals in the early Christian movement and throughout Christian history goes back to the table fellowship of Jesus. In the Christian tradition, of course, the meal has become a ritualized sacred meal, no longer a real meal. But for Jesus, these were real meals with real outcasts.[26]

This suggests a vast undercurrent in the gospels, which surfaces and finds symbolic resonance in many of the miracle stories. Following this current leads us away from critical scholarship and, for scholars like Borg, theologians such as Schillebeeckx, and like-minded churchmen such as Bishop John Shelby Spong, into a new appreciation of the gospels, one in which the historical and the spiritual resonate off one another. Consider, as a way into it, what is perhaps the most beloved of all the miracles:

> When it grew late, his disciples came to him and said, "This is a deserted place, and the hour is now very late; send [the people] away so that they may go into the surrounding country and villages and buy something for themselves to eat." But he answered them, "You give them something to eat." They said to him, "Are we to go and buy two hundred denarii worth of bread, and give it to them to eat?" And he said to them, "How many loaves have you? Go and

> see." When they had found out, they said, "Five, and two fish . . ." Taking the five loaves and the two fish, he looked up to heaven, and blessed and broke the loaves, and gave them to his disciples to set before the people; and he divided the two fish among them all. And all ate and were filled; and they took up twelve baskets full of broken pieces and of the fish. Those who had eaten the loaves numbered five thousand men.[27]

It is worth quoting this well-known story at length because it falls into two interesting categories. As a nature miracle, it is universally considered fanciful by Bible exegetes. But it is also one of the rare stories that appears in all four canonical gospels, which indicates how important it was for the early church.

Now, imagine that we are living in the early morning of Christianity, after the crucifixion but before the gospels were written. The "resurrection" has happened (what matters here is not whether it literally happened, but that the early believers had an experience of it). Let's say we are among these believers; we have participated in some transcendental religious experience that has moved us to recognize divinity in a murdered human being. We have decided that he is Daniel's Son of Man: the prophet who will bring about the end of history. We are packing our bags, expecting him to return shortly. We are thrilled with our new awareness. We want to tell the world.

The question is: *How do we transmit this experience to others, who have not shared it?*

We remember episodes from his life, and ponder what special significance they might have. John Meier speculates that what underlies this miracle story is an actual event in Jesus' life, "some especially memorable communal meal of bread and fish, a meal with eschatological overtones celebrated by Jesus and his disciples with a large crowd by the Sea of Galilee."[28]

In attempting to communicate the significance of Jesus, we have, first of all, this actual memory of Jesus sharing a meal with a crowd of his followers. If we are Jews, it may bring a piece of Scripture to mind, a passage from the Second Book of Kings involving one of the great prophets, with whom it would be meaningful to compare Jesus:

> A man came . . . bringing . . . twenty loaves of barley and fresh ears of grain in his sack. Elisha said, "Give it to the people and let them eat." But his servant said, "How can I set this before a hundred people?" So he repeated, "Give it to the people and let them eat, for thus says the Lord, 'They shall eat and have some left.' " He set it before them, they ate, and had some left, according to the word of the Lord.[29]

Now remember that we find meaning by associating the present with the past. But we are convinced that Jesus was not simply equal to Elisha—he was more than the prophets, he was their culmination. So instead of one hundred people, it becomes five thousand. Instead of twenty loaves, five. Jesus' miracle is more miraculous than Elisha's. And the ending is the same, for what God said of old still holds: "They shall eat and have some left."

Something like this may have been the first stage of development, the first step in translating the inexplicability of Jesus Risen to those who had not experienced it firsthand. But there was more. Mark's final product contains telltale phrases. The apostles are concerned about the people going hungry, and Jesus orders: "*You* give them something to eat." This is chain-of-command talk; the early church is telling the faithful who is in charge: *we twelve.* Stick with us and we'll take care of you. Why *twelve* baskets of leavings? The twelve apostles, of course: heads of the twelve tribes of the new Israel. So also within Mark's final miracle story is a bit of political maneuvering.

Of course "Who feeds the people?" answers the question of authority, but the deeper questions are: What are the people hungry for? What are they given to eat? Why are we talking about food in the first place?

Because it is what *he* talked about. Eating together was one of his ways of showing the kingdom. Shared meals were the kingdom of God on earth. Why? What is eating but accepting an outside being into the body: con-suming, being one with? If God is Being par excellence then God's unity comprises all objects, and by blessing and consuming this object I am making myself aware of that mystery: I am accepting God into myself, reacquainting myself with Being. The early church was aware that Jesus emphasized this special way of looking at the act of eating. We know they were aware of it because of the many different ways food and eating feature in the gospels: the multiplication of loaves and fishes (so important to Mark and Matthew that it happens *twice* in their gospels), turning water into wine, parables about banquets, a prayer to "give us each day our daily bread," the commandment to eat with others, to exchange healing for food.

And, with the exquisite structure of a Greek tragedy or a Hindu mandala, it all comes to a climax in—what else?—a last supper. In which, finally, the object to be consumed, to be accepted joyfully into the body, becomes *his* body. He becomes, finally, the particularization of God's Being. If the kingdom can be reduced to an essence, he is it.

As this thinking proceeds during those early decades, as the soft light of early morning gives way to the hot sun of high Christology in the Gospel of John, this idea becomes intoxicating, even ghastly:

> . . . unless you eat the flesh of the Son of Man and drink his blood, you have no life in you. Those who eat my flesh and drink my blood have eternal life, and I will raise them up on the last day; for my flesh is true food and my blood is true drink. Those who eat my flesh and drink my blood abide in me, and I in them. Just as the living Father sent me, and I live because of the Father, so whoever eats me will live because of me.[30]

So the miracles would seem to be a collaboration, a joint venture on the part of the historical Jesus and his followers. Finally embracing him, probably in a way quite different from what he intended, they threaded and rethreaded the stories of his life with the wonder they had discovered. So, as Bishop Spong points out, the same four verbs that are the key to the Last Supper scene—he *took* bread, *blessed* it, *broke* it, and *gave* it—are found in this miracle story. The gospels are not biographies but symphonies, with overtures, recurring motifs, variations on themes.

One need not be a supernaturalist, a believer in ghosts or bodily resurrections, to appreciate that these co-creators of Christianity experienced something truly reality-altering—something that did indeed cut across social boundaries—in a human being. And that in their ecstatic creativity these early followers made *him* into the ultimate nature miracle. A man invites people to a place he calls the kingdom of God; healing them, making them whole again, is his way of leading them up to the front door; sharing meals takes them across the threshold. And they are so smitten by the experience, and by him, that within a short time they have transformed him—symbolically, essentially, world-historically—into the meal itself.

CHAPTER EIGHT

NEW GOSPELS

We have looked at two bunches of evidence surrounding the career of the historical Jesus, which might be labeled "words" and "deeds," or "parables" and "healings." From these we saw that when Jesus talked he seems to have been most interested in what he called the kingdom of God. And while his acts were certainly compassionate and indicate a person who was unusually attuned to the spiritual, one could also see them as political: attacks on the class system of Jewish Palestine.

But how can we bring all of this together? *What did he mean?* That is the Holy Grail, so to speak, of Jesus research. It is not, of course, the apex of Christian theology. The two-thousand-year mystery that Christianity has both revered and tried to fathom is the resurrection: What does it mean to say that "the Son of God" died for me? The words and deeds of a first-century prophet run a distant second in importance. But to Jesus researchers, the words and deeds are everything. And while there is impressive agreement on what words and deeds to consider authentic, when it comes to how they should be interpreted, the neat scholarly consensus falls into ruin. Voices rise in pitch; normally dry and polite academics start to shout over one another. And everyone insists that it matters very much which view is correct. After all, we are talking about nothing less than who and what Jesus of Nazareth thought he was.

The more one studies the field of historical Jesus scholarship, the less it seems possible to arrive at a dispassionate answer to this central question, which leads one back to the autobiographical nature of the search for Jesus. Facts are cold, but an arrangement of facts is a hot-blooded thing. A story, any story, is not just a recitation of events but involves a worldview. "The king died. The prince believed his uncle killed him. He couldn't decide what to do about it." The difference between these "facts" and *Hamlet* is the worldview they are set into. How do I find meaning? Does evil exist? Is it up to me to see that justice is done? A few centuries before Shakespeare, these questions would have come with ready-made answers. But in *Hamlet* the modern consciousness is beginning to break through the medieval fortress of certainty. The prince is us: we are all trying to decide what to do.

The writers of the four gospels had another worldview in which to set their "facts." And within this worldview each represented variations. Mark, writing just after the destruction of the Temple, seemed to believe that the apocalyptic scenario was about to unfold, and he viewed Jesus' actions through this lens. Luke's gospel was written later, and suggests a less literal sense of the world coming to an end. The vicious anti-Jewish spin that Matthew gives to the pieces of the story shows the need of his community to divorce itself from the greater mass of Jews who rejected

Jesus. John's gospel, written latest, portrays a distant, ethereal Jesus, far removed from the earthy figure in Mark.

Historians today, people today, have different needs. Implicit in the whole historical Jesus enterprise is the idea that what worked for the gospel writers doesn't quite work for us anymore. We need to take the pieces and move them around, into a different story. Historians may like to think that they are working with clinical detachment, like scientists in a lab, and this may be true when they are simply isolating the data to focus on, but when it comes to interpreting the data they are creating stories. In trying to decide what Jesus meant, each scholar is writing a gospel, just as much as Matthew, Mark, Luke, and John were.

Nearly all of the researchers work from the same toolbox, which has resulted in basic agreement on the information in the previous two chapters. One of these tools, which we have already examined, is the criterion of embarrassment: any incident in the gospels that would have been a source of embarrassment to the early church must be authentic and too well established for the gospel writers to expunge it. Another is the criterion of multiple attestation, which judges that an incident or saying is more likely to date to Jesus if it appears in two or more independent sources.

Beyond the use of these tools, and several others like them, there is basic agreement on the layers within the gospels. Since the mid–nineteenth century, scholars have concurred that the striking similarities among Matthew, Mark, and Luke are due to the fact that Matthew and Luke each had a copy of Mark in front of them when they composed theirs. The priority of Mark is one of the guiding lights of New Testament research.

Further, as soon as this insight is accepted, something else becomes apparent. If you erase Mark from Matthew and Luke, you still have an enormous amount of similar material, including vast sections that are nearly word for word. In the era of the tape recorder this would be unremarkable, but in first-century Palestine these parallels suggest something else: that Matthew and Luke shared a second source besides Mark. Nineteenth-century German scholars called this other source Q for *Quelle,* or "source." Q thus becomes another tool: it has been an accepted component of New Testament scholarship ever since.

So these are some of the basic implements scholars apply to the New Testament in their search for the historical Jesus. It is thanks to them that we have something like a core of material that most experts consider authentic. For example, the reason the first three beatitudes are universally considered authentic is that they appear in Q: that is, in both Matthew and Luke. Others (e.g., "Blessed are the peacemakers") appear in only one gospel, which increases the possibility that they were added at a later time.[1]

This is a simple, judicious example of the use of these tools. But they can be applied in all sorts of ways, with some astonishing results. For instance, in recent decades, some experts have become so enamored of Q that they have concluded it represents nothing less than an entire hidden gospel. The thinking is that if Matthew and Luke shared a common written source, that source must have been written down for a reason, and the only good reason would be to support a community of Christians. This document, then, must represent the beliefs of the earliest Christians, those who lived in the decades prior to the composition of the canonical gospels; it might even represent on-site reporting of people who actually sat at Jesus' feet as he preached. And when you consider that this mysterious document contains some of the most hallowed chunks of Jesus lore, including the Sermon on the Mount, the Lord's Prayer, and many of the parables, it begins to seem that it may be the key to the whole puzzle.

The Q effort came to a head in the 1980s. An International Q Project was formed. In the alphabetical listings of course catalogs at seminaries, the "Q" section suddenly became fat. Q authorities came into being. Within a remarkably short time, Q became the cutting edge of Jesus research.

Q's popularity was helped by the increasing interest in another formerly unknown gospel. In 1945, when two brothers searching for fertile soil on a desert mountainside near Nag Hammadi in Upper Egypt found a hoard of manuscripts that had been preserved in an earthenware jar, scholars soon realized that among the trove of twelve leather-covered papyrus books was an intact Coptic version of a gospel referred to by the early church fathers but long since thought vanished: the Gospel of Thomas.

As with the Dead Sea Scrolls, the Nag Hammadi find was so rich that it took some time to digest, in part because so few people were fluent in Coptic. But as the decades wore on, it began to seem that here was a major new source of insight into the earliest days of the Jesus movement, and perhaps into the mind of Jesus himself. The Gospel of Thomas dates from the second century and embodies the teachings of the Gnostics, a sect that rivalled orthodox Christianity. Many scholars also detect an earlier layer in it that may date to the mid–first century.[2] If that is the case, then Thomas would be a lost gospel whose contemporaneousness, and thus claim to legitimacy, would equal that of the "big four" in the New Testament. The reason it was excluded from the canon, according to some, had more to do with the developing theology of the church in the fourth century, when the canon became fixed, than with its authenticity. In other words, Thomas shows us a different Jesus from the one portrayed in the Bible, and this other portrait may have just as much claim to "accuracy."

Now, when these scholars looked at Q and Thomas together, another realization dawned. These two documents—the hypothetical one deduced from the canonical gospels and the unearthed one that represented a community of early followers of Jesus that didn't survive the centuries—have a similar structure. They are both batches of sayings: unlike the canonical gospels, there is almost no linking or narrative material in either one. They are just strings of utterances linked by "Jesus said . . ." While this may be only moderately interesting to a layman, to those steeped in the intellectual traditions of the ancient world it was like dynamite. Sayings collections were a popular form of literature in the Greco-Roman sphere. Could it be that the earliest form of the gospels fit this type?

In Europe and the United States, new studies were undertaken: Q and Thomas were combed through and examined alongside examples of ancient "wisdom literature." In 1987, John Kloppenborg published a study analyzing sayings collections from around the ancient Mediterranean. He concluded that Q represented one of the common forms in which information was packaged in hellenistic times: reducing the teachings of wise men to pithy one-liners and compiling them into books. This was the way Greek culture, as it spread into diverse and far-flung areas, was made portable.[3]

Wisdom literature also had a history in Judaism, perhaps thanks to the centuries of Greek influence in Palestine. Examples in the Old Testament are the books of Proverbs, Ecclesiastes, and Job. In fact, as Marcus Borg points out, two kinds of wisdom are apparent: conventional, which prescribes the rules by which society is organized and functions, and alternative, which in essence warns that conventional wisdom isn't all it's cracked up to be. Proverbs is a sayings collection of conventional wisdom—"A slack hand causes poverty, but the hand of the diligent makes rich"—but the warmer voice of Job counters these finger-waggings; much of Job is like a tennis match in which various seemingly wise friends lob aphorisms at Job, the archetypal man who played by the rules but lost anyway, who bats them back with the savagery of the truly bitter:

"Your maxims are proverbs of ashes, your defenses are defenses of clay. . . . How then will you comfort me with empty nothings? There is nothing left of your answers but falsehood." In the end, ironically, God rewards Job for speaking the truth about the folly of conventional wisdom.

There is, then, as Borg says, "a tension or dialectic within the wisdom tradition itself. Indeed, Ecclesiastes and Job can be understood as a radical questioning of the easy confidence of the conventional wisdom of Proverbs that if one lives right, all will go well."[4]

Thanks to Q and Thomas, some scholars now saw Jesus as part of this wisdom tradition—that is to say, the alternative wisdom tradition. Pulling back to a wider perspective, Borg argues that as a teacher of alternative wisdom, Jesus is in close company with Lao-tzu and Buddha. Like them, he promoted not a conventional Ten Commandments kind of truth by which society would function and the just would be rewarded, but a countercultural wisdom. Socrates also fits into this tradition, though his alternative wisdom employs the concepts of philosophy and the tricks of Greek rhetoric rather than the parables of a Jewish sage. In his 1989 best-seller *The Trial of Socrates,* I. F. Stone chastised Socrates for undermining the democratic inclinations of the Athenian state. Stone, the great journalistic champion of democratic principles in the twentieth century, seemed to find it troubling that generations of university students have idolized this Greek who advocated the morally inferior concept of absolute monarchy, especially in an age when democracy was all the rage. "Socrates and his followers were totally out of step with their time in advocating kingship of any kind," Stone charged.[5]

But Stone missed the point. Socrates is not a Hammurabi or a Jefferson; he isn't revered as an explicator of conventional wisdom but as a model of the countercultural radical whose wit and rhetorical parrying cut through the pieties of his day. Stone does not seem to consider the possibility that if the prevailing spirit of Athens had been for monarchy, Socrates might very well have advocated democracy. Generations of historians have drawn parallels between Socrates and Jesus. The most important one may be that both challenged the social norms of their day. The fact that both were put to death suggests what a risky business that was.

One major view of Jesus' "program," then, encompasses the importance of the Q document and the Thomas gospel, and the idea that Jesus and his followers were operating within the "alternative wisdom" tradition of the ancient Near East. How far can these hypotheses be taken? If you dig deeply into Q, keeping in mind the notion that Jesus was a wisdom teacher, where do you end up?

THE GOSPEL ACCORDING TO MACK

You end up with the first of three modern "gospels" that are representative of contemporary scholarship. This is the most radical of the three, and it is one of the most intriguing and provocative reconstructions in the history of critical scholarship. Burton Mack, professor emeritus of the School of Theology at Claremont, represents the far fringe of the broad spectrum of scholars who give primacy to Q. His method has been to try to separate Q into various layers of tradition so that, as one peels back these layers, one edges closer and closer to the first followers of Jesus, the people who actually heard his words from his own lips, stored them in their minds, and passed them along for others to write down. He ends up with a Jesus who fires off tart one-liners—"Love your enemies," "Sell your possessions"—and an imagined group of followers who wove these into a new model for living.

In a series of books starting with *A Myth of Innocence* in 1988, Mack has outlined a bold thesis: that the four canonical gospels contain almost no historically authentic material about the life of Jesus. There is no virgin birth in Mack's picture of the historical Jesus, no miracles, no Temple incident, no Last Supper, no death and resurrection. From this perspective, Jesus may never even have died on a cross, for the crucifixion stories, in this view, are later, and therefore suspect. And while he demolishes the historicity of all of these elements, Mack also unearths a Christian equivalent of the lost city of Atlantis: a whole community of people previously lost to history, the original followers of Jesus.

If Mack is right—if Q is the earliest layer of the Jesus tradition, if this kind of wisdom collection predates not only the four gospels but Paul's writings as well—then the historical Jesus and Christianity itself must be radically rethought. Mack is about as sweeping as one could possibly be: "The discovery of Q may create some consternation for Christians because accepting Q's challenge is not merely a matter of revising a familiar chapter of history. It is a matter of being forced to acknowledge an affair with one's own mythology."[6] Mack charges the media with the task of bringing this new insight to popular attention. Christianity, Mack claims, began not with a historical figure of divinity or a man with insights into the divine, but with a simple teacher along the lines of a Greek sage. This was the "real" Jesus. His followers tried to keep his countercultural wisdom alive, but as soon as it spread, it degraded into a "religious society on the model of a hellenistic mystery cult,"[7] featuring a divine hero with all the attributes familiar to a Greek audience: a miraculous birth, miraculous powers, a miraculous return from death. Christianity stole Jesus away from the people of Q. Burton Mack thinks it's time that we acknowledged that.

This is the extreme position. Think of the gospels as four ancient paintings that have become beloved icons, and Jesus scholars as art historians who study the surfaces and conclude that there is a great deal of later accretion—grime, old varnish, and plenty of retouching. They use their tools to strip off these later layers, to try to get at the original image. Burton Mack uses the same tools as everyone else but applies them with more gusto, and he thinks he has revealed an entirely different picture beneath the ones we have revered for centuries. It's a totally different subject, painted in a different style, with a different intent. Or maybe the better way to carry the metaphor is to say that Mack uses his tools to scrape the canvas entirely clean, and then stands back and says, "Look, there's nothing there!"

THE GOSPEL ACCORDING TO CROSSAN

John Dominic Crossan, an intense, sprightly, almost elfin Irishman, a onetime Catholic priest who quit after one-too-many confrontations with the Vatican over his stands on abortion and priestly celibacy, is one of the most respected and controversial New Testament scholars. His 1991 book *The Historical Jesus* quickly became a modern classic in the field, and the lectures and radio, TV, and on-line appearances he has made since his retirement from teaching in 1995 attract remarkable public attention. This is partly due to his crisp Irish wit, but also to the kind of Jesus he comes up with.

Like Burton Mack, Crossan takes Q and Thomas seriously, but Crossan also thinks that there is much in the canonical gospels that dates to Jesus' time. Crossan believes that Jesus was a Jewish holy man who was steeped in the Greekness of the Mediterranean world. Perhaps it came during childhood trips to Sepphoris, perhaps it was simply in the air, something so pervasive that it would have been impossible for an intelligent young man to miss, but as far as Crossan is concerned, a definite hellenistic influence is apparent in the authentic words of Jesus.

The precise form of this hellenistic influence, Crossan believes, the precise way that the alternative wisdom tradition affected Jesus, is Cynic philosophy. The Cynics were thinkers who, rather than engage in the great questions of the day, as Greeks of former generations had done, "despaired of the world, and felt that, though they themselves knew what was needed, there was no hope of its being brought about," as Bertrand Russell put it. Cynic philosophy was not what we now think of as cynicism; it was a highly developed system of personal virtue. The world may have gone crazy, the Cynics said, but at least I can remain virtuous. They saw hypocrisy in conventional Greco-Roman society; people dressed and behaved as though they were virtuous, but secretly cheated, stole, and exploited in order to make their way in an increasingly chaotic world.

The way out of this societal mess was through rising above it. By freeing oneself from conventions, one attained happiness. If the Empire was led by Roman aristocrats who ruled with arrogant despotism and driven by ethnic entrepreneurs who exploited their neighbors in their zeal for success, the Cynics were dropouts who stood on street corners thumbing their noses at the rich and mocking the empty values of the merchant classes. By the first century they had become fixtures throughout the Empire. The city of Gadara, only thirty miles from Nazareth, was a major center of Cynic thought.

The Cynics had a code: carry only a walking stick and a wallet, live in no fixed abode but wander from town to town begging. A Cynic handbook advised: "Wearing one chiton is preferable to needing two, and wearing none but only a cloak is preferable to wearing one. Also going barefoot is better than wearing sandals. . . ."[8] They begged ". . . not for a free gift . . . but for the salvation of everyone."[9] How should the Cynic face the inevitable scorn of others? "[H]e must needs be flogged like an ass," wrote Epictetus, "and while he is being flogged he must love the men who flog him, as though he were the father or brother of them all."[10]

Even those with only a passing familiarity with Jesus' words and deeds as recorded in the New Testament will find this code familiar:

> Love your enemies, and pray for those who persecute you . . .
>
> Do not resist an evildoer. But if anyone strikes you on the right cheek, turn the other also; and if anyone wants to sue you and take your coat, give your cloak as well . . .
>
> Blessed are the poor.
>
> It is easier for a camel to go through the eye of a needle than for someone who is rich to enter the kingdom of God.[11]

So the classic aphorisms of Jesus read like a Cynic primer, or seem to. And according to both Mark and Q, Jesus mandated a kind of Cynic code for his disciples as he sent them out on healing missions: "He ordered them to take nothing for their journey except a staff; no bread, no bag, no money in their belts; but to wear sandals and not to put on two tunics."[12] The sole difference between this list and the Cynic one, according to Crossan, is significant: Jesus forbids even a purse. A Cynic, proud of his beggary, needed a purse to hold out to accept coins. Jesus' followers would not beg but exchange healing for food and shelter. This is the cement that would bind the new community: "a shared egalitarianism of spiritual and material resources."[13]

Crossan believes that Jesus' genius was in fitting the Cynic code—the code of the down-and-out—to a Jewish context. The success of the Empire was at the expense of the vast majority of the Mediterranean world: whole populations at the bottom of the economic ladder for whom even hope was impossible. The Cynics gave dignity to their oppression. According to Crossan, Jesus and his disciples brought this dignity—the pride of poverty—to Jewish peasants: "They were hippies in a world of Augustan yuppies."[14]

Crossan's "gospel" follows Mack's much of the way. Both see Jesus as a Greco-Jewish sage. But Mack is convinced that the "real" story ended there, that the rest is a lie. Crossan, for all his radical ways, is a Christian, and this colors the story he tells. His Jesus is a radical social visionary who uses parables and healings to enact the ideal justice of Israel's God; he is, or can be seen as, God's son, the means by which God brings healing grace to humanity. Is the Jesus of Crossan's "gospel" divine? As Crossan says, "Divine means, for me, that somebody finds God at work in Jesus."

THE GOSPEL ACCORDING TO SANDERS

Crossan's views are influential today, but not everybody is influenced by them. His work—and that of Marcus Borg and the Jesus Seminar—relies heavily on Q, Thomas, and the idea of Greek influence on first-century Judaism. What it seems to leave out, according to critics, is Judaism itself.

What would happen if you started your examination of the data not with the sayings but the deeds? What if you used first-century

Judaism as your backdrop and plugged into it the puzzle pieces that seem most reliable: that Jesus' career was framed on one end by his baptism at the hands of a prophet of Jewish eschatology and at the other end by his action against the Temple, which seems a direct response to ancient Jewish claims about the coming restoration of Israel? According to E. P. Sanders, whose 1985 *Jesus and Judaism* is for many scholars the major Jesus study of our time, you would have a fairly recognizable account of a first-century Jewish prophet, one that squares with other known data about the time and place, and one that doesn't have to resort to hypothetical documents and relate these to hypothetical intellectual movements. In other words, Sanders uses the same toolbox, but by favoring some tools over others he finds that quite a lot of the gospel portrait stays intact.

Most importantly, in Sanders' view Jesus comes across quite clearly as an eschatological prophet, one in the mold of the Baptist and the priests at Qumran. He believed the world was coming to an end, and soon. According to Sanders, "The hard evidence is this: he talked about a kingdom; his disciples expected to have a role in it; they considered him their leader; he was crucified for claiming to be a king."[15] It wasn't an ordinary kingdom, however, for many of the early references to it speak of God parting the clouds and the righteous being swept up to some aerial nirvana.

The crucial question in New Testament studies, then, the one that all scholarly battles center on, is a deceptively simple one: What exactly does "the end of the world" mean? Is it the end of the space-time universe? A change of individual consciousness so radical that a new age can be said to have begun? Or is it downright supernatural: Was Paul copying the notion from Jesus when he looked forward to being "caught up in the clouds . . . to meet the Lord in the air"?

Sanders thinks that a hard look at the gospel evidence, coupled with an understanding of Jewish history, indicates that the kingdom Jesus expected was of-this-world. His symbolic destruction of the Temple, his choosing of twelve disciples, his apparent discussions with disciples about what place each would occupy in the new kingdom all lead to the conclusion that Jesus saw the Old Testament prophecies about to be fulfilled by him, on earth. And the Dead Sea Scrolls support this: the scrolls speak of the apocalypse coming on the heels of an army that would be divided into twelve units, one for each of the twelve tribes. The scrolls were also explicit about how the Temple would be rebuilt in the new age.[16] Here was a community of mystics living in Jesus' time who also clearly believed that this new age would take place in the world.

So forget about Greek influence. Throw Q in the trash. A sober application of the historian's tools to the gospel portraits, Sanders argues, reveals a figure close to what we find on the surface: a Jewish apocalyptic prophet, who lacks only the showier supernatural flourishes.

MAKE YOUR OWN GOSPEL

If Sanders is right—and he represents a major wing of scholarship, which includes John Meier, Geza Vermes, and many other renowned authorities—then Jesus expected God to perform some miracle that would inaugurate a new holy rule in Israel. This is radically different from the view of the new brand of thinkers—Crossan, Borg, Robert Funk, and most members of the Jesus Seminar—who find the kingdom of God most clearly pointed to in the parables: a state of awareness rather than a visible kingdom.

This is the fault line; here is where, it seems, ordinary people must choose a side. What is at stake is the character of Jesus. What kind of man was he? Even seemingly dispassionate academics who insist on separating Jesus the man from the Christ of faith quiver as they face this issue, for in answering it they are making a profound statement about Christianity. On the face of it, it would seem that the Crossan position is the more radical, for it paints the man as a mystic whom, over time, the church confused with the spiritual realm he pointed to. The eschatological prophet of Sanders, by contrast, seems fairly close to the gospel portrait. If one wanted to be safe, it would seem, one could line up behind Sanders.

But Paula Fredriksen, who models her own argument on Sanders's, outlines what she sees as the theological agenda of the other side. "These people have painted Jesus in recognizably modern, politically pleasing colors," she says. "He's a Jesus who is a social reformer, a maverick wiseguy. Basically what they're doing is relieving themselves of the embarrassment of having a Jesus who is so terribly wrong about something."

As far as Fredriksen is concerned, Jesus was a Jewish apocalyptic who expected a cataclysmic intervention of God into history . . . and was devastatingly wrong. Christianity, then, amounts to a series of attempts to deal with this staggering error, most notably the doctrine of the Second Coming. Looked at this way, the seeming radicals of the Jesus Seminar, with Crossan at their head, turn out to be apologists: they try to get Jesus out of his bind by claiming that he never proclaimed an imminent end. They are doing theology, creating a new gospel, trying to prove their beloved religious figure relevant today and for all time. So while many critics decry the Jesus Seminar for trying to undo Christianity, for pulling out such supporting beams as the virgin birth and the bodily resurrection, Fredriksen charges that in fact they are a newfangled, secular-humanist sort of apology for the whole Christian myth; that they are attempting to cover up the fact that Christianity has based itself on that most tawdry of religious figures, an unprophetic prophet.

Is this a fair charge? Everyone in the field can be accused of having a personal agenda. Burton Mack is moved by a need to unmask Christianity, Sanders by a need to shore up the New Testament picture, Fredriksen by a need to "convert" Jesus to Judaism. The facts themselves don't speak: the person interpreting them does. We all create our own gospel, we each have our own way of making sense of things.

That is one way of viewing this work: that it is a search for personal truth as much as historical truth. As a way to test this, consider: Does the staggering amount of attention being paid to this one historical figure itself affect the results? Don't the scholars expect to find Jesus saying and doing some earth-shakingly important things? If an utterly dispassionate examination of the evidence resulted in a Jesus who was just one more first-century fist-shaker who uttered a few profound sentiments, made an elaborate (and incorrect) apocalyptic prediction, and died anonymously, would we accept that? Would most scholars even allow their work to proceed along such lines? Are we ready to follow the advice of Mack and make the historical Jesus a footnote, a marginal personality who, through whatever series of accidents, was turned into a god? Or does the very scope and depth of the search reveal that this is not a dispassionate analysis of evidence but a theological agenda?

The widely divergent pictures suggest that total detachment from the evidence is impossible. The portrait inevitably takes on some features of its painter. Maybe it is not useful to think of the historical Jesus as a hard-and-fast thing, as an image that is slowly being revealed or an artifact being excavated. Maybe he turns out to be more like a musical instrument. The scholarship has succeeded in reconstructing this instrument so that it has certain definite features, but when it comes time to play, everyone plays a different song.

If every historical Jesus scholar is in effect writing his or her own personal gospel, why can't the rest of us? We can, and we do. Telling stories—about our family, our country, ourselves—is how we make sense of the world. Getting to the "real truth" behind a personal story is a tricky business, as any psychoanalyst knows. Perhaps it would be naive to think that when it comes to the historical Jesus we are doing anything more definitive than retelling an old story in a way that makes the most sense to us. By following the work of the scholars, perhaps we are searching for a basic template that we can tailor to our needs.

One thing most scholars, and many Christian observers, seem to agree on is that it matters very much what view of Jesus emerges victorious from this scholarly debate: apocalyptic firebrand, Greco-mystic, or some combination of the two. But does it? Is it really possible that we will someday get to a more definitive understanding of his mind, that we will discover some new clue that will show that the "real" Jesus expected the world to collapse when he upset tables in the Temple, or that the "real" Jesus was a counterculture guru? This work is profoundly important for getting us to this stage, from which we can observe the historical Jesus acting and speaking; but surely it is up to each of us to interpret the actions and words, just as it was up to his disciples to do so. The historical critical method can take us this far; beyond, we're on our own.

But while we study the various templates offered to us by the experts, there are also other possibilities—the sorts of puzzle solutions that critical scholars by nature and training tend to ignore. For one, most reflection on Jesus' Message sees it just like that: with a capital letter, as if it came to him fully formed, a total package direct from God. Little consideration is given to the simple notion that his thinking evolved over time. Say, for example, that along with John's baptism he took the idea that an apocalyptic end to history was imminent. This fired his religious awakening. Perhaps when he first healed a sick peasant he experienced another revelation: he saw this expected Power, this coming Spirit, at work here-and-now, through him. So he had it both ways: the kingdom was coming, and the kingdom was present. This may not make clear, rational sense, but it seems obvious that Jesus was not a man who cared much for the rational. Trying to imagine his understanding of the kingdom of God logically may be like trying to figure out logically why Beethoven went from one phase of his career to another. Surely a religious genius, like a musical genius, works by different rules.

This is not a new insight. As early as 1937, the historian Henry Cadbury wrote a book called *The Perils of Modernizing Jesus,* in which he argued that "the sense of purpose, objective, etc., as necessary for every good life is more modern than we commonly imagine. . . . What I wish to propose is that Jesus probably had no definite, unified, conscious purpose, that an absence of such a program is *a priori* likely and that it suits well the historical evidence."[17]

This serves not as the final word on Jesus' work, but as a reminder that we are dealing with someone who lived in what, to us, is a truly ancient, truly primitive age. As Fredriksen said to me, "No first-century person is under obligation to make immediate sense to us. If our parents hardly make sense to us, and they are not that much older than us, it's ridiculous to think that a first-century person will be transparent to us ethically and religiously."

For this reason, we should perhaps be skeptical of coherent reconstructions of Jesus that ignore important chunks of evidence. The evidence of Greek influence on ancient Palestine—archaeological, literary, historical—seems strong and clear. But a moderately critical examination of the deeds of Jesus as recorded in the New Testament—one that considers only those deeds generally thought to be historical—suggests a man who was operating in a fundamentally Jewish context. If all of this is solid evidence, both the Greek and the Jewish, then it would seem the picture of who Jesus was and what he thought he was doing has to encompass all of it, whether or not what results makes immediate sense to us. To paraphrase Sherlock Holmes, if you have exhausted all of the probable scenarios, whatever is left, however unlikely, becomes the new hypothesis.

Consider, then, a blend of ideas from the seemingly conflicting views of contemporary scholarship:

First, everyone agrees the historical Jesus was a radical prophet who knew God, directly and intimately, and who believed that divine truth was open to all of Israel. He attempted to bring this divine truth to ordinary people via parables and healings.

Second, he may have seen himself as a prophet in the tradition of Elijah and Elisha, a freelance healer, working outside the Temple system. He could even have referred to himself as a "son of God," though the phrase "*the* Son of God," meaning a divine being, doesn't exist elsewhere in the Judaism of Jesus' time and seems to be a later creation.

Third, he could have genuinely believed that God was literally about to split open the blue sky above and rain lightning bolts down upon the wicked. He could have believed this was going to happen in his lifetime. He could have believed he had a central role to play in this great event. If this is so, however, then he seems to have modified this belief, for he spoke of both a present and a coming kingdom of God. Perhaps he held both concepts in his mind at the same time; perhaps his beliefs evolved over time.

He could have consciously or unconsciously blended apocalyptic eschatology with Greek philosophy to achieve his insights. This blending of cultures may have contributed to the uniqueness of what he did and said.

Most of these statements fit the evidence. They all have a

degree of probability attached to them. But it doesn't seem possible that we will get much closer than this, unless someone unearths Jesus' personal diary. The picture, then, is of a man of the first century, a Palestinian Jew who lived in an age of Greek influence, a profoundly spiritual person who felt called to bring his revelation of divine insight to others.

But Jesus wasn't entirely of a spiritual cast. If there is one other point that the various scholars agree on, it is that he must surely have been aware of the political implications of what he was doing, even if he was not himself a militant. In the rigid social, political, and economic system of ancient Palestine, someone who said the things he said and did the things he did, and gathered a large following in the process, would have been seen as a sower of disorder.

The proof of this is in the final fact about his life. The Romans were methodical and efficient rulers. They generally liked to have a reason, real or perceived, before sentencing someone to death by public execution.

CHAPTER NINE

MURDER MYSTERY

A man is dead. A killer has been identified, tried, and punished. The chain of events outlined by the prosecution is compelling: motive, means, and will are all established. Add to this the fact that the defendant is on record as confessing to the deed, and the unusual twist that the victim is reported to have returned from the dead to corroborate these details, and you have a pretty tight case.

All this is ancient history. But now comes a generation of detectives who claim to have discovered important new evidence—evidence that exonerates the long-suffering defendant and points to cover-up and gross misrepresentation of the facts. Ladies and gentlemen of the jury, what lies before you is nothing less than the most egregious wrong ever committed in the history of criminal justice.

The victim, of course, is Jesus of Nazareth. The defendant is the Jewish people, a race that has endured centuries of punishment, from Constantine to Hitler, directly or indirectly related to the widespread belief that "the Jews" were responsible for Jesus' death. And the detectives are the current generation of historians, archaeologists, and experts in other related fields who believe they are chipping away at the rock-face of time to reveal the outlines of a historical figure.

As historical Jesus work proceeds, it is becoming clear that there is a current and crucial issue behind this chapter of it, for many scholars are convinced that in the construction of the final act of the Jesus saga, the Jews were framed by the gospel writers.

To understand how that might have happened, consider the structure of a gospel. Matthew opens with a short infancy narrative, proceeds to a series of disjointedly connected episodes—healings, preachings, seemingly disembodied strolls through grainfields or by the lakeside, sudden trips to Nazareth or Tyre or Caesarea Philippi—before finally settling down into a single, fully developed narrative action, which culminates in death. This drama, which takes up more than one-third of the gospel, is where the writer has focused his art and energy. This, clearly, is what mattered to him—and this is where the other three gospels are most focused also.

They are called the passion narratives, from the Latin *patior,* "to suffer." Here, as elsewhere, comparing the four gospels reveals a wealth of inconsistencies, but the basic features are the same in all, and all are deeply concerned to present Jesus' ultimate suffering—his entry into Jerusalem, Last Supper, agony in Gethsemane, arrest, and execution—in a carefully wrought frame of significance. For Jesus' followers, his death on the cross was the most devastating and unexpected of events; the passion narratives—certainly among the greatest literary works of all time—reveal more than anything the anguish and shock of a community peering into the void, then turning slowly to one another and their tradition in a hungry search for meaning. Blame, it seems, was to be one element of that search. Punishment was another.

Trying to determine the origins of the notion of Jewish guilt for the death of Jesus is a major issue surrounding current research into the trial and crucifixion accounts in the gospels. The other, which underlies all else, has to do with historical truth in general. How much of the action in the passion narratives really happened? And if the answer is "not much," where did all those glorious details come from?

A clear, concise answer to the first question is possible. The vast majority of scholars agree that the nearly certain facts can be summed up in a few prepositional phrases. Jesus was killed:

a. by crucifixion
b. in Jerusalem
c. at a place called Golgotha
d. during Passover
e. under the authority of Pontius Pilate
f. probably around 30 C.E.

Conservative scholars agree on this list. The comparatively radical exegetes of the Jesus Seminar, at their Santa Rosa meeting, voted these details as nearly certain as well. Supporting the gospels on these bare facts are the independent testimonies of Josephus and the Roman historian Tacitus. This is our bedrock.

The consensus begins to fray when we delve into the details, but there is one overall point of agreement, albeit nervous agreement. Simply put, most scholars are convinced that the passion narratives are at least in part fictions based on Old Testament references. A few basic, well-established facts, it is held, were embellished in the way that first-century Jews found most meaningful, with details borrowed from Scripture. The difference between the conservative wing of scholarship and the liberal is only one of degree; where the one argues that *some* of the passion narrative is woven from Old Testament references to the Hebrew Scriptures, the other says *most* of the passion narrative is woven from Old Testament references. As the Catholic scholar Raymond E. Brown puts it, using the Hebrew Bible to develop the passion stories "is quite understandable if we remember that followers of Jesus were interested in the significance of what happened: How was Jesus' death on the cross meaningful in the divine plans for God's people? The only language in which they could answer that question was scriptural . . ."[1]

Where does this sweeping reversal of two millennia of tradition come from? How can Catholic, Protestant, and other authorities calmly claim that much of the passion may not have literally happened?

To begin with, there is the non-evidence of the earliest sources. In Paul's copious writings, so fervently focused on the redemptive death of Jesus Christ, there is no mention of the saga that we all know so well: the triumphal entry on an ass, the crown of thorns, the confrontation with Pilate. If Paul, writing only a decade or two after the crucifixion, knew about such theologically potent details as Jesus' prayer in Gethsemane or his dying words on the cross—"Father, into your hands I commend my spirit"—how could he not have expounded upon them? The answer that comes to mind is the same one that comes to mind with the virgin birth story: he didn't know the features of the passion story because they hadn't been invented yet.

Again, this is not to say that all scholars believe all elements of the passion story are fiction. Most hold that certain incidents echo a historical memory; disagreements are over which do and do not. The devil, so to speak, is in the details.

But, one might counter, we already have four different accounts of the passion. How many do we need before we can call it reasonably authentic? The problem with this argument is that we don't have four *independent* accounts. Matthew's and Luke's passion narratives are clearly dependent on Mark's; John's may be as well. Suddenly we have not four basic sources for the events leading up to and including the crucifixion, but two, or possibly only one. So our earliest source, Mark, was written probably around 70 C.E., or nearly forty years after the crucifixion, and John, even if independent, was nevertheless written nearly seventy years after the crucifixion, and in all that time no other letter or document mentions any of the details that these gospels so lovingly and insistently toll, details that have become the pith and substance of Christian liturgy.

Now take as a final piece of evidence something that was recognized as early as the second century: that a remarkable number of the elements of the passion saga have clear, often verbatim Old Testament parallels. It begins to look as though someone filled in gaps by mining the ancient texts. This was, of course, a standard method for finding meaning in ancient Judaism. We saw it at work in the Hebrew Bible, where Moses' ability to part the waters is bequeathed to Elijah, and in the birth narratives of Matthew and Luke, both of which are woven around a kernel from the Book of Isaiah, the idea that an *almah,* read as "virgin," would give birth.

Some writers have used the Hebrew term *midrash* to refer to this practice. Properly speaking, *midrash* was a technique employed by Jews of the first seven centuries of the common era for interpreting current-day events in light of scriptural passages. Jacob Neusner, the renowned scholar of Judaism, in describing *midrash,* gives an important clue to how an ancient Jew would have seen events in his own time through the lens of history. "People commonly suppose that when Judaic or Christian authorships turned to Israelite Scripture, it was in search of proof-texts," Neusner writes.

In fact, the ancient Jews believed their Bible was so irradiated with divine wisdom that a wise writer could take pieces of it out of context and recombine them to create new meaning: "Scripture formed a dictionary, providing a vast range of permissible usages of intelligible words. Scripture did not dictate the sentences that would be composed through the words found in that (limited) dictionary."[2]

So the gospel writers would have pored through their Bible not out of a desperate need to shore up their position, but in a sincere search for insight. Others in Jesus' time did something similar. For the Dead Sea Scrolls sect, the way to understand the deep relevance of their present circumstances was to do a meticulous, line-by-line reading of a portion of Scripture and draw parallels between the incidents and people found there and incidents and people in their own time. Through this technique, called *pesher*, the Essenes saw their desert settlement as spiritually related to the desert camp of the Israelites under Moses. Just as the Israelites were preparing for a great war for the Holy Land, the Essenes prepared for the great battle to end history and bring in God's new reign. To reinforce the parallel, the Essene hierarchy named itself after the heads of the twelve tribes.

There are overt indications in the gospels that a related technique is being used. In Luke's gospel, the Risen Christ actually tells the disciples where to look for scriptural passages that they should relate to him:

> Then he said to them, "These are the words that I spoke to you while I was still with you—that everything written about me in the law of Moses, the prophets, and the psalms must be fulfilled." *Then he opened their minds to understand the scriptures,* and he

> said to them, "Thus it is written, that the Messiah is to suffer and to rise from the dead on the third day . . ."[3]

Daryl Schmidt of Texas Christian University analyzes this text: "Luke's perspective is not that Scripture merely 'says' things that are now coming true, but that it requires 'open minds' and a 'hermeneutic' in order to see these things."[4] Why does it require "open minds"? Because nowhere in the Hebrew Bible does it say anything about a Messiah suffering and rising from the dead on the third day. The suffering motif was gleaned from a passage in Isaiah about a suffering servant who is vindicated. It is one of the favorite citations of literal-minded Christians, for it seems so clearly and irrefutably to prefigure Jesus on the cross. The problem, however, is that until the creation of the gospels Judaism never expected a Messiah to suffer.[5] A Messiah was a warrior, a king, an absolute victor on the battlefield. In retrospect, the meek, humble Jesus of the gospels seems a perfect fit with suffering servant imagery, but the gospel writers had to really work at it to fit "servant" and "Messiah" into the same box. They have recruited none other than the Risen Christ himself to aid them.

No one today knows how literally or metaphorically a Jewish audience would have understood these biblical allusions in the gospels. But it seems clear that a change came during the following decades, when Christianity became not only a religion in its own right but a Gentile religion, for the Gentiles knew nothing of *midrash* or *pesher*. And so what was originally a self-conscious way to associate Jesus with King David and with references from Isaiah and the psalms became literalized. So that, for example, with Matthew's detail of Jesus on the cross, "they offered him wine to drink, mixed with gall,"[6] its clear echo of Psalm 69—"And they gave for my bread gall, and for my thirst they gave me to drink vinegary wine . . ."[7]—became lost on the Gentile Christians, and the reference—a combination of poetic allusion and mystical fusing of the past into the present—hardened into a real event. The same goes for the words Jesus cries out from the cross—"My God, my God, why have you forsaken me?"[8]—an exact quote of the opening of Psalm 22.

But why would it have been necessary to flesh out the story in this way? Surely the followers of Jesus were vitally concerned with his execution at the time it was happening. Surely those who had stayed at his side during his strolls through Galilee remained with him as events built to a climax in Jerusalem that fateful Passover, and were thus able to supply the actual details of the terrible event.

Ah, but they didn't, they weren't. The gospels are clear on this: "All of them deserted him and fled."[9] So what pro-Jesus witness was left to observe the unusual nighttime meeting of the Sanhedrin, where Jesus was supposedly brought before the high priest Caiaphas? Would Caiaphas have allowed such a witness—a peasant nobody—to attend, even if he or she had not fled with the others? Are we to suppose that Caiaphas himself gave the account to a reporter afterwards, making himself look like a shrill fool? Who witnessed Peter's three denials of Jesus? Who observed the trial before Pilate and recorded the details?

Of course, no one did. No one even knows whether a trial of Jesus ever took place. Raymond E. Brown has written the most comprehensive study of the passion narratives, the two-volume *Death of the Messiah,* a work that switches back and forth between theological commentary and historical examination of the texts. It is more tentative in its conclusions than most recent works on the subject, but Brown is quite matter-of-fact on the question of historical truth. The passion accounts are not history, they are "dramatic narratives." Evidence for this is everywhere: "For instance, an impressive number of happenings occur in threes," Brown writes. "After he has prayed, Jesus returns three times to find the disciples sleeping. In all the gospels Peter denies Jesus three times. . . . Jesus is mocked three times as he hangs on the cross. . . . The use of 'three' is a well-known feature in storytelling, most familiar to English-speaking audiences in jokes (English-Irish-Scot, priest-minister-rabbi, etc.)."[10]

So even Catholic scholars readily admit that the passion narratives are dramas, literary creations, not histories. They were created not to put down the facts for posterity but to try to explain what at first seemed to Jesus' followers as inexplicably cruel and horrifically meaningless. They believed in a just God, a God who worked through history. And they believed that Jesus of Nazareth somehow represented that God and was leading them to something he called the kingdom of God. How, then, was it possible that he had died—so suddenly, so summarily, so shamefully?

That is the question the gospels were written to answer. To be more precise than this is impossible, but many historians try. One theory gaining in prominence today is that the gospels, and especially the passion narratives, are in effect transcriptions of the first Christian liturgies. According to this view, soon after Jesus' death, groups of his followers began to perform ritual services of remembrance, in which details from his last days, elaborated with scriptural imagery, were recited. The gospel writers, then, did not create the passion stories but rather combined elements that were circulating—stories of miracles performed, collections of sayings, and this ritual "performance" of Jesus' suffering and death—into one text. In this reading, Mark was not the first creator of a Jesus story, but the first compiler of all the parts into a whole. If this is even close to what happened, then it explains some of the contradictions that, as we have seen, theologians and historians have long wrangled with. Why does Jesus seem at times to be primarily a healer, at other times primarily a subversive sage, and then ultimately an almost godlike being aware of and approving his own approaching death? These are really three different people; how do they fit together?

They fit together only because they were forced together by Mark. What we seem to have is a situation in which several different groups of people viewed Jesus in distinctly different ways. One—represented by the Q document and the Gospel of Thomas—collected wisdom sayings. Another—represented by a "signs gospel" that is embedded in Mark and John—collected miracle stories. And the followers of an apocalyptic prophet, whom they believed was preparing them for the New Age, who felt abandoned by his death and strove for understanding, developed a liturgical ritual as a way to highlight the significance of his death, to turn earthly defeat into spiritual victory.

This division of the followers into three is surely too neat and simplistic; some could have seen him as a sage *and* a healer, or a healer and an apocalyptic. The point is that Mark, the writer of the first gospel, was removed from all of them, and while he has done us the great service of putting it all down in writing he has also obscured this diversity.

He was fairly brusque in combining these three images of Jesus, but he did make some attempt to harmonize them. The Jesus of the first two groups—the storyteller and the miracle-worker—has been given knowledge of his end. While still in Galilee, "He was teaching his disciples, saying to them, 'The Son of Man is to be betrayed into human hands, and they will kill him, and three days after being killed, he will rise again.' "[11] The disciples don't get it; "they did not understand what he was saying and were afraid to ask him." Later, he tries again, even more explicitly: "See, we are going up to Jerusalem, and the Son of Man will be handed over to the chief priests and the scribes, and they will condemn him to death;

then they will hand him over to the Gentiles; they will mock him, and spit upon him, and flog him, and kill him; and after three days he will rise again."[12]

By thus highlighting the apocalyptic, Mark reveals where he stands: he himself is looking for Jesus to return and usher in the kingdom. But other groups continued to exist. The New Testament itself makes it clear that James, Jesus' brother, was the leader of one of these. James was not one of the disciples, and apparently kept his distance from his radical brother along with the rest of the family, as the gospels suggest in several places ("For not even his brothers believed in him."[13]) But after Jesus' death, James emerged as the leader of the Jewish followers of Jesus in Jerusalem. His group seems to have honored Jesus as a prophet and a reformer of Judaism. (When James was stoned to death in 62 C.E. under orders of the high priest, his uncle Cleopas inherited his position, which seems to indicate that the Jerusalem faction also had in mind a hierarchy based on blood succession.)

As we turn from Galilee to Jerusalem and move into the passion narrative, we are leaving behind the Jesus we have been observing up to now. The historical Jesus—a teacher, a healer, a prophet—is the subject of the first part of each gospel. As we approach the gates of Jerusalem, however, he vanishes, and another figure takes his place. Even before he is crucified, the Jesus of the gospels is transforming into the Christ of faith, the Son of Man, who will come again to judge the living and the dead.

Mark is operating in two roles at this point, as a dramatist and a theologian. The dramatic question before him is, "How do I get my tragic hero from Act Two to Act Three?" Or, put in other words, "How does Jesus get to Jerusalem, where he will die?" Mark's solution is a theological one: Jesus goes to Jerusalem precisely because he knows he is going to die.

Historians, however, aren't content with this foreknowledge.

They ask different questions: "What really brought Jesus to Jerusalem, and why was he executed?" Searching the surface of the gospels for answers, we find the wandering Jesus moving closer and closer to his fate: into Judea, to Jericho, then to the Mount of Olives, and so into Jerusalem, to celebrate the feast of Passover. The Synoptics seem to imply that this was his first trip here as an adult, but this is unlikely. All able-bodied Jews were expected to make a pilgrimage to Jerusalem three times a year: for the festivals of Pesach or Passover, Sukkot or Tabernacles, and Shavuot or Pentecost. This was a practical impossibility for most peasants, but it indicates that travel to Jerusalem was a part of Jewish life. Paula Fredriksen surmises that John's gospel is more accurate in this regard. John has Jesus coming to Jerusalem not once but *five times* during his ministry. Perhaps he did come repeatedly, each time preaching in the Temple, each time upsetting the authorities a little more. Being of the apocalyptic camp, Fredriksen believes the historical Jesus had a purpose in mind on this fifth visit: to proclaim that the apocalyptic kingdom would arrive *now,* this Passover, complete with divine justice raining down on pious Jews.[14] And it was his openly and riotously proclaiming this end of the current regime and coming of a new kingdom, amid the volatile atmosphere of Passover, that led to his arrest.

This eschatological view has the advantage that it gives Jesus an intention: he goes to Jerusalem with a very specific purpose in mind. Non-eschatological scholars can posit no such clear purpose. Maybe he went to celebrate Passover, as he had many times before, and things simply got out of hand.

But consider the events leading up to the Last Supper, as the gospels give them. First we have Jesus and his disciples in the village of Bethany on the Mount of Olives, preparing to enter Jerusalem. Jesus instructs them to go into the village, where they will find a colt tied, and bring it to him. Jesus then rides this colt into the city, and suddenly people are tossing branches into the road in front of him and shouting, "Hosanna! Blessed is the one who comes in the name of the Lord! Blessed is the coming kingdom of our ancestor David!" Jesus goes immediately to the Temple, where he simply "looked around at everything," and then leaves.

All of this is rather strange if seen as actual human behavior. But if seen as drama that is meant to enact Scripture, the pieces fall into place. Zechariah 9:9 is the controlling text, which both Matthew and John quote explicitly: "Shout aloud, O daughter Jerusalem! Lo, your king comes to you; triumphant and victorious is he, humble and riding on a donkey, on a colt, the foal of a donkey."

Did the historical Jesus actually ride in on a donkey, to associate himself with this piece of Scripture? This has been one of the most furiously debated questions in the hundred-year history of historical Jesus research. Why? Because it shows intent. *Did* he see himself as the Messiah? *Was* he overtly challenging the Jewish and Roman authorities? Or is this devout fiction, created after the fact to associate Jesus with messiahship?

There are no hard facts to sway the matter one way or the other. What anyone believes will be based on one's overall image of Jesus. Sanders thinks Jesus was an apocalyptic prophet; to him it makes sense that Jesus would enter the city on an ass, consciously associating himself with Scripture. But Sanders himself sees a problem with this reading: If Jesus entered as a king while crowds swarmed around him to acknowledge his kingship, why wouldn't the Romans have nabbed him at once as a dangerous upstart?[15]

Crossan thinks the whole episode makes more sense if seen as pious fiction. He points out that the Book of Zechariah was not exactly on the bestseller list in antiquity; it wouldn't have occupied a place in popular consciousness that the stories of Moses and

David had, so it seems unlikely that anyone seeing Jesus riding in on a donkey would see this as symbolic of anything (especially since riding a donkey was about as commonplace as riding in a Toyota is today), and therefore it doesn't make sense that it would even have occurred to Jesus that riding into the city on a donkey would make a big religio-political statement.[16]

In the minds of the gospel writers, the entry into Jerusalem is directly tied to one of the most crucial events in the life of the historical Jesus, an event that almost everyone agrees really happened: Jesus goes into the Temple and causes a disturbance of some kind, which leads to his arrest.

The first thing to note here is, as any visitor to the Temple Mount today can attest, the absolute enormity of the Temple. Today you proceed from the crowded, dim, cacophonous warren of the Old City, through one of several small portals, past an armed guard, and emerge awestruck into an astonishingly vast expanse of shimmering grass and ancient stones. Bright sunlight overwhelms you; the trees bend and sigh in a steady, rushing wind. The Dome of the Rock, with its massive gold dome and blue, white, and green tiled walls, dominates all. Surely more history and reverence is packed into this breathtakingly peaceful place than anywhere else on earth. This is supposedly Mount Moriah, where Abraham raised the knife to kill his son Isaac but was stopped by the Lord, and also the spot from which Mohammed, astride his horse Buraq, ascended to heaven one night in the seventh century. It is the site of the first Temple, built by Solomon in the tenth century B.C.E., and of the destruction by the forces of Nebuchadnezzar of Babylon in 586 B.C.E. And, of course, this was the center of Herod the Great's colossal building program, and the focal point of the

Roman invasion of Judea in the war of 66–70 C.E., which brought an end to ancient Judaism.

But, most importantly of all for our purposes, this was the holiest spot in the world for first-century Jews, a massive, teeming complex with no parallel in the modern world, a combination sanctuary, slaughterhouse, and state treasury.

Look again at a piece of Mark's gospel quoted in brief above: "Then he entered Jerusalem and went into the temple; and when he had looked around at everything, as it was already late, he went out . . ."[17] The next day Jesus goes right back to the Temple and "began to drive out those who were selling and those who were buying . . . and he overturned the tables of the money changers and the seats of those who sold doves . . ."

What we seem to have here, if there is any history behind it, is a premeditated act. Jesus goes to the Temple, but it is late and most people have gone home: he doesn't have an audience, so he leaves. The next day he enters again, and immediately gets to work raising a ruckus. As a pious Jew, he would be familiar with the Temple and its money changers, so the argument that he was surprised and shocked by the money changers' presence makes no sense. He knew what he would find here, and he waited until the time was right to do what he had come to do.

Scholars and theologians once held that Jesus was "cleansing" the Temple, keeping God's place free of crass commerce, as his words imply ("Is it not written, 'My house shall be called a house of prayer for all the nations'? But you have made it a den of robbers"). Sanders, however, makes the persuasive point that this Jesus would have been a virtual stranger to Judaism. The Temple was an integral part of every Jew's life; even the Essenes, who loathed the Temple priests so fiercely that they had exiled themselves to the desert at Qumran, still sent offerings to the Temple. Nearly all scholars consider the "den of robbers" lines to be the product of a later writer.

So what was Jesus doing in upsetting the tables? There are two possible scenarios. For those inclined to an apocalyptic Jesus, the action is clear. Jesus, like John the Baptist, believed that the end of history was rapidly approaching—maybe that it was going to come at this very Passover. In his religious fervor, he was attempting to usher in the new kingdom, following the prophecy of Tobit, which suggested that the apocalypse would begin with the destruction of the Temple: "And the Temple of God . . . will be burned to the ground. . . . But God will again have mercy on them . . . and they will rebuild the Temple of God . . . and will rebuild Jerusalem in splendor . . ."[18]

The problem with this reading is a practical one. How did this apocalyptic Jesus think his action would ignite such a cataclysm? Did he believe other Jews would follow suit and a riot would ensue, which would then turn into a mass uprising against the Jewish authorities and the Romans? Or is it possible that he believed he was so connected to God that he would become a conduit for the supernatural: flames shooting from his fingertips, the earth splitting open at his feet?

The other scenario, the non-apocalyptic one, sees the act as more of a righteous protest of the sort staged by various prophets of old. It wouldn't, however, have been a protest against the Temple per se, for the Temple was the heart of Judaism, and what we know of the historical Jesus indicates that he was a devout Jew throughout his life.* And it wouldn't have been a protest against the money changers and animal sellers. These were part of the

*Besides that, if Jesus had had a problem with the Temple per se, surely his followers would not have continued to worship there after his death, as Acts makes clear repeatedly: "One day Peter and John were going up to the Temple at the hour of prayer . . ." (3:1). "And every day in the Temple and at home they did not cease to teach and proclaim Jesus as the Messiah" (5:42).

ordinary functioning of the Temple. Jews came to make sacrifice to God in order to atone for sins; the Bible required that only "clean" animals be sacrificed, and the animal sellers simply assured that their product fit the bill. As for the money changers, their job was to exchange the various kinds of coinage people brought to pay the Temple tax into the one coin acceptable in the Temple precinct.

No, in this view the protest was against the priests, the ruling elite, who had steadily increased taxes on the peasants and whom ordinary people were coming to see as corrupted by their alliance with Rome. This ruling elite had amassed an enormous fortune, which was kept in the Temple treasury. It wasn't the middlemen sitting before him with their caged birds and stacks of coins whom Jesus was pointing the finger at, nor was it the Temple itself, which was after all God's house; it was the ones in charge, who had turned the people's piety into an economic noose.

Now, as stated, the Temple platform was and is vast: twenty football fields would fit neatly inside it. The money-changing activity and the freelance preaching went on in the colonnade that ran around the perimeter. Imagine this enormous area jammed with tens of thousands of people and Roman guards ranged along the walls. Jerusalem was normally under Jewish control, but during the big festivals, when the population went from thirty thousand to three hundred thousand, the Romans brought in their own troops.[19] Passover in particular was a festival of high spirits and high tension.

So you have thousands of Jews gathered together in what Sanders describes as "a kind of combination of state fair, silent worship, butchery of animals, eating red meat—a rare treat—and drinking wine."[20] You have Roman troops looking down nervously from the walls, under orders to pounce on anyone who gets too rowdy. You have simmering enmity between these troops and these worshipers, going back to Ptolemy's scandalous march into the inner sanctum of the Temple in 63 B.C.E., an enmity that could at any moment explode into violence. An instance of such an eruption during Passover is recounted by Josephus. About twenty years after the death of Jesus, a Roman soldier standing guard on the wall "pulled up his garment and bent over indecently, turning his backside toward the Jews and making a noise as indecent as his attitude."[21] The Jews' indignation turned into a riot; Roman reinforcements poured into the Temple compound and slaughtered thirty thousand. Even allowing for Josephus' tendency to exaggerate atrocities, this incident suggests how edgy things could get during Passover.

And now comes this Galilean peasant, preaching, perhaps to a large crowd, a crowd growing larger by the minute, for he may well have become famous in Jerusalem by this time. And then, in righteous protest, he charges at some of the tables, overturning them, sending coins flying, pigeons squawking, merchants cursing.

This would have been enough to get him arrested and executed. He had probably been marked as a troublemaker for some time, perhaps ever since his association with the Baptist. The data suggests Jesus was an honest-to-God radical who tried to make impossibly idealistic social and political changes. The authorities may have been constantly watching him, waiting for the slightest excuse to get rid of him.

But, at the same time, Sanders's point is still persuasive: Jesus was a man of his time. It's all well and good for a twentieth-century mind to see things in terms of political protest, but that simply isn't the way they thought back then. Jesus did, however, live in a world in which apocalyptic expectation was real.

So might both sides of this argument be right? If Jesus saw and felt the increasingly exploitative nature of the Temple, he would have seen and felt it in his own terms, which could have meant *wickedness is on the rise; the End is at hand.*

This is another perfect academic argument: perfect because unwinnable. Just as it is impossible to know what he meant by the kingdom of God, we will never know for sure what he had in mind when he attacked the Temple. As with the kingdom of God, there is room in the Temple to accommodate all comers.

Whatever led him to lunge, he did lunge. Jesus caused a commotion, enough to bring the authorities to act against him.

But there is a twist: somehow, he got away. All the gospels separate the act from the arrest. Maybe the Romans were slow in responding. Maybe, given the size of the crowds and the vastness of the complex, it was a simple matter of blending in. Whatever the case, Jesus was presumably a wanted man from then on. It was only a matter of time before they found him. And the main action that occurs between the Temple incident and the arrest is, of course, the Last Supper.

Was there a Last Supper? Of course there was. But, as Crossan once quipped during the Jesus Seminar's deliberations, "Everyone has a last supper—the trick is knowing about it in advance." Scholars seem to be divided on this question. Knowing about it in advance doesn't necessarily involve having supernatural awareness; any criminal holed up in a room with the cops closing in might have such knowledge. But believing in the historical truth of the entire Last Supper scene is another matter. It is generally considered that the body-and-blood ritual—in which Jesus has the disciples identify bread and wine with his body and blood—is later Christianizing.

A moderate position might be to imagine that Jesus and his followers did indeed have a final Passover seder, overhung with the sense of impending doom, and that, especially since shared food was so vital to him, he invested the meal with more than usual significance. But to accept all of the language attributed to him as historical would mean believing that this mortal man invented the entire Christian construct of Messiah as Lamb of God, saw himself in that role (that is, reimagined the Jewish idea of Messiah/warrior king as a grand sufferer who redeems sins and conflated this figure with the Passover ritual of sacrificing and eating a lamb in remembrance of the lambs sacrificed the night before the Exodus from Egypt), and, to cap it all, stage-managed his arrest.

Some scholars see no reason to distrust the gospels' order of the ensuing events, and the action seems trustworthy enough on the face of it. After the seder, Jesus and his associates cross the Kidron Valley and climb partway up the Mount of Olives to a place called Gethsemane. Depending on exactly where in the city the dinner was held, this could be a walk of twenty to forty minutes. Why would they have gone this distance? Why to this particular garden?

According to a theory by New Zealand authority Joan Taylor, it wasn't a garden they were going to at all. The Synoptics, in fact, never mention a garden, only "a place called Gethsemane." Taylor argues that it is to a cave adjacent to the garden that the disciples went: that, in fact, they were lodging here. Archaeological surveys have determined that this cave held an olive press; "Gethsemane" seems to derive from the Hebrew *gat-shemanim,* "oil press." Taylor speculates that the owner of the cave rented or loaned it to the Galilean rabbi and his associates during the Passover, when accommodation was at a premium. According to the literary record, it was the cave that was the site of Christian pilgrimage in the early centuries of the common era; it wasn't until the twelfth century that pilgrims began to consider the adjacent garden as the site of Jesus' arrest.

John's gospel does mention a garden, but doesn't refer to it as Gethsemane. However, as Taylor shows, a close reading suggests more precisely what this place might have been. Jesus and his followers went "across the Kidron valley to a place where there was a garden, which he and his disciples entered." We learn that "Jesus often met there with his disciples." Soon Judas shows up with soldiers. Jesus "went out" to meet them but, significantly, is still "in the garden." All of this seems to indicate a property that consists of a cave with an enclosed garden just outside it. Jesus "went out" of the cave and met the soldiers in the garden.[22]

The cave is still there, still a site of pilgrimage, though it is bypassed by most tourists as they rush to the garden. So this would seem to be both a twist on the traditional story and a confirmation of its basic historicity: there was and is a place called Gethsemane, which would have been a logical indoor shelter for financially pressed out-of-towners during the high season. This, surely, was the site of Jesus' arrest.

But some scholars don't like it. What's wrong with this story is not its details, but its overall structure. By focusing on the texts only we are forgetting that the gospel writers were Jews desperately searching for some significance to Jesus' death, and, in the manner of Jews of the period, they worked back and forth from the Scriptures to find it.

According to one argument, put forth most recently by Crossan and Koester but stretching back at least to the 1930s,[23] while the death of Jesus under Pilate is considered historical fact, the entire framework for the passion—from Gethsemane to crucifixion and resurrection—never actually occurred as written but is based on a section of the Second Book of Samuel having to do with King David. For ancient Jews, David was a sort of combination of George Washington and, well, Jesus: he was the father of his country and also the original Messiah. Those who looked forward to another Messiah were looking for David redivivus. Whatever

Jesus' original followers thought of him, those who came to believe in him after his death quickly saw him as just this, "Son of David," so much so that Matthew's gospel opens by tracing Jesus' genealogy back to David, and then, for good measure, from David back to Abraham.

So it was natural that those who were seeking to find meaning in Jesus' horrendous death would do so by relating him to David. Jesus, it was decided, was a Messiah who had been betrayed and suffered, but who, through his resurrection, snatched transcendent victory from the jaws of defeat and proved that God was in him.

This is precisely what occurs to David in the fifteenth to the eighteenth chapters of Second Samuel. In those chapters there is, first, suffering, brought on by the fact that David's son, Absalom, is in rebellion against him. Next there is betrayal: Ahithophel, a trusted follower, abandons the Messiah/king and joins the son, who is massing an army to attack his father. The parallel in Jesus' story is Judas's betrayal.

Next, when David learns of the plot against him he goes from Jerusalem up to the Mount of Olives with his followers, where he weeps and prays to God, saying submissively, ". . . let him do to me what seems good to him." This is exactly what Jesus does: goes with his followers to the Mount of Olives, prays at first to be released from what is to come, then submits with the words "not what I want, but what you want."

Then both Messiahs go to their bitter fates: David in battle against his own son, Jesus to be crucified by, according to the gospels, his own people. But both are victorious: David wins the battle, Jesus is resurrected. The final parallel again concerns the two betrayers: both Ahithophel and Judas end by hanging themselves.[24]

According to this reasoning, there was no historical incident in

Gethsemane—whether garden or cave. There was no ascent up the Mount of Olives to pray and await the arrest. This whole chunk of the saga represents a way to link Jesus with David.

It should be emphasized this is only a theory, and a minority position. Even if the Jesus–David parallels strike one as forceful, it doesn't necessarily follow that the entire episode is invention. Perhaps, after the Temple incident and the seder, Jesus and his friends did go up the Mount of Olives. If so, then, later, as people reminisced about it, the David parallel would naturally come to mind. And once established, the Old Testament story could provide some of the details, such as Jesus' prayer in Gethsemane.

But this is only the beginning of this deconstruction of the texts. The sequence of events after the prayer in Gethsemane is as follows: Judas comes with soldiers, points out Jesus as the one they are after, the soldiers take him away. There is a hastily arranged nighttime trial before the Sanhedrin, the Jewish council, led by the high priest, Caiaphas. Everyone is eager to convict Jesus of a capital crime, though no one can find one to pin on him. Some people give testimony against him, but their stories do not agree. Finally, the high priest, in frustration, simply stands up and puts it to Jesus: "Are you the Messiah, the Son of the Blessed One?" Jesus answers: "I am," and then quotes Scripture: " 'You will see the Son of Man seated at the right hand of the Power,' and 'coming with the clouds of heaven.' " The priest declares this to be blasphemy; everyone jeers; and they agree to hand him over to Pilate.

Most scholars agree that this scene never happened. Lurking beneath it is the figure of Judas, the betrayer. While he is generally accepted to have been an actual follower of Jesus, the details of his betrayal are thought to have been suggested by Scripture, including his receiving thirty pieces of silver for his act, which comes from Zechariah: "So they weighed out as my wages thirty shekels of silver."[25] As for the trial, an earlier version of it may lie in a text called the Gospel of Peter. Fragments of this document were discovered in the nineteenth century; most scholars believe them to be a ninth-century copy of a second-century manuscript. Some of the material, however, may reflect even older traditions. The odd thing about this account of Jesus' last day is that it contains a composite trial, at which Herod, Pilate, and the Jewish priests are all present. While Jesus is condemned by all of these, once Jesus dies they all witness the resurrection and so come to realize the enormity of what they have done. At this point, the priests beg Pilate to cover up this resurrection sighting, saying, "For it is better for us to make ourselves guilty of the greatest sin before God than to fall into the hands of the people of the Jews and be stoned."[26] So in this alternative account "the Jews" are clearly not assigned guilt for the deed; it is the priests who are responsible. If this section of the Gospel of Peter is earlier than the canonicals, then assigning blame to the Jewish race was a later development.

But this is not to say that the events in Peter are any more historical than those in the canonicals. It is unimaginable that there would have been a trial that brought together the leaders of Judea and Galilee. And if there was a trial before the Jewish authorities, none of Jesus' friends were there to report it.

What we are left with in the canonical texts is two separate trials. And so we come to the next sequence, and the heart of the anti-Judaism in the gospels: the trial before Pilate. Again, that such a trial ever happened is questionable. Jesus may have been too minor a figure for the Roman prefect himself to bother with. We know very little about Roman legal administration with regard to peasants in its client states. In all likelihood, this is because there was no codified system for dealing with them; this level of human life was not deemed worth the law's protection. It may be that Jesus was taken to a low-level Roman functionary, who would have quickly ratified whatever decision the local authorities had reached. If the Jewish leaders wanted him dead, why fight them?

But there is still the text. It is high drama: Roman prefect versus Son of God, the embodiment of earthly power versus the embodiment of heavenly power. Who will win? Both will, in their different ways, but in the end the heavenly power will be proved superior.

But there is a twist, for Pilate does not engage Jesus like a true antagonist. He ducks; he offers an out. He doesn't want this confrontation. Against all logic and against everything known about Roman administrators, he relinquishes his role in the matter and hands it over to a crowd of Jews to decide. The reason given—"at the festival the governor was accustomed to release a prisoner for the crowd"[27]—is total fiction. Pilate was known from other ancient sources as a particularly ruthless administrator.[28]

So the crowd is in an anti-Jesus frenzy, whipped up by the Jewish priests. Here a figure called Barabbas enters the story. Most scholars consider him a creation of Mark. *Bar-abbas* means "son of the father"—it isn't a Jewish name but, apparently, a kind of placeholder, like John Doe. Pilate asks whom he should free, the bandit Barabbas or Jesus. The crowd ask for Barabbas. Pilate then loses all sense of judicial reserve: "Why, what evil has he done?" he asks, practically pleading for acquittal. (In John, he goes even further: "I find no case against him."[29]) But the nearly hysterical crowd will have none of it.

Pilate then does his famous clean-up, literally washing his hands of the affair. His accompanying words were carefully crafted by the writer: "I am innocent of this man's blood; see to it yourselves."[30] A fascinating point is made here by Raymond Brown: ". . . Pilate acts and speaks as if he has read the [Old Testament] . . . and is following Jewish legal customs."[31] The washing of hands is called for by Deuteronomy 21 in case of a discovered death. The elders are to wash their hands and declare, "Our hands did not shed this blood, nor were we witnesses to it. Absolve, O Lord, your people Israel, whom you redeemed; do not let the guilt of innocent blood remain in the midst of your people Israel."[32]

The creator of this fanciful narrative, then, has taken a prayer that was meant to absolve the Jews from the sin of murder and used it *against* the Jews. It is the Roman who properly carries out the Law, the Jews who reject it.

And Matthew makes certain that they reject it. The people "as a whole" respond to Pilate with a phrase that has rung through the ages:

His blood be on us and on our children!

Actually, the Greek sentence contains no verb; a direct translation would be "His blood on us and on our children." It copies quite precisely, according to Brown, "a formula of Israelite holy law dealing with responsibility for death."[33] This phrase appears many times in the Old Testament. Leviticus contains a litany of evils that call for the death penalty and applies this formula in each case to mean that the responsibility for the death of the guilty ones is their own. Hence, one who curses his parents must be put to death, and "his blood upon him." If a man has intercourse with his father's wife both must die, and "their blood upon them."[34]

Some scholars, mostly evangelicals, continue to argue that this scene with Pilate presenting Jesus to the crowd is historical, but try to squirm out of the anti-Semitic implications by reductionist logic: the only responsibility is on those Jews actually present at the time. As evangelical scholar Craig Blomberg put it: "It's easy to look at that [passage] and shout 'anti-Semitism.' But if you look at it in context, I think it makes better sense than if you attribute it to the early church. If you put it in the context of a small crowd of people standing outside Pilate's headquarters, it becomes an idiomatic way of saying, 'If you turn this man over to us we accept responsibility for his death.' "

Clearly, however, this section of the passion narratives is an intricately woven piece of fiction, a parody almost, in which a Roman official absolves himself of guilt in the manner of a Jewish high priest and the Jewish population ritually curses itself and its offspring. Mark created the primary layer; the other three gospels picked it up and embellished it. The characters might be of the 30s C.E., but the subtext is of several decades later, when the early church is engaged in a bitter divorce from Judaism proper. In 70 C.E. the Romans sacked Jerusalem and destroyed the Temple. Jews were casting around wildly for answers. Why had this happened? What had they done? Who was to blame? They were leaderless since the power of the Sadducees, regulators of the Temple, had collapsed with the structure itself. In the confusion, one group, the Pharisees, gathered at a place called Jamnia and held a council on the future of the Jewish religion.[35] There they laid the groundwork for a new form of Judaism, the one still practiced today, in which study of Scripture and holy works took the place of Temple worship and animal sacrifice.

This new rabbinic program of the Pharisees was peaceful, but it blamed free thinkers within Judaism for the troubles that had come, and insisted on rigid conformity to the Law of Moses. There were clashes with the Jesus followers, who by now formed a significant presence in synagogues around the Empire. The gospels were therefore constructed around two agendas: to point the finger of blame for Jesus' death at the Jews, and to deflect blame away from the Roman Empire, under which they had to continue living. Perhaps it wouldn't have mattered if this had stayed an intramural argument between two sects of Judaism. But three centuries later, one of those sects became the religion of the entire Roman Empire. Christian writers and Christian warriors looked at the scene before Pilate and at Matthew's line about "his blood be on our heads," and seventeen hundred years of persecution began.

So here is a place where historical Jesus work has something straightforward to say. If you don't agree with the argument that the virgin birth is a myth, fine. If you insist that the resurrection was a literal, bodily event, you have every right to. If you find it farfetched that the story of David's betrayal in Second Samuel provided the raw material for the Gethsemane incident, that is quite understandable.

But the idea that "the Jews" killed Jesus and that an entire race is therefore worthy of contempt is something that, according to the overwhelming consensus of New Testament authorities, has to be acknowledged as a fiction perpetrated by people who were themselves largely Jewish and who had no idea what the consequences of their words would be. In *The Origin of Satan,* Elaine Pagels shows how the modern pastime of identifying one's enemy with Satan derives from this very strain in the gospels. In ancient Judaism, Satan was a disembodied force, an obstructor; but as you proceed through the gospels you find "the Jews" more and more equated with evil, until, in John, Jesus tells "the Jews": "You are of your father, the devil." Theologians have for years tried to downplay or excuse this sort of talk, but that won't do. "John's decision to make an actual, identifiable group . . . into a symbol of 'all evil' obviously bears religious, social, and political implications," writes Pagels. "Would anyone doubt this if an influential author today made women, or for that matter Muslims or homosexuals, the 'symbol of all evil'?"[36]

The earliest extant piece of a gospel is a papyrus fragment of John dated to about 125 C.E. and containing, ironically, the words

Pilate puts to Jesus in 18:38: "What is truth?" In John's gospel, Jesus doesn't respond, and silence may be the smartest answer to most of these historical questions, but not this one, for its implications have been too great. Jesus was indicted not by "the people" but by the authorities—Jewish priests and Roman overlords—as a troublemaker who threatened their order. Case closed.

CHAPTER TEN

"THE MOST WRETCHED OF DEATHS"

It is undoubtedly because the most famous person ever to be crucified met his punishment at the hands of the Romans that we tend to associate crucifixion exclusively with Rome. But the Assyrians, Persians, and Phoenicians resorted to it centuries before the rise of Rome. As the Roman Empire spread, crucifixion was adopted as an effective way to deal with unruly slaves; at first, however, it wasn't a means of execution but of humiliation. The offending slave had to walk through the streets of the city with a beam lashed to his arms while he called out his crime. By the first century B.C.E., this had evolved into a stake-and-crossbeam torture, which ended in death.[1]

Roman citizens were rarely crucified; if they incurred the state's wrath they were poisoned or beheaded—quicker, less agonizing deaths.

Slaves, enemies caught in battle, and political prisoners were the main groups subjected to this supremely degrading kind of end, for it was above all a public act, a commercial advertising Rome's thorough vanquishing of its enemies. However, this punishment wasn't necessarily rare. Gerard Sloyan points out that it was common enough that *crux* later became a slur one would hurl at an enemy, meaning something like, "May you end up on a cross."[2] Crucified figures were a frequent enough sight on the landscape that there were popular nicknames for them: *Patibulatus,* which Sloyan translates as "Crossbar Charlie," and *Corvorum Cibaria,* or "Food for Crows."[3] During the Jewish War of 66–70 C.E., the Romans seemed to take particular delight in torturing and crucifying captured Jewish rebels; Josephus records that at one point five hundred people a day were being hideously tortured and hung up on crosses: "The soldiers themselves through rage and bitterness nailed up their victims in various attitudes as a grim joke, till owing to the vast numbers there was no room for the crosses, and no crosses for the bodies."[4]

Over centuries of incorporation into Christian art, crucifixion has become so highly stylized—a thing of beauty, even—that it is difficult to imagine the true horror of it. Just as the outrageous social behavior and dangerously transcendent parables of the radical from Galilee have been domesticated by the church, the cross has been tamed too. But the reality was something else. Consider, first, the horror it meant in a society where personal dignity—even a peasant's dignity—was the highest virtue. To be made a public spectacle—convicted of a crime, exposed naked, and dying in agony—was punishment far beyond mere execution.

Then there was the torture. It generally included being bound to a post and flogged, either with a flagellum, a short whip consisting of several leather tongs beaded with lead or bone tips, or with sticks. The victim was usually mounted to the crossbar on the ground and it was then hoisted up and attached to the upright. Nails were usually driven through the hands or wrists, and the feet. Sometimes the arms were tied to the bar with ropes, either in addition to the nails or in lieu of them; presumably, if the arms were not tied, the nails were driven through the forearms rather than the hands, as otherwise the hands would tear off the cross. The body was supported by a wedge at either the feet or the buttocks. Seneca writes of some people being impaled with a spike through the genitals. Josephus, an eyewitness to more than his share of crucifixions, called it, matter-of-factly, "the most wretched of deaths."

Remarkably, in 1968 an archaeological team working at an ancient cemetery in northeast Jerusalem known as Giv'at ha-Mivtar unearthed the remains of a crucified man of the first century, in his twenties, who was executed in or near Jerusalem: an astonishingly close match to Jesus. It was Jewish custom to bury a body for a year, then to dig up the bones and put them in a stone ossuary, or bone box, either alone or together with those of family members. In this case, the ossuary contained the bones of a man, a woman, and a child of about three years. It was decorated with rosettes and, conveniently enough, contained an inscription that identified the man as one "Jehohanan the potter."

It is certain that Jehohanan died of crucifixion because the right heel bone was pierced by a four-inch spike, and fragments of wood were found still clinging to it. The original excavator drew several conclusions about the manner of crucifixion; however, a 1985 team from Hadassah Medical School and the Israel Department of Antiquities identified errors in the original work and issued a reappraisal.[5] It is clear, from their analysis, that the crucifixion position so familiar to us all from countless icons and rosaries was not the only one used by the Romans. Jehohanan evidently had his arms tied to the crossbar, legs straight down, and feet straddling the upright so that the heel bones were nailed into either side of it.

One puzzling detail was that not one but two different kinds of wood were found attached to the nail and heel bone. The probable solution is that the Romans used a small plug of wood as a kind of washer on the outer side of the foot, to prevent the victim from pulling his foot free of the nail. We have no idea what variation on this ghastly theme was employed in Jesus' case.

Death from crucifixion came not from nail wounds but gradual loss of oxygen. As the autopsy team put it, "Hanging from the cross resulted in a painful process of asphyxiation, in which the two sets of muscles used for breathing, the intercostal muscles and the diaphragm, became progressively weakened." With no support at all one would die from lack of breath in a very short time. But the whole point of crucifixion was to provide a vivid, lengthy public spectacle of how an enemy of Rome ended up; therefore the use of a support under the feet or buttocks was not meant to ease the suffering but to prolong it. Indeed, the buttock "seat" was often a spike, which Seneca seems to refer to in the line "You may nail me up and set my seat upon the piercing cross."

In 71 B.C.E., the Romans crucified six thousand slaves who had followed Spartacus in rebellion; some of these were still alive and talking with soldiers after three days. But this Roman tradition would have caused particular problems in Palestine, where it was against God's law to leave a body exposed after sunset. Hence the account in John 19:32, where the soldiers break the legs of the two thieves crucified on either side of Jesus, long seemed to suggest that the Romans honored that custom; without leg support, they would die quickly. The evidence of Jehohanan may back this up. The leg bones are indeed broken, and although the breaks came after death, this could paint a picture in which soldiers on crucifixion detail in Palestine routinely smashed the victims' legs at a certain hour before sunset to hasten death, then hauled down the bodies before evening to appease the locals. In the case of Jehohanan, they would have broken the legs without bothering to check whether he was already dead.

Pilgrims from other parts of the Mediterranean world were selecting sites of veneration related to Jesus' death by 333 C.E., and probably much earlier. Around 1100, a Russian abbot recorded the site of the trial before Pilate as being the Antonia Fortress, where Rome stationed its troops in Jerusalem. Since the place of execution had long been known—a rocky outcropping known as Golgotha in Aramaic and Calvaria in Latin—medieval pilgrims began to make a procession between these two points, retracing what they believed was the procession of the cross. Over time, various events recorded in the gospels as having happened along the route of crucifixion, and several from popular tradition, were given specific sites. By 1400, the Via Dolorosa—the "Way of Sorrow," Christendom's most sacred road—was well established.

Today the Via Dolorosa is lined with kitsch: shops selling olive-wood crosses, painted-velvet Pietàs, "Israel: Uzi Does It" T-shirts, postcards, posters, menorahs, "Thai boxing" trunks, baklava, after-shave, Afghan bread, and soccer balls. There is a Holy Rock Café and a Holy Cow Hospice. Along these alleyways, ancient stone walls shining golden in the harsh sun, the faithful or curious stroll, pilgrims in nun's habits, safari outfits, or Reeboks and jeans, while signs shout down at them in multiple languages: "En Este Negocio Iconos Originales Rusos," "Wir Haben Echte Alte Russische Ikonen," "We Have Russian Icons."

But there is an astonishing amount of dignity here as well. At the second station of the cross, where tradition holds Jesus was scourged and given his cross, white-habited Franciscan nuns quietly and diligently oversee the peaceful Churches of the Condemnation and the Flagellation, seemingly oblivious to the barking and hawking going on all around them. Station four, a stately little Armenian church, no bigger than a closet, marks the spot where, it was decided centuries ago, Mary stood watching as her son passed with his burden. The words Pilate speaks to the crowd in John's gospel—*Ecce homo!* "Behold the man!"—are also given a geographic fix: an ancient archway just off the road. Never mind that the arch has since been proved to date from two centuries after Jesus; the Ecce Homo Basilica, a white marble structure built around the arch, radiates with soothing white light, its priests moving noiselessly as they go about their business, heads bent, robes swishing on the stone floor.

A rationalist would be in a rush to make clear that archaeological and historic evidence suggests that Pilate was not headquartered at the Antonia Fortress but at Herod's Upper Palace, on the other side of the Old City, and that therefore this route was probably not the one Jesus would have taken with his cross. But here, as at other stages of this inquiry, the rationalist is stilled by something else: not exactly religion, but the force of myth—myth in its grandest sense, a sense lost to us most of the time. A myth is not a story told among people too primitive to understand the truth. It is a try at loading a world of real but inexpressible experience into a single object or event. If millions of people, day after day, century after century, have embraced the myth of these stone streets and stone chapels, and in embracing it have comprehended it in some preverbal way, taken it into themselves, how can mere rational inquiry contradict it? And in what way are we limiting ourselves if we let it?

Or, as the Via Dolorosa tourist pamphlet properly if somewhat defensively puts it: "What is a Holy Place? It is not the exact spot where Jesus walked, but it is a place where the Church venerates a mystery of Christ's life [and] a place made holy by the prayers of the faithful."

Herod's Upper Palace was located at what is today called the Citadel, near the Jaffa Gate. James Charlesworth of Princeton Theological Seminary, who has synthesized much of the archaeological work related to the New Testament, gives it as consensus that this was where Pilate based himself; therefore, whether or not there was an actual trial before Pilate, this is where Jesus would have been brought before Roman justice. Which would mean that, in fact, the procession with the cross would have been from the other direction than that trod by the tourist hordes: from the west, not from the east.

The more historically correct way of the cross, therefore, begins at the plaza just inside the Jaffa Gate and alongside the Citadel, which today is a starting point from which many tourists launch their assault on the Old City. Plastic tables and chairs spill out onto it from cafés; the sign at an unauthorized money changer announces "Authorized Money Changer." This is where Pilate would have presented Jesus to the crowd, if there is any history to that part of the story.

A procession was indeed part of the Roman crucifixion tradition—at least for political prisoners (mass executions were more summary). Jesus would likely have been given not an entire cross to walk with, but the crossbar only. And so he would have set off toward the area just outside the city walls that was reserved for crucifixions: Golgotha, "Place of the Skull." The straightest path today takes one down David Street, not a street at all but a narrow, stepped alleyway lined with shops selling rosaries, loaves-and-fishes plates, and other tourist ware. Nothing was the same two thousand years ago, except everything: it was a city, teeming with people going about their business. And the topography, that would have been roughly the same: a steady downhill walk from the Upper City to where David Street intersects what later became known as the Cardo—Main Street of Roman Jerusalem. To the right, a section of the Cardo has been renovated and restored in the style of its Roman/Byzantine period. Sections of the original arches and columns are set between tony shops selling art and jewelry; it is paved with the original block paving stones.

But Jesus would have turned left. Today this left turn takes you out of the tourist district and into a teeming Arab market. Veiled women cluster around stalls offering tennis shoes, gym socks, hair ribbons, cheap plastic toys. The smell of grilled lamb hangs in the air; men sit on stools sipping tea.

The street follows the course of what was the northern wall in Jesus' time, and somewhere not far along it was the Gennath Gate. Golgotha was just outside the gate. Turning left, one proceeds up a flight of steps, and there it is: the dome, the Church of the Holy Sepulchre, and Golgotha. This, one can't help but think, is what Jesus did: turned, looked this way. Only instead of an ancient muddle of architecture topped by a dome, he would see only a hill, stony and bare.

The Church of the Holy Sepulchre, ground zero for Christendom, has a long and bizarre history; the original building, dedicated in 335, was raised over the traditional sites of both the crucifixion and the tomb; it was claimed by the six divisions of the ancient church: Roman Catholic, Greek Orthodox, Armenian Orthodox, Syrian Orthodox, Coptic, and Ethiopian. Power struggles between these sects began almost at once; they partitioned the sacred buildings into sovereign territories, which to this day are zealously guarded against invasion by priests of the other denominations. It is surely one of the ugliest churches in the world. Anyone for whom the phrase "Old World church" brings to mind Notre Dame or Chartres cathedral would be shocked by this tortured pile of bricks and columns that looks more like a military outpost of some grim Hun-like tribe than the holiest place in the Christian world.

Just inside the doorway is the first object of adoration: a marble slab on which, according to legend, Jesus' body was prepared for burial. On this day a heavy, middle-aged woman in a floral dress is outside the doorway, approaching the slab on her hands and knees, stopping at each pace to kiss the floor and pray. Tears stream down her face. Robed Franciscan monks pass by her, chatting and holding plastic shopping bags. Some in the cluster of tourists stare at her, but not for long as there is a lot of this sort of behavior hereabouts. At the slab itself, a group of women, some of them weeping, are wiping at it with alcohol swabs, to absorb some of the particles of sanctity. A wrinkled, gnome-like woman angrily beseeches her terrified granddaughter in Spanish, *"Tocala! Tocala!"* Touch it!

One sympathizes with the girl. To actually touch the deeper realities of this place seems terrifying. It means letting go of reason. The old women gathered around the stone have no problem with this. To someone who does, it feels safer, having reached the actual spot where the climax to the historical Jesus' life played itself out, to turn to reason itself for answers.

The crucifixion is a near-certainty, and that it occurred at this place is highly probable. Can history tell us anything else about the circumstances of Jesus' death?

A remarkable number of the details of the scene in the gospels seem to come directly from Psalm 22. As early as the second century, Tertullian spoke of this psalm as "containing the whole of Christ's passion." Look first at the picture the gospels convey. Mark gives the following details:

- As Jesus died, the soldiers cast lots for his clothes.
- Two "bandits" were also crucified, one on either side of him.
- While he hung on the cross, people taunted him.

- Jesus cried out as he was dying, "My God, my God, why have you forsaken me?"

Now consider Psalm 22. It was traditionally considered a "psalm of David," and it is a hymn of agony, death, and vindication—so that it mirrors the suffering of Jesus in its overall framework. If Jesus' followers were looking for a piece of Scripture related to David that matched what Jesus endured and suggested his eventual triumph, this was a good choice.

Now look at the details:

1.) As mentioned before, the psalm opens with the words, "My God, my God, why have you forsaken me?"—the very words spoken by the dying Jesus.

2.) The speaker in the psalm is "scorned by others" and says, "All who see me mock me." This person is clearly in agony: "All my bones are out of joint . . . my mouth is dried up like a potsherd." And most tellingly for purposes of comparison is the line "My hands and feet are pierced." At least "pierced" *was* considered the appropriate translation of the Hebrew, both in the Septuagint, which the gospel writers used, and in English in the King James Version; however, it has since been decided that the Hebrew may more likely mean "shriveled." While this change in translation weakens the comparison today, in the text the gospel writers worked from, "pierced" must have jumped right out at them.

3.) The sufferer in the psalm says, "Dogs are all around me; a company of evildoers encircles me." This, it is widely believed, inspired the creation of the two thieves crucified on either side of Jesus.

4.) The sufferer says of his enemies: "They divide my clothes among themselves, and for my clothing they cast lots." This, obviously, led to the creation of the detail of soldiers casting lots for Jesus' clothing.

It is clear to most scholars that Psalm 22 was the creative force behind the details of the crucifixion scene. Raymond Brown believes that "the earliest appeal to the psalm was to enable Christians to see the relationship between what happened and God's plan."[6] Brown also outlines the ways the gospel writers used this psalm: "(1) To concentrate on certain details, e.g., the presence of co-crucified wrongdoers, the pierced hands (and feet), the division of clothes; (2) to dramatize the mocking hostility shown to Jesus by those around the cross, challenging his claim to have God's help; and (3) to highlight the reversal in an abandoned death and subsequent victory."[7]

Beyond this, Brown notes that the use of Psalm 22 gives a "strong sense of desolate isolation" to Mark's account of Jesus on the cross. Mark actually highlights this by placing the words "My God, my God, why have you forsaken me?" on Jesus' lips at the *end* of the suffering, whereas the line comes at the beginning of the psalm. It's as though Mark wanted to stress the hopelessness at this lowest ebb. Screenwriters talk of bringing a heroic character, at the climax of the action, to "the negation of the negation"—the farthest possible point of despair—before initiating the action that leads to victory. As at the beginning of his gospel, which starts with the baptism as the action that launches Jesus' adventure, Mark climaxes his story with a screenwriter's sense of drama.

There is one other possible use to which Psalm 22 was put, which is suggested by Brown's point (3) above. The last part of the psalm is a hymn of vindication and thanks: somehow, this sufferer is relieved of his torment and praises God. Various scholars have suggested that this switch from suffering-and-death to sudden praise helped give the early followers of Jesus a sense of Jesus' victory over death, helped give rise to the idea of resurrection. One possible indication of this use of the material in the post-resurrection section of the gospels, Brown notes, is the psalm's line

"All the families of the nations will worship before Him."[8] In Matthew, the Risen Christ says to his amazed disciples, "Go therefore and make disciples of all nations . . ."[9] If the historical Jesus never spoke of extending his work beyond Israel, this line from the psalm could have suggested to his followers that it was now time to do so.

Other Old Testament texts are considered likely to have been mined for crucifixion details. The soldiers offering him "wine to drink, mixed with gall" seems to come from Psalm 69: "And they gave for my bread gall, and for my thirst they gave me to drink vinegary wine."[10] And one non-detail also may come from Scripture: while the legs of the two thieves are broken, Jesus' legs are not. This seems to relate to the Jewish rules given in Exodus about preparing the paschal lamb: ". . . you shall not break any of its bones," especially since John overtly refers to it: "These things occurred so that the Scripture might be fulfilled, 'None of his bones shall be broken.' "[11]

The soldiers' abuse of Jesus contains elements from Isaiah 50:6 and Zechariah 12:10, which speak of a sufferer being scourged, spat upon, and pierced. Most intriguingly, according to theories proposed by Crossan and Koester, the ancient Jewish scapegoat ritual, derived from Leviticus, was a major creative force behind the abuse scenes in the gospels. The scapegoat was a real goat, onto the head of which the ancient Israelites deposited their sins before they sent it off into the desert to die. Various traditions have the goat *spat* upon, caught among *thorns*, and *pierced* in the side. All of these elements find their way into the gospels: Jesus is spat upon, fitted with a crown of thorns, and pierced in the side with a spear.[12] Here then is the root of a powerful theological notion: just as the goat bore the sins of the community, the early Christians, faced with an incomprehensible death, decided that Jesus was the ultimate sacrifice, who would bear the sins of the world.

It is important to stress again that this scriptural interpretation really was the means by which ancient Jews discovered the meaning in current events. The Hebrew Bible, they believed, contained not just the past but the seeds of the present and future. Jacob Neusner writes that the ancient Jews' faith was "a faith under construction," a faith that required constant exploration: "They did not write *about* Scripture, they wrote *with* Scripture, for Scripture supplied the syntax and grammar of their thought . . ."[13] So that in the Genesis *Rabbah,* a fourth-century interpretation of the book of Genesis, Jewish sages rather radically reconceived the stories of the patriarchs in a way that shed light on the plight of the Jews of their time: the time when the Empire itself became Christian, and Jews found their traditions under attack.

The application of scriptural details to Jesus' death, then, was a way to find meaning in that death. How literally they would have been taken by a first-century Jewish audience is impossible to say. But it is certain that early Christians took them as historical events, noted the Old Testament parallels, and insisted that Scripture prophesied Jesus' death. The second-century Christian bully Justin Martyr wrote a long tract against the Jews in which, among other things, he scorned them for not appreciating the amazing coincidences between Psalm 22 and the details of the crucifixion.

So many, perhaps most, of the details of the crucifixion scenes in the gospels are the invention of devout followers hungry to find meaning in Jesus' death. Believers today who hunger for a newspaper-like report on "what really happened" could strip away these theologically derived touches. But what are they left with?

With one fact, which nearly all critics agree on. And as you stand in the sacred, touristed darkness of the Church of the Holy Sepulchre, you are staring up at it. There are no signs or plaques, and the whole thing is covered by an enclosure and an encrustation of holy objects, so it's difficult even to know at first what it is.

There is a steep stairway: nineteen high steps. Going up, you begin to feel dizzy: the throng of devout tourists is at its thickest here, pressing on all sides; incense and candle smoke devour the oxygen. Gold mosaics cover the vaulted ceiling like randomly applied patches. Lamps and braziers hang low.

Slowly, as the throng processes, you are thrust toward an altar of wrought silver and iconic saints flanking what seems a cardboard Christ on the cross. Up and down the walls and across the low ceiling are fairy-tale images of angels and stars, so primitively executed that they are not so much childlike as childish: a crazy, smothering jumble of holiness. The center of the Christian universe is illustrated with the dreams of children.

The people just in front now are in tears or are staring transfixed. They give way to reveal a Plexiglas covering just below the Christ figure, and finally you realize that you have ascended Calvary, and you are looking at an angry gray jutting of rock. This is not a mount or a hill but a single solid rock fourteen feet high, now covered with devotion and enclosed in a massive and unwelcoming building, and you are on top of it.

Skeptics and believers alike agree on one point: this is the place. Mark Twain visited the Holy Land in 1867 and wrote a book about the experience, *The Innocents Abroad,* which occasioned an uproar in America for its wisecracking dismissal of so much reliquary. But even Twain felt something as he stood on this spot. "With all its claptrap sideshows and unseemly impostures of every kind," he wrote, "it is still grand, reverend, venerable—for a god died here."

For a god died here. Twain, modern before his time, was able to lighten the tone with an indefinite article, but it seems to make it even more profound. How many different gods are worshiped on earth? And for how many of them is a specific spot and a specific time in history given for their earthly end? Where else can you say with utter conviction "a god died here"?

One more experience climaxes the pilgrim's ritual. Below the cross is a brass ring on the ground with a hole in its center. The visitor kneels down and puts a hand into this hole. Your arm sinks up to the elbow: Golgotha has swallowed your arm. This, presumably, is the very receptacle of the cross, the hole cut into the rock for placement of countless cross uprights, including *the* cross upright. Along with Twain, one may find it easy to grin at most of the legends associated with this place—that when Jesus died the stone cracked (see, you can still see the fissure, here at the base, through this glass panel); that Adam himself lies buried beneath the rock. But this action of dipping one's arm into a hole sweeps away reason. You have personally violated what millions of people believe to be the most profound act in history. You have penetrated Golgotha.

The full impact does not necessarily register at the time. It is only afterward, as you contemplate the associations and try to connect all your disparate images of this event—from Matthew, Mark, Luke, and John, from DeMille and Zeffirelli, from some droning Sunday school teacher, from the children's Bible—try to connect all of these with *here, this* place, *this* pile of rock, that you begin to feel the strangeness. As if, suddenly, you have participated a bit too much. You have come for an experience, but not *the* experience. It was better when it was a distant imagining in the mind of a small child, an act residing safely in the land of myth.

The one indisputably unique thing about the man-God Jesus Christ is that he straddles the mythic and the historic—he was once of our world, a creature of a certain time and place, and yet he is eternal. If there is an actual geographic spot where these two irreconcilable realities come together, this is it. But, of course, they never really can. One may have spent years studying the subject from the perspective of history and science, but standing at the raw heart of it all, reason finally collapses under the strain. This is the absolute farthest it can take you: if you will proceed further, it must be by some other means.

The Greek monks who painted the walls with infantile images had it right after all. The mythic, the preverbal: that, truly, is where this place belongs.

CHAPTER ELEVEN

RESURRECTION

The apocalypse came in April 1993. It had come before, and doubtless will come again, but for eighty-six people in Waco, Texas, the moment when FBI and ATF agents rammed the walls of their "Ranch Apocalypse" with tanks and a mysterious fire began to engulf them, the words of Revelation must have been playing in their heads: "The first angel blew his trumpet, and there came hail and fire, mixed with blood, and they were hurled to the earth; and a third of the earth was burned up, and a third of the trees were burned up, and all green grass was burned up."

David Koresh's Branch Davidian cult occupied a spot on the far radical fringe of Christianity, but in an important sense it was quite mainstream. Jesus will come again to usher in the kingdom of God: that was the doctrine the Branch Davidians held close to their hearts, and it is also the backbone of institutional Christianity. Koresh may have been psychotic, but the main tenet of his theology was as Christian as Kingdom Come.

Matthew Fox is as far removed from Koresh as it is possible to be on the Christian spectrum; he is the anti-Koresh. He was trained as a Dominican priest, but over the past two decades he has evolved a global, pan-religious spirituality. Through twelve books, the most famous of which is *The Coming of the Cosmic Christ,* he has followed the stream of New Testament theology out into the great ocean of human consciousness. Perhaps inevitably, his work is not church-based but instead has become a continuing-education road show in which he lectures on "Creation Spirituality." Through his organization, the Institute in Culture and Creation Spirituality, and magazine, *Creation Spirituality,* he promotes "the Creation Spirituality movement, which integrates the wisdom of Western spirituality and the global indigenous cultures with the emerging scientific understanding of the universe and the passionate creativity of art."

Mystical experience as a way to individual knowledge is the core of Creation Spirituality. The Cosmic Christ is universal consciousness: the mind of Being. Fox's writings are dense with cross-cultural associations and mix systematic theology with pop psychology ("Jesus employed his *right brain,*" "All too many Christians have been led to believe that Christ is not present in lovemaking"). Fox has a huge, worldwide following and, while his name is virtually synonymous with New Age, his specialty boutique in the great shopping mall of contemporary Christianity has an ancient pedigree—just as ancient as David Koresh's cult, and, like that more militant strain, its roots may go back to the historical Jesus himself. These two extremes, the apocalyptic and the nondoctrinaire-contemplative, are represented in the earliest Christian literature;

they reflect different ways in which the followers of Jesus interpreted his message.

Clearly, the apocalyptic strain won the day. Its texts became enshrined in the New Testament canon. But both variants continued to exist for several centuries after the crucifixion. The death of the more individualistic and mystical form of Christianity can be assigned a date: October 28, 312. On that day the armies of two competitors for the title of Roman Emperor clashed on a bridge ten miles north of Rome. The night before the battle, the would-be invader had a dream. A voice said to him, "By this sign you shall be the victor." The sign was a cross intersected by the Greek letters *chi* and *rho:* the symbol of the orthodox Christians. In the morning, the general ordered this sign to be painted on the shields of his troops. That day, in the Battle of the Milvian Bridge, Constantine's invading army crushed the larger force of Maxentius, defender of Rome. Constantine became emperor. The Empire became Christian. The world changed.

The bishops of the orthodox church, who had been persecuted by Rome as recently as nine years before, now controlled the most powerful army the world had ever known. They set out at once to secure their position. This meant that Jews began suffering for their "folly" in not recognizing Jesus as the Messiah; and it meant the death of gnostic Christianity.

One of the major results of scholarship of the past few decades has been the determination that gnosticism was not an oddball heretical development of the second and third centuries, as had been believed, but in fact has a pedigree that extends back as far as that of orthodox Christianity. The reason the one is now considered "Christianity" while the other died out as a heresy has more to do with Constantine's dream and subsequent rise to emperor than with any authoritative claim to represent the authentic message of Jesus.

But why would the orthodox bishops have been so keen to eliminate this variant sect? What gnostic doctrine threatened them so much that they branded the leaders "agents of Satan" and declared that anyone who followed their teaching would burn in hell? What one issue divided these early followers of Jesus so bitterly?

> For I handed on to you as of first importance what I in turn had received; that Christ died for our sins in accordance with the Scriptures, and that he was buried, and that he was raised on the third day in accordance with the Scriptures, and that he appeared to Cephas, then to the Twelve.[1]

This is Paul's concise summary of core Christian belief as it had evolved by the 50s C.E. This was, for him, what anyone who sought to join the movement had to profess. This man, whom Paul had never met in life, had died and then returned, signaling his special status. And, just as vital for the early church, he had appeared in resurrected form "to Cephas, then to the Twelve."

But what was this resurrected form? Was he a dream in the mind of the beholder? A ghost? Was he pure spirit?

Many people today might wonder what difference it makes. Those who saw him were convinced of his reality—so fervently convinced of it that they spawned a movement that almost instantly swept beyond the borders of Palestine and into the wide Roman world, a movement that in a remarkably short time developed into something the historical Jesus would have found completely bewildering—an unprecedented mix of Jewish and Greek religious imagery and Roman administration, an interlocked set of *ekklesiai* with bishops, deacons, and priests. No one, not the most skeptical skeptic, denies that some of Jesus' followers had an experience of him after his death. So who cares what form that resurrected being took?

The early Christians cared. And institutional Christianity today cares. The Catholic church cares. The Eastern Orthodox churches care. Evangelical Christians care. Nearly all mainstream Christian institutions insist that Jesus rose *bodily* from the tomb, that after three days of decay, his flesh revivified, his heart began pumping blood, his lungs began taking in air; that after three days' experience of the grand mystery of death this human consciousness reawakened in its shell of living tissue and ventured out again among the living. All four gospels go out of their way to affirm this:

> They were startled and terrified, and thought that they were seeing a ghost. He said to them, "Why are you frightened, and why do doubts arise in your hearts? Look at my hands and my feet; see that it is I myself. Touch me and see; for a ghost does not have flesh and bones as you see that I have."[2]

As if this weren't enough to make it clear that this is Jesus-in-the-body, Luke underlines it:

> "Have you anything to eat?" They gave him a piece of broiled fish, and he took it and ate it in their presence.[3]

The Doubting Thomas story also serves this purpose. Thomas misses Jesus' first appearance, and when the others tell him Jesus has come back, he can't believe it. "Unless I see the mark of the nails in his hands, and put my finger in the mark of the nails and my hand in his side, I will not believe."[4] So the next time Jesus comes he orders Thomas to touch his wounds, and Thomas believes.

It is clear that the gospel writers—fathers of the nascent Christian church in the latter days of the first century—thought this a terribly important point. But did the actual followers of Jesus? A number of scholars and theologians think not. They believe that by carefully reading the resurrection accounts in both the canonical texts and in extracanonical sources they can detect evidence of the way the actual followers described their experience. This primary stage consisted of "luminous appearances," in the words of James Robinson of the Institute for Antiquity and Christianity at the Claremont Graduate School, one of the pioneers of the new understanding of the relationship of gnosticism to early Christianity. The most notable of these luminous appearances is Paul's conversion on the road to Damascus:

> While I was on my way and approaching Damascus, about noon a great light from heaven suddenly shone about me. I fell to the ground and heard a voice saying to me, "Saul, Saul, why are you persecuting me?" I answered, "Who are you, Lord?" Then he said to me, "I am Jesus of Nazareth whom you are persecuting."[5]

Paul's experience predates the gospel accounts, and so is our earliest evidence for an experience of the Risen Christ. And while Paul is often thought to affirm a bodily resurrection, nowhere does he refer to it as such. It is only by reading Paul in light of the gospel accounts that he seems to have in mind a bodily resurrection; but to read him this way is to confuse the timing of the writing of the gospels with the timing of their story. If Jesus died around 30 C.E., and Paul wrote in the 50s C.E., and the gospels were written after

70 C.E., it stands to reason that Paul should not be read through the prism of the later gospels. When he says, "Christ has been raised from the dead, the first fruits of those who have died,"[6] it cannot be automatically assumed that he means a resurrection of the body. And by "the first fruits of those who have died," he is expressing the Jewish eschatological belief that at the End Time all those who have died will be raised. This appears to have been a commonly held belief, and it is likely that the experience of Jesus as raised from the dead further fueled this eschatological image of him. He was the "first fruits of those who have died"—his resurrection signaled that a general resurrection was to follow.

But this doesn't answer the question of precisely what "resurrection" meant in first-century Judaism. And those who use this passage from First Corinthians 15 to buttress their arguments for a bodily resurrection tend to gloss over what comes later in the same chapter:

> But someone will ask, "How are the dead raised? With what kind of body do they come?" . . . If there is a physical body, there is also a spiritual body. . . . What I am saying, brothers and sisters, is this: flesh and blood cannot inherit the kingdom of God . . .[7]

Here Paul is clearly differentiating between a spiritual and a material body. He seems to believe that when the physical body dies the soul inhabits a kind of ghostly version of it, and it is this that walks through the gates of paradise. At any rate, Paul certainly does not provide hard evidence for an early tradition that held that Jesus' physical body returned from the dead.

The next piece of evidence in support of the theory that Jesus' followers experienced something other than a physical presence after his death comes from the gospels. While all four evangelists take pains to stress Jesus' material body, in certain places they reveal traces of other appearance stories that may reflect the actual experiences of the followers and not the overlay of the evangelists.

Twice in John's gospel, Jesus appears suddenly in the room with the disciples even though "the doors of the house where the disciples had met were locked for fear of the Jews." Clearly this Jesus has ghost-like properties. John also has him appear to Mary Magdalene, but when she tries to touch him he tells her not to "because I have not yet ascended to the Father," which seems to indicate some sort of semi-earthly presence and at any rate contradicts his behavior in the Doubting Thomas story. Luke tells of Jesus appearing to two disciples on the road to Emmaus whose "eyes were kept from recognizing him." He walks with them and they tell him all about Jesus, who has just been crucified, unable to believe that this stranger hasn't heard of him, and it is only when they all sit down to eat, after the mysterious stranger "took bread, blessed and broke it, and gave it to them"—the precise formula for the Last Supper ritual—that the disciples suddenly recognize him. Whereupon "he vanished from their sight."[8]

These stories suggest a tradition within the gospels of disciples encountering a Jesus who was something other than material. But why does it matter? Why insist on a bodily resurrection? Why was there this curious development over time, with Paul showing no overt interest in presenting the resurrection as bodily, then the gospels taking pains to indicate that it was a physical body while still allowing some stories that suggest otherwise, and finally the second-century church father Tertullian making it absolutely and viscerally clear that Christian faith must be in a resurrected body composed of "flesh . . . suffused with blood, scaffolded of bones, threaded through with sinews, intertwined with veins"?[9]

In 1979, Elaine Pagels published *The Gnostic Gospels,* a book that did for the gnostic texts found at Nag Hammadi in 1945 what

Edmund Wilson had done for the Dead Sea Scrolls twenty-four years before. Wilson brought the ancient library of Qumran texts, which threw open the doors to our understanding of ancient Judaism and early Christianity, to a broad public. Pagels, professor of religion at Princeton University, tuned the public in to a debate that raged through the first two Christian centuries, a debate that reveals the deep divisions among the followers of Jesus over the most basic notions of what it meant to be a Christian.

Foremost among these was the debate over Christ's resurrection. Besides its religious significance, Pagels wrote, "the doctrine of bodily resurrection also serves an essential *political* function: it legitimizes the authority of certain men who claim to exercise exclusive leadership over the churches as the successors of the apostle Peter."[10] What seems to have developed in the first decades of the new movement, following the stories of the appearances of Jesus to his disciples, was a veritable rash of further appearances. The luminous Jesus was turning up all over the Mediterranean. This soon became a problem. The original disciples were busy trying to establish a network of believers, which entailed establishing doctrine and authority—i.e., a church. When questions arose, someone had to answer them; those who had experienced the Risen Christ were deemed to be in this position of authority.

But now all sorts of people, in Ephesus and Antioch and Alexandria, people who had never known Jesus in life, were insisting that they had been visited by him after his death. Why were their visions any less authoritative than others? Why could they not find their own way through Jesus? What special sign of power did the disciples possess?

Somehow, between the years 30 and 70, an answer to this problem was decided on. We see it enshrined today in the New Testament. Jesus appeared *bodily* to Peter, then to the other disciples. He stayed on earth in *bodily* form for forty days after the resurrection, and then he ascended *bodily* into heaven. And that was that: no other appearances were to be considered authoritative. By appearing in a resurrected physical body to Peter and certain others, he conferred a special status on them. They were to lead his church. And this doctrine of bodily resurrection redounds to us today, for in Catholic tradition the Pope still derives his authority from Peter; the sitting Pope wears "the shoes of the Fisherman." Every mainline Christian institution similarly claims a place in the relay of authority from Christ to Peter to the early fathers and so on.

The proto-gnostics were left out in the cold by this formulation, for they insisted that belief based on a bodily resurrection was a "faith of fools." For them, individual ecstatic experience of Christ was all that mattered. The receiver of Christ became initiated into the mystery of God, a secret wisdom; no broker or middleman was required. As it developed, gnosticism went even further in the direction of a radical spiritual individuality and away from the traditions of Judaism. As Pagels writes: "Orthodox Jews and Christians insist that a chasm separates humanity from its creator: God is wholly other. But some of the gnostics who wrote these gospels contradict this: self-knowledge is knowledge of God; the self and the divine are identical."[11] The Jesus of the gnostic Gospel of Thomas makes this clear: "Whoever drinks from my mouth will become like me; I myself shall become that person . . ."[12]

I don't need a church to broker my faith; I can know God immediately. And if I know myself, I know God, for God and I are one. If this sounds somehow modern it isn't because many gnostic churches have opened up in the 1990s, but because the idea behind gnosticism—individual inspiration supersedes human institutions—never died out. In revolting against Pope Leo X, Martin Luther was playing it out fourteen hundred years later. The sharp rise in pentecostal congregations in the United States in recent years is in the same spirit, as is the East-West mysticism of Matthew Fox. And if this idea of a personal relationship with God also sounds anciently familiar, it should. "The kingdom of God is within you": What set the historical Jesus apart from the crowd of first-century prophets if not his radical message that individuals could come to experience God directly? That gnosticism mirrors this basic notion of Jesus is also an argument in favor of its direct link to him. As James Robinson puts it, "[T]he left-wing trajectory out of which second-century Gnosticism emerged must have been contemporary with the Pauline and Johannine schools and could well be a major factor in influencing them."[13]

This postulated proto-gnostic influence on Paul is another area that has made orthodox Christian theologians uncomfortable for centuries. If, as they have claimed, Paul inherited the tradition that we see in the gospels—if, in other words, early Christianity sprang fully formed from the well-orchestrated plan of Jesus—and if what later came to be known as gnosticism was just a heretical misreading of Jesus' message, why does Paul break out in some places into what sounds very much like gnostic mysticism? Paul writes of entering a trance and being taken up to heaven, where he "heard things that are not to be told, that no mortal is permitted to repeat." Elsewhere he differentiates between two kinds of Christian knowledge: the ordinary knowledge of Jesus' death and resurrection, and a "secret and hidden" knowledge which is only for the advanced.[14]

Orthodox Christianity is democratic in its faith: it insists that there are no secret insights reserved for the elders. Gnosticism, as it developed in the second century, became consumed with secrets that it believed were passed from Jesus to various disciples or others; it is this secret knowledge that the name gnosticism ("knowing") refers to. So what is Paul doing professing to hold such secrets? Christian theologians have written off these passages, but to scholars like Robinson they add further proof to the theory that a wisdom tradition dates to Jesus' own lifetime—that those who compiled the first version of the Gospel of Thomas were also among Jesus' followers, had just as much authority as Peter and the others, and have just as much likelihood of having gotten to what Jesus "really meant" as the orthodox tradition.

When it came time for Mark to put stylus to parchment, he would naturally tend to shun stories and traditions of a gnostic nature and instead favor those that reflected the way his community understood Jesus' message. And the same held true for the other writers of what would become the canonical gospels.

Edward Schillebeeckx sees beneath the gospel resurrection stories evidence of two separate traditions, which the writers fused together. One includes the stories of the appearances of the Risen Christ. The other, Schillebeeckx argues, is a separate "empty tomb" tradition. We see this in its primitive state in Mark, which contains no appearance stories at all, and ends, in its earliest version, with Mary Magdalene and other women going to the tomb to prepare the body but instead finding "a young man, dressed in a white robe," who tells them Jesus has been raised and orders them to go tell others of this. The first gospel therefore has no appearance stories, and a tomb empty of a body but with this curious figure in it.

Schillebeeckx argues that what happened historically was something like the following. Some of the disciples had an experience of the Risen Jesus. As these stories made the rounds of the followers of Jesus (many of whom had presumably given him up for dead), a renewed interest in him took hold. What had once been devotion turned to awe; perhaps they had in mind already the connection between "resurrection" and the End Time. It was a Jewish tradition to revere a special holy place that one associates with divine revelation. It is a matter of intense debate whether the Romans would have allowed Jesus—a lowly peasant and a political prisoner—to be put in a tomb. Some members of the Jesus Seminar think it more likely he would have suffered the common fate of crucifixion victims: to be thrown in a ditch, where wild dogs would have made the whole idea of bodily resurrection a moot point. (An ancient poem suggests this was the usual practice, saying that these victims ended up ". . . an ugly meal for birds of prey and grim scraps for dogs."[15]) Even if Jesus had been buried, it is debatable whether his followers (who had fled to Galilee, probably in fear for their lives) could have located it. In keeping with the custom of associating a wondrous event with a specific place, however, some tomb would have been found. And there, Schillebeeckx argues, a ritual expression of faith in the Living Christ developed. That man in white in the Mark story is an angel; he signifies that God has done something wondrous. But beneath Mark's story, according to this view, is an actual early liturgy—the first truly Christian ceremony—celebrating the belief of these Jews that the man they revered as leader and prophet had somehow become—not divine, but touched by the Divine (the wording in Mark is not "He arose" but "He has been raised").[16]

The idea that behind the empty tomb story lies a primitive liturgy is gaining currency today. James Charlesworth adds another piece of evidence for it. Golgotha, the site of both the crucifixion and the supposed tomb of Jesus, was known to be an abandoned stone quarry. A line of Psalm 118 reads, "The stone which the builders rejected; this has become the head of the corner." Acts records a scene in which Peter, taken prisoner by Caiaphas and other members of the Sanhedrin, defiantly refers to Jesus as "the stone that was rejected by you, the builders; it has become the cornerstone."[17] This same line appears in Mark's gospel; it is spoken by Jesus at the end of a parable. Charlesworth speculates that its prominent inclusion in both Acts and Mark suggests that this piece of Psalm 118, so evocative of the place of reverence, was part of the liturgy that the followers recited at the tomb.[18]

Another piece of evidence in support of this theory comes from the recent Ph.D. thesis of Ellen Bradshaw Aitken of Harvard Divinity School. Aitken notes the seemingly obvious but heretofore overlooked point that the texts that form the structure of much of the passion and resurrection accounts in the gospels—Psalm 22, with the casting for lots and other crucifixion details, Psalm 69 with the "gall and vinegar" detail, and Psalm 118 with its possible echoes of the site of the tomb—are all psalms. And what is a psalm but a song? A ritual of celebration of victory over death would naturally contain song, might even be totally comprised of chanting and singing.[19]

Bishop Spong imagines a ritual procession culminating at the tomb—"a primitive version of what came to be called the stations of the cross"—where the celebrants would encounter "a liturgical functionary who wore a white vestment to play his liturgical role in this drama"—the role of an angel.[20] Once the procession arrived, Spong suggests, a ritual dialogue took place:

> LEADER: "Whom do you seek?"
> PEOPLE: "We seek Jesus of Nazareth, who was crucified."
> LEADER: "He has risen. He is not here. See the place where they laid him."

This is essentially the dialogue in Mark's empty tomb story; and since it is women who come to the tomb in the gospel story, Schillebeeckx surmises that this ritual may have been celebrated by women.

The important point is that the belief came first, and the tomb second. The empty tomb was not a proof for skeptics; it was a symbol that developed later for those who already believed. Evangelical theologian William Craig has recently written a "historical proof" of the resurrection—part of a wave of ultraconservative reaction to contemporary biblical scholarship, especially the Jesus Seminar—which includes a ten-point argument that demonstrates "the historical fact of the empty tomb," and which concludes, "Although the empty tomb may have proved at first ambiguous and puzzling to the disciples, today we know that most alternative explanations are more incredible than the resurrection itself (for example, the disciples' stealing the body, Jesus' not being dead, the women's going to the wrong tomb, etc.)."[21] Craig does not explain why it makes more sense "today" to believe that a dead body revivified and walked away than that it was stolen. Such attempts to *prove* that there really was an empty tomb imply that this was needed, and is still needed, as proof that Jesus lives on. Surely devout Christians are not all Doubting Thomases; surely religious faith does not depend on physical evidence.

In fact, another writer who finds layers behind the empty tomb story, Thomas Sheehan of Loyola University, thinks this story in Mark is not there as proof of the resurrection but serves precisely the opposite point; after all, the women who encounter the tomb and the angel aren't convinced by this "proof" but instead run away in fright. Sheehan believes the story acts very much like one of the parables of Jesus: it "subverts its own apparent theme." It is written not to convert the skeptical but to assure those who already believe that their faith does not rest on mere evidence.[22]

If the tomb was not originally a piece of evidence but a negative symbol of the transcendence of the divine—"Because Jesus is alive, he is not to be looked for in a sepulchre, the place of death!" is how Schillebeeckx translates the myth into words—then those who first experienced the Risen Christ did not find themselves faced with a physical body; they did not wonder, "If his body is here, what is in his tomb?" They did not carry out a body search. The original experience had to be something other.

But this ineffable experience had to be communicated to other people, and in this process it became literally incorporated into myth: the story took on a body, a corpse, which leaves its tomb. Perhaps Mark was responsible for this, or perhaps the ritual at the tomb had already become mythologized, and Mark simply copied the myth onto the end of his gospel. To this the other gospel writers added the various appearance stories, which gave authority to those figures they revered. And the foundational documents for an institution were established.

According to this reading of the first stages of Christian (i.e., post-Jesus) history, then, not one but several groups of Jesus' followers preserved what he did and said, in different ways, depending on their differing backgrounds. We know there were more than just the two that came to be the orthodox church and the gnostics. One other group centered around James the Just, the brother of Jesus. It remained based in Jerusalem and held to the conviction that Jesus was a reformer of Judaism, not a rebel from it. As Judaism itself underwent a crisis following the war of 70 C.E. and emerged in the rabbinic form we know today, this group died out. Burton Mack suggests that the Q document that underlies Matthew and Luke bespeaks yet another group, which, like those who collected the sayings in the Thomas gospel, considered Jesus a wisdom teacher. This group would have eventually become integrated into the rapidly growing apocalyptic movement represented in the writings of Paul.[23] This would indicate that the gnostics were the only non-orthodox followers of Jesus to survive very far into the second century. It was to consolidate its authority and repel this rival that the orthodox church came to insist on a bodily resurrection.

The nature of the resurrection; the relationship between the divine and the human; the authority of the church: with so many areas of profound disagreement it isn't surprising that the gnostics and the orthodox Christians became mortal enemies. But they did agree on one important point. Both groups devalued the historical Jesus. What mattered for both was the experience of the Risen Christ, and what becomes less and less significant as one moves forward in time from the crucifixion—what becomes lost in the impassioned theology of resurrection and redemption from sin and in the acquisition of secret wisdom—are the words and deeds of the peasant from Nazareth. Paul, the founder of Christian theology, says almost nothing about the life of Jesus, so focused is he on the death, and church fathers, right down through Luther, follow his lead. It isn't until quite recent times, and the elevation of rational inquiry, that a curiosity arises about the life, deeds, and circumstances of the man who ignited this world-historic force.

CHAPTER TWELVE

THE HISTORICAL JESUS GOES TO CHURCH

All arms are up high and waving, fingers seemingly wanting to caress the ceiling. The woman in the purple dress keeps her eyes squeezed shut as she leads the song, strong voice pouring into the microphone and filling the room:

> The name of the Looord is . . .
> a hiiiigh tower.
> People go innnto it . . .
> and theeey are saved!

Around and around the verse goes, the musicians gradually upping the tempo. Some arms come down and begin flapping or windmilling. The chanted lyrics become confused, syllables stick and repeat, until finally the woman in the purple dress is leading in a staccato jabber of pure ecstasy, unsullied by syntactic sense. A huge black man roams the aisle banging a tambourine with blissful fury. A woman doubles over in her seat, shoulders twitching. The view out the windows of this third-floor office building is a grim one: midtown Manhattan, graffitied walls, forlorn parking lots, and right across the street that bleak temple of transience, Port Authority Bus Terminal. The white coat of the blizzard of 1996 only partially blankets the grime and despair. Here inside the Healing Stream Deliverance Church, however, the mood is all up, and the reason is in the window—the tall neon lettering delivering good news to the neighborhood known as Hell's Kitchen: JESUS KNOWS. There isn't much of a sermon—a brief story of how prayer to Jesus overcame the evil of homosexuality. For the most part the congregation—mostly black, Chinese, and Latino—are happy to sit in or dance around rows of formed plastic chairs, shrieking, moaning, swaying, hugging. Talk isn't really necessary: Jesus knows, and in order to realize it, all you have to do is jump into the rushing current of the spirit.

A few dozen blocks uptown on this same Sunday morning, at the United Methodist Church of St. Paul and St. Andrew, a stately old Upper West Side institution, a young man in a gray suit stands at a lectern delivering opening remarks to a congregation that is whiter, seemingly wealthier, and, judging from their discussion, more educated. A hymn to the "Great Spirit" is sung, then the statement-and-response litany begins, a staple of Christian institutions, but here with a difference:

LEADER: We will enter into relationship with other communities of faith to deepen our understanding of God and our respect for each other.

CONGREGATION: We will encourage openness, and in so doing

> advocate and embrace diversity—of age, race, ethnicity, gender, economic status, abilities, sexual orientation, marital status, etc.—which is God's gift to the human family.

Then there is a vow to help others, "just as Christ did," to speak out for the voiceless, "just as Christ did," and to embody Christ's love and compassion.

What is notable here, besides the overt inclusiveness, is that at no time during the entire service is mention made of Jesus' redemptive death and resurrection, of his having died for our sins. Instead, it is the deeds of Jesus during his life that this congregation models itself on. And the meaning of the vow of inclusiveness becomes apparent when one learns that this is a Christian church only half of the time; three days a week it becomes B'Nai Jeshurun Temple. The church's pastor, James Karpen, has become so much a devotee of historical Jesus studies that he has embraced Jesus' own faith and enrolled in a doctorate of rabbinic studies program at Jewish Theological Seminary. When the local synagogue's roof collapsed five years ago, he invited its rabbis to share the church. The two congregations now co-sponsor a homeless shelter and have joint classes, at which they discuss such loaded topics as the Christian and Jewish interpretations of "Messiah."

"Historical Jesus work has been really important to me," says Karpen. "I've struggled with what Christianity is. It's very difficult to know what Jesus was up to, but it's clear to me that it's unlikely he was trying to form a new religion. He was up to some sort of reform of Judaism, emphasizing certain aspects of the many Judaisms that were floating around in the first century. So for me, to think of Christianity without thinking about it as some form of Judaism is missing the intentions of the founder."

Karpen and his fellow pastor, Edward Horne, and their very

socially active congregation haven't stopped at Christian–Jewish dialogue. Last year they included a local mosque in their discussions, examining the dense matrix of texts and history centered on first-century Israel from the perspective of all three major faiths. Beyond that, their embrace of recent trends has extended to reciting prayers to "our Father God and our Mother God."

These two churches—the Pentecostal Healing Stream Deliverance and the Methodist St. Paul and St. Andrew—represent two very different versions of American Christianity in the 1990s. To say that the first is predominant would be an absurd understatement: it is rapidly becoming the dominant Christian experience worldwide. Not only in the United States but in virtually every country, traditional, mainline churches—the kind with steeples and stained-glass windows—are losing membership. According to Gallup polls, the percentage of American Roman Catholics who regularly attend mass fell from seventy-four percent in 1958 to forty-six percent in 1993.[1] In thirty years, the Episcopal church has lost twenty-three percent of its members. Lutheran, Baptist, Methodist, and Presbyterian denominations are all in steady decline. In England, the Anglican church has lost ten percent of its rolls in five years;[2] fewer and fewer Italians and Spaniards and Latin Americans entrust their eternal spirits to the Vatican.

And yet Christianity is on the rise. The explanation, of course, is the astonishing worldwide phenomenon of newfangled churches variously termed charismatic, pentecostal, or evangelical—churches that often aren't housed in traditional structures, whose congregations have grown so fast and furiously that they meet in tents or abandoned movie theaters or airport hangars. They have taken hold not just in traditionally Christian countries but across Asia and Africa, where they do not so much borrow elements from local religions as freely mix traditions—ancestor worship, shamanistic rituals, and evocation of the spirits of the earth and water alongside the Eucharist and baptism. The largest single church in the world is the Yoido Full Gospel Church in Seoul, with a mind-numbing figure of 800,000 parishioners, whose services include ritual chants to ward off the spirits of meddling ancestors and who send their prayers to "Hananim," the pre-Christian Korean deity. As Harvey Cox put it in *Fire from Heaven,* his exploration of global pentecostalism, "The delicate question of which divinity is absorbing which is not always clear. Is Hananim displacing the God of the Bible? Or is Hananim just the name Korean Pentecostals apply to that God? What is clear is that Korean pentecostalism has become a powerful vehicle within which hundreds of thousands of people who might be embarrassed to engage in the 'old-fashioned' or possibly 'superstitious' practice of shamanic exorcism can now do it within the generous ambience of a certifiably up-to-date religion, one that came from the most up-to-date of all countries, the United States of America."[3]

Clearly, traditionalists would scarcely recognize this as Christianity at all. And the forms it takes in this country are nearly as exotic. The most elaborate evangelical churches in the United States feature color brochures detailing the services they provide, outdoor speakers broadcasting the sermon to passersby, parking lots named Peace and Love. Most combine a conservative theology in which Jesus is seen as the Redeemer of mankind, the one and only hope for the world, with worship that includes rock, country, or even rap music, and in some cases a menu of different services featuring music tailored to particular tastes, as well as dancing and scripted skits. Some favor practical advice sermons, others tend toward writhing on the floor and speaking in tongues. Practices that would have brought in the Inquisition at one point in the Christian era are now common. Indeed, more than common. According to a 1995 Gallup poll, no less than forty-three percent of the United States population characterizes itself as "born-again" or "evangelical" Christian, up five percent in five years.[4] Apart from a slight drop in 1988, when the televangelistic antics of Jim Bakker and Jimmy Swaggart left the public with a momentary distaste for big-business evangelism in general and the Assemblies of God church in particular, the trend has been steadily upward.[5]

Needless to say, the historical Jesus is of little interest in this realm—or rather, Christians of this type would consider that the Jesus in the gospels *is* the historical Jesus: that the gospels present an accurate picture of Jesus the man, from his divine birth to his supernatural defeat of death.

Ecstasy, then, seems to be replacing drab social duty as the predominant form of Christian expression, and historical Jesus scholarship doesn't even rate an asterisk. But the explosive rise of evangelical sects is not the only significant trend. Conversations with ministers around the country reveal that another, quieter revolution is taking place as well, for more and more churches—mostly small, mainline Protestant institutions like Karpen's St. Paul and St. Andrew—have been welcoming an important new member. Within the past several years, the historical Jesus has started going to church. Typically it begins with a minister who can't let go of his or her seminary training. Many complain that in their seminary days they were exposed to the full brunt of critical scholarship on the New Testament, often becoming excited about its implications for faith, but were then sent into the ministry with no guidance on how they might present it to their congregations. Indeed, most training grounds for clergy seem to operate under the principle that, since biblical scholarship won't go away, it is necessary for their recruits to be familiar with it, but that making it accessible to ordinary Christians would only be asking for trouble.

However, some ministers have nursed the feeling that in withholding the fruits of scholarship from their congregation, they were being dishonest. C. Blayney Colmore is rector of St. James-by-the-

Sea in San Diego, one of the largest Episcopal churches in southern California. In three decades as a clergyman he never forgot the perspective on Jesus he got from his seminary days, but only found the outside support he needed to present critical scholarship to his parishioners once he became an associate of the Jesus Seminar four years ago. "There are a group of us who never recover from it," he said. "When I got to seminary it was like being immersed in the Jesus Seminar for three years. I didn't know that people in the institutional church were doing this kind of thing. It never occurred to me that that was why they were in the seminary—because they couldn't do it in the church. But what happens is, five years out of seminary you're criticizing the professors at the seminary for not knowing where the real issues are."

Colmore now includes issues from contemporary biblical scholarship in his Bible study classes and sermons. "I've tried to indicate that I think Jesus was a normal human being, the same as everybody else in the Bible, and when we talk about the Christ we talk about an ongoing process of salvation," he said. Almost inevitably, a portion of his congregation considers him heretical. "I had a delegation two or three months ago who came to test my orthodoxy. One of them asked, 'Do you believe in the literal, bodily resurrection of Jesus as attested to in the New Testament?' I said, 'I believe in the resurrection of Jesus but I don't believe the New Testament portrays it the way you just said it.' "

Colmore believes that study of the historical Jesus is more than just an interesting footnote to faith. "It has renewed or will renew a lot of people's hope that the issues about Jesus really have something to do with the critical issues of their own life. The way Jesus is normally portrayed by the church leaves vast numbers of people, including me, thinking, 'Who cares?' I think the people in the historical Jesus movement who are really digging are asking questions that have to do with the way we live our lives. There are people in my congregation who really get it when I preach. They get all churned up and excited. Like me, they are naive enough to think it's going to infect the whole congregation."

Marianne Niesen is a former Catholic nun who is now a United Methodist pastor in Helena, Montana. She has oriented her ministry around the historical Jesus, focusing especially on the work of Marcus Borg, who has made himself into a kind of new wave missionary, bringing to churches the message of his scholarship, that the historical Jesus was not a uniquely divine being but a "spirit person," in the mold of Lao-tzu, Moses, the Buddha, and Mohammed. The result of historical Jesus scholarship, according to Borg, has been "to undermine the conviction that Christianity is the only way of salvation."

"I think one of the very helpful things that [Borg] talks about," Niesen said, "is that the Christian movement isn't so much about believing *in* Jesus but in taking seriously what he took seriously. It's about a relationship with Jesus, with the divine. That's where the work the historical Jesus people are doing is so helpful to us. As they begin to illuminate the historical Jesus as a real figure who dealt with real issues, we are freed to say, 'In the spirit of Jesus, how are we going to deal with this particular problem?' But you have to think it through. You can't just open your Bible and get an answer, because Jesus didn't give answers."

This is the kind of talk that makes conservative Christians feel their worst fears about critical Jesus scholarship are justified. Ministers like Niesen and Colmore are crossing a line that hasn't been crossed before: they are Christian clergy who openly declare their belief that Jesus is not the point of Christian faith, but more of a messenger, a road sign pointing the way to truth. Niesen feels very strongly about this. "Jesus has been used," she said. "You see it on bumper stickers: 'Jesus is the answer.' Well, Jesus *isn't* the answer. Jesus was a person who sought for answers and, I think, gave us a way to do the same. But he didn't give us answers. He couldn't conceive of the kinds of issues we're dealing with."

Richard Watts, a Presbyterian pastor for thirty-six years, took the dramatic step a few years ago of founding a new church in Illinois specifically for Christians who no longer believed in traditional teaching about Jesus. "I think there are an awful lot of people out there who, hearing only a theological construct about Jesus—language about a divine being who comes from eternity to save a sinful humanity and then ascends into heaven—find that those categories are not credible," he said. "And when these people are introduced to what we can know about the historical Jesus, they say, 'Gosh, this is interesting stuff.' And they get reconnected. They say things like, 'I didn't think I could be a Christian anymore but now I think there's a place for me in the church.' "

Watts initially ran radio ads for parishioners: "If you're shopping around for a church that makes sense . . . we're a new, growing community of people from many church backgrounds who are committed to loving God with our minds as well as our hearts, who take the Bible seriously but not literally . . . who believe that authentic faith has nothing to fear from contemporary knowledge." His perspective on Christian origins affects not only Watts's sermons but his liturgy. The practice of communion is ordinarily tied to the Last Supper, mirroring Jesus' breaking bread, giving it to the disciples and saying, "This is my body . . . do this in memory of me." Watts finds it more meaningful to stress not the transubstantiation of the bread into Christ's body, but another theme, which Jesus research highlights as deriving from the historical Jesus: the open table. "I'll introduce the communion with the words of the feeding of the five thousand," Watts said, "or reading from Acts, where it says they took their meals in one another's homes with glad and great hearts." As with Karpen's congregation in New York City, Watts emphasizes the example of the historical

Jesus: his breaking down of social barriers by sharing meals with the lowest of the low gets more attention from him than the "theological construct" of the redemptive death on the cross.

The Rev. Wade Renn of Grace Church in Nutley, New Jersey, has been pursuing his own revisionist approach to Christianity for several years. He dispenses with sermons altogether in favor of question-and-answer periods in which he and his congregation do their own deconstruction of the gospels. Renn takes it for granted that the gospels are political documents meant to reinforce the position of one group of Christians, and that appreciating the underlying spirit means first stripping away the politics. "I see that the canonical gospels were written with certain concerns to be addressed," he said. "People were falling away from the faith because Jesus was not returning." The answer was to objectify the spiritual truth of the resurrection so that instead of "we are all born anew through the new awareness of God's love that Jesus has shown us," we have "Jesus literally came back from the dead." "Like in the Old Testament," says Renn, "they wrote very sensational stuff to try to make real these things so people would believe. So you find the resurrection sensationalized in the gospels. That makes nice stuff for Easter that people can understand: the women went to the tomb and it was empty, and so on."

Renn has written his own Sunday school curriculum "that tells kids the truth." He holds workshops for other ministers who are interested in getting behind the texts. "People in America take things at face value," he complains. "It's only when you get behind the surface that you see the radical truth of Jesus."

And what is that truth? "People think when he broke the bread and gave it, it was himself. But the bread is you and me. Jesus takes you and me and gives thanks to God. I tell people, '*You* are the body of Christ.' That's radical."

It isn't entirely radical—the church has always preached that the

Christian congregation is the body of Christ. But this new breed of clergy takes this view to the extreme. Blayney Colmore found that some in his congregation began to consider him a heretic not when he questioned the historicity of certain parts of the gospel story but when he declared himself a universalist, when he preached that God's love covers everyone, whether or not they are Christians, whether or not they go to church. "People started to say, 'He's misguiding people and encouraging them to sin by telling them that God will find a way to save everybody. That means that you don't have to worry about how you act.' "

Richard Rhem, a Reformed Church minister in Spring Lake, Michigan, got into trouble with his denomination's hierarchy for proclaiming similar beliefs. When he refused to recant before the regional governing body in 1996, the tribunal censured him and considered trying him for heresy. Rhem resigned, and his congregation voted to secede from the denomination—all over an issue nominal Christians might well think beyond argument: whether there is room in heaven for non-Christians. That it is still very much of an issue perhaps has to do with the inherent tension that comes from trying to maintain an organization whose foundational figure was himself suspicious of organizations. The root message of the historical Jesus, as far as these ministers are concerned, is that you need no broker to gain God's love and attention. This message was so volatile it had to be contained at once, and so the gospel writers refocused its beam, trained it onto the figure of Jesus as Christ. He became the medium. The great irony of Christianity, according to these radical clergy, is that the man who preached an unbrokered relationship with God was himself made into the ultimate broker.

Attempting to point out that irony can be risky. John F. Paulson, pastor of Grace Lutheran Church in Corvallis, Oregon, invited Marcus Borg to speak to his congregation, and the result was a bitter dispute that ended with many parishioners leaving and Rev. Paulson taking early retirement. "We had people calling Borg an instrument of the devil, Satan personified," Paulson said. "It was a negative thing for our congregation. It hurt us financially and hurt our spirit. But I wouldn't do anything different. This work takes away some of the absolutist character of the church. The church has all of these treasured truths, but I've been taught ever since seminary that all of these truths are nothing, the only truth is Jesus Christ. Everything else is subject to revision or improvement."

It is perhaps inevitable that clergy who hold such views will always be looked on as radicals—beloved, perhaps, even revered, but always radicals. They are soldiers demonstrating against war, corporate executives declaring capitalism evil. "Religion is the great sin," says Renn. "I fight against any form of religion."

The explosive interest in the historical Jesus—a minor explosion in comparison with the rise of pentecostalism and evangelicalism, but an explosion nonetheless—surely has to do with this anti-religion sentiment, the sneaking suspicion that in protecting its own status the church has shielded people from the very ideas that are its reason for existing. Christians of this type seem to feel that the church has brokered Jesus into irrelevance, buried his blatant spiritual insights, and given us instead a primitive idol—born of a virgin, floating around among the clouds like some medieval blimp—that is an insult to our modern intelligence.

The fascinating thing is that this same sense of having been duped by the church, this same radical individualism, seems to underlie the larger trend in Christianity. The two movements—the smaller, "liberal" one that digs through the gospels in search of truth and the larger "conservative" one that finds truth aplenty on the surface—tend to view one another with suspicion, but they are cousins. For one thing, both are products of the baby-boom era.

Barry Kosmin and Seymour Lachman, in *One Nation Under God: Religion in Contemporary American Society,* analyze statistical data on religion and characterize this generation and its tendencies: "They increasingly question all authority, hierarchy, and domination. They show less loyalty to denomination and congregation, and are less likely to acknowledge the church as the source of religious insight or its authority on matters of religious truth and doctrine. It is as if they have collectively imbibed George Bernard Shaw's statement that 'every profession is a conspiracy against the laity.'" Above all, for these people, the authors note, "religious insight is increasingly based on personal experience . . ."[6]

All of this applies equally well to members of the Healing Stream Deliverance congregation and the United Methodist Church of St. Paul and St. Andrew. The difference, ultimately, may be a matter of temperament. As Catherine Kurs, a New York theologian, put it, "There are people who wouldn't be caught dead playing tambourines and waving their arms, but they still have a need to get closer to Jesus."

Taken together, these two trends—stripping away layers of theology and finding a direct personal connection to the Divine—are also reminiscent of the first great heresy declared by the church. Indeed, Harold Bloom believes that American Christianity is so far along on this path that it has ceased to be Christianity at all: after all these centuries, Bloom argues, gnosticism has finally won the day. "Salvation, for the American, cannot come through the community or the congregation," he writes in *The American Religion,* "but is a one-on-one act of confrontation."[7] This intense personal struggle outside the traditional institutions is not the Christianity organized by Peter and Paul; it is not what drove the Crusaders into the desert or what gave the American pioneers their backbone. We have become, according to Bloom, "an obsessed society wholly in the grip of a dominant Gnosticism."[8] We are all mystics, or would-be mystics, wandering in the desert, forever wriggling free of the shackles of orthodoxy.

This is apparent even within the larger movement itself. The new churches springing up all over the country resist simple definition and keep splitting and rearranging at a remarkable rate: conservative evangelicals distinguish themselves from evangelicals, who aren't the same as charismatics, who hold pentecostals at arm's length, who are different from Wesleyan, Foursquare Gospel, Christian Reformed and Vineyard. And this pervasive American trend isn't confined to Christianity. Kosmin and Lachman find the same wandering in search of insight among Jews, American Indians (who seem to be reclaiming their ancestral religions), and various sects of Buddhism and Hinduism in the U.S. New Age adherents—Wiccas, goddess worshipers, New Thought metaphysicians, Eckankarites, etc., etc.—express this tendency by their very existence. Rampant individualism seems to be on the rise across the board.

This is not to say that Christians who value historical Jesus research are essentially the same as those who adhere to an evangelical doctrine. If they spring from the same generational trend, they spring in opposite directions. The basic difference is clear. The conservatives insist that Jesus is *the* way, the only way. The historical Jesus crowd are pluralists. In each other's eyes, the former are hidebound dogmatists and the latter are pie-eyed heretics. Both see the other as dangerously misinterpreting the meaning of Christianity.

No one expresses the new Christian pluralism—which seeks to "rescue" Christianity by deconstructing its foundational texts—more eloquently or more controversially than John Shelby Spong, Episcopal bishop of Newark, New Jersey, one of the premier popularizers of biblical criticism. The titles of his books say it all: *Born of a Woman: A Bishop Rethinks the Virgin Birth and the Treatment of*

Women by a Male-Dominated Church, Rescuing the Bible from Fundamentalism, and *Resurrection: Myth or Reality?* He has been called "wildly offbeat," "a political and ecclesiastical windmill," and "an enormous embarrassment to the rest of the church." *Time* announced the arrival of one of his books with the headline "More Spongtaneous Eruptions." Twice he has faced down presentment—the preliminary to an official charge of heresy. He has taken heat for ordaining an openly gay man to the priesthood and for espousing the view—put forth by various scholars through the years—that St. Paul was a repressed homosexual.

His office in downtown Newark is a comfy mix of old wainscoting, indoor/outdoor carpeting, book-stuffed shelves and furniture that looks old but decidedly not antique. He appears anything but offbeat. A tall, lanky, craggy sixty-four-year-old with a deep, sugar-magnolia Southern baritone, he comes across remarkably like Honest Abe. When he sits, his limbs flow over and around the chair. He grips a coffee cup with long, bony fingers. He takes in his visitor with a relaxed, meditative stare.

The first thing to understand about Spong is that he is not your typical East Coast liberal. He was born into a fundamentalist Christian family in Charlotte, North Carolina, where Billy Graham was a neighbor. He served for a time as rector of an Episcopal church in Lynchburg, Virginia, where he first encountered an up-and-coming Southern conservative named Jerry Falwell. Spong's fundamentalist background instilled in him a deep passion for the words of the Bible; but, unlike many of his colleagues, he came to find that this very focus led to difficulties. How was it possible to believe in the literal truth of the Bible when the Bible says that the earth is flat, that women are property, that epilepsy is caused by demon possession? The young priest found himself in a spiritual quagmire; the way out turned to be through reading the book *Honest to God,* by Anglican bishop John Robinson, which argued that since God is by definition beyond our capacity to comprehend, all attempts to encompass him—even those in the Bible—are only rough metaphors. Robinson's book, which built upon the work of the German-born theologian Paul Tillich, helped fuel a modern revolution in Protestant thinking. Spong read it three times, and began to see the Bible in a new way.

Spong has now written fourteen books of his own on the need to creatively interpret the Bible in order to keep it relevant. He has taken part in civil rights marches, championed the cause of women and gays as priests, and dueled with the Vatican over its stand on these issues. In 1989, he and Jerry Falwell faced off once again, this time on the set of ABC's *Good Morning America.* This brought him a whole new level of fame, which he has since exploited in a one-man effort to counter the Religious Right's version of the Christian experience. He has appeared on *Oprah* and *Politically Incorrect.* When *People* covered the furor over his ordination of a gay priest, he cheerfully posed for a photo in full bishop's regalia. He has been lampooned in *National Review* and the evangelical *Christianity Today,* which he seems to consider badges of honor.

Spong is no biblical scholar, but a theologian who respects scholarship and considers it an important tool for Christian faith. Indeed, some of the theories on Christian origins that he outlines in his eloquently folksy prose make some scholars cringe, such as his idea that Judas was a fictional creation of the early church, a fall guy meant to represent the Jewish race ("Judas . . . bears the name of the whole Jewish nation. One suspects that his naming is neither a coincidence nor an accident"[9]). Many scholars shake their heads over such notions, countering that since the early church was still largely comprised of Jews, it hardly makes sense that they would conceive of such a scapegoat. Besides that, Judas was one of the most common Jewish names; Jesus himself had a brother of that name.

So Spong's importance may be less for the details of what he writes than the fact that he is writing it at all. One prominent New Testament historian put it this way: "If he was not a bishop, his writing wouldn't be important, but since he is a bishop it is absolutely important. He has the courage to say these things." Meaning that having one of the most prominent figures in a major Christian church incorporating the results of biblical scholarship into his faith—and actually redefining his faith—has a profound impact. Spong says he has received thousands of letters over the years, coming in at a rate of twenty-five to thirty per day: "I get enormous mail from people who say that I've given them a way that they can stay inside the Christian church with integrity." These correspondents include priests and ministers who confess to deep doubts about basic facets of their faith, doubts that his books have helped to set in a new light, if not to erase.

These thorny issues include the virgin birth, the resurrection, the nature miracles. Must a Christian believe in these things as literal events in human history? Must Jesus be seen as a supernatural divinity? Or is it an abuse to insist that the language of the Bible be taken literally? Spong argues that to do so diminishes the Bible and threatens to make it irrelevant for our time. He takes it for granted that any human utterance comes prepackaged with certain prejudices, and that the job of a truth-seeker is to free language from old prejudices, to reinvent myth.

The ultimate myth, for him, is God, which he elaborated in conversation:

"I am a white, male, heterosexual American Christian. God is none of those things. When I in my particularity try to describe what I mean by God, I can only use the language of a human being. I was one of the consecrating bishops for Desmond Tutu, and he once said we don't realize how subjective English is, how much it's a white man's language. He pointed out by way of example the phrase 'I was tickled pink.' It's a white language, and it's a male language. So it's a prejudiced language. So whenever you use English, you're talking subjectively about that which is not able to be subjectified. That's what I mean by mythology. No description of God will ever be 'real.' All I can do is deconstruct the mythology of yesterday so that it can make sense to me today. I'm not deliberately setting out to create a myth. I'm saying that every word I speak about God is limited by my limitations. I take seriously the people who wrote the creeds and the Bible and shaped the tradition, but I don't want to idolize it. My job is to take their experience and translate it into my world so that it makes sense to me. And I hope my heirs will do the same for their generation. My words can no more be eternal than anybody else's."

But isn't the eternal significance of these particular words precisely the point? "That's what the church doesn't understand because the church is in the control business. That's why the church claims that it is the source of infallible authority. 'We've got a lock on God—if you want God, come to us.' I don't want to feed into that. My Christian faith says that I'm on a journey into the mystery of God, and every day I take another step and I see God from a different angle. So I can't take the words that were real yesterday and suggest that they will be real tomorrow. I've got to look at God from that new angle. That means that I'll never be secure, but I see security as an idol, a heresy. I think if I can make you secure, I've taken away your humanity. I think we're supposed to be insecure, that's what it means to be human."

Security may be the root of the difference between Christians who favor Spong's approach and those of a more traditional bent. The Jesus Seminar meeting in Santa Rosa included a round table for ministers who were trying to broaden their message to include some of these concepts; one summarized what must be a basic issue: "I have professional people in my congregation who understand that in their disciplines things evolve, that truth is changing, but these same people want to think that in my field truth is the same, always and forever."

Throughout the whole history of Christianity, clergy have borne the burden of being possessors of eternal, definitive truth. Lately, some—fortified by recent scholarship and emboldened by the example of people like Bishop Spong—have slipped off their suits of chain-mail certainty and breathed a sigh of relief. They and their faith stand proudly defenseless, willing to admit limitations. For some, this represents the finest fruits of historical Jesus scholarship, a step that could carry Christianity fully into the modern world.

To other observers, however, it shows how misguided the whole enterprise has become.

CHAPTER THIRTEEN

THE CASE AGAINST

Good Friday 1995. The program is *CNN*'s *Talk Back Live,* the subject "Jesus: Man or Messiah?" The guests are Jesus Seminar fellow John Dominic Crossan, William Craig, an evangelical theologian who has made a mini-career out of vilifying the Jesus Seminar, and Rabbi Joseph Potasnik, a radio talk show host. The studio is tricked out for maximum effect: a neon logo, a couple hundred audience members sitting in a close circle around the stage, TV monitors and computer terminals, cameramen roving for dramatic angles. An 800 number and a fax number are flashed repeatedly across the bottom of the screen. Terribly concerned to be online and in-touch, the show is linked to its audience by fax, phone, e-mail, and visual satellite downlink from American University. There is so much going on, and the host, Susan Rook, is doing such a determined Oprah Winfrey impersonation that it's difficult to follow the discussion.

But it is a fascinating discussion, in part because this live nationwide program is an indication of how hot the historical Jesus has become, and also because it reveals the confusion and alarm it is causing within some conservative Christian circles. The different way that Crossan and Craig handle the questions shows something else: that the promoters of the historical Jesus still operate by the rules of academia, while their conservative opponents understand *realpolitik*. Throughout, Crossan consistently responds to earnest questions about whether Jesus was or was not divine by stressing that divinity is not a historically provable concept. For Craig, the supernaturalist, the matter is much more straightforward:

CRAIG: I'm concerned that there are good historical grounds for believing that the Jesus we see portrayed in the gospels is in fact a credible historical figure and not the product of myth and legend that skeptical scholars like John Dominic Crossan take him to be.

ROOK: So you're saying that it's historical fact that he was a divine being.

CRAIG: Yes, and that we have good grounds for believing that.

Here Rook thrusts her microphone in the face of a startled audience member.

ROOK: Jean, what do you think: historical figure, fact, or fiction?

JEAN: I think . . . it's both, fact and fiction.

ROOK: Divine being?

JEAN: Yes, somewhat. But he also was human too. And I agree with this man [Craig].

ROOK: Dominic, talk to Jean. She disagrees with you.

CROSSAN: I thought she said exactly the same thing, Susan: Jesus is fully human . . .

ROOK: But she says Jesus is a divine being.

CROSSAN: "Divine being" is a statement of faith. Nobody can make that as a fact.

Rook looks puzzled at this; clearly, she had been prepped to expect this scholar to adopt an anti-Christian line to counter Craig's pro-Christian stance. Crossan's answers are too subtle; he doesn't give good TV. Craig, however, does not disappoint: "I think this is a false dichotomy," he declares, "this idea that something is either fact or faith. It's either a fact that Jesus was divine or he wasn't. Believing ain't gonna make it so."

The audience bursts into applause. Here is something to appreciate: a straight, sinewy, graspable statement. Craig develops his theme as the program goes on: "I think that there are three major factors that undergird the belief in Jesus' resurrection as a fact of history: the discovery of his empty tomb, his post-mortem appearances to his disciples, and the very origin of the Christian movement itself. The consensus of New Testament scholarship is that each of these three facts can be independently established. And I know of no better explanation of those three facts than the fact that Jesus historically rose from the dead."

Once again, applause. Now, whatever one's beliefs, the idea that it is the "consensus of New Testament scholarship" that the resurrection "can be independently established" is preposterous: it is precisely because the consensus is quite otherwise that Craig is here in the first place. But this statement reveals that Craig has come to get a job done. He is here to counter this new wave of scholarship, or rather this newly public wave of scholarship. He will do that by attempting to meet it on its own terms—giving not a theological response but a critical one, beating the historians at their own game. It's not enough to say that Jesus scholarship is misguided, that the resurrection is a profound spiritual truth that the scholars, for all their emphasis on history and science, seem blind to. No, it is important to Craig that the methods of critical scholarship *prove* his view of Jesus as Messiah. This is a strange and surprising new turn in conservative theology, one that, like historical Jesus research itself, seems to have arisen out of our reverence for science, our feeling that historical truth is, if not the only truth, at least the most primary truth. In other words, where once Christian fundamentalists rose to challenge modernism, which had enthroned reason above belief, this approach embraces reason, looks to rationalistic inquiry to support belief.

Behind this new tack is a fear that historical Jesus scholarship is about to "prove" that the Jesus of the gospels is not identical with the Jesus of history. If this could be shown, the thinking seems to be, then Christian faith would collapse. So a full-fledged counterattack is necessary, which takes the same form as historical Jesus scholarship. And, since we all value scientific and historical truth so highly, it follows that once the empty tomb and the post-mortem appearances are proven to be real, historical events, humanity will have no choice but to see Jesus as the Christ, the Son of God, the only savior of the world.

There is one problem with this neatly tied bundle, and Rabbi Potasnik spots it. "What troubles me about William's presentation is, I wonder what room there is for Judaism?" he asks. "He seems to express this exclusive doctrine that doesn't leave room for any other belief. I wonder what William has to say to Jews who do not accept Jesus as the Messiah?"

Craig has a response to this: "What that question prompts in my mind is, what do *you* do with Jews who *do* accept Jesus as the Messiah?"

This practiced response avoids an answer—the only possible answer Craig can make is "Jews and Muslims and those of all other religions are simply wrong," which would not be politically correct—by deflecting the question back onto the rabbi, neatly suggesting that conversion is the appropriate response to these unassailable facts. Crossan doesn't like this argument, and he tries once again to point out logical flaws: "I would like to take up Bill's consistent confusion of fact and faith. Faith, as far as I am concerned, is in the meaning of a fact—it sees through the fact to something else. I really agree with the rabbi. To say that these were facts and not acts of faith means that anyone who does not believe in them must be blind or willfully refusing to see the obvious, and that is very dangerous."

Crossan has made his point, but there is no applause. By this time, meanwhile, Craig has given those Christians who may be concerned about historical Jesus scholarship a brickbat to use against it: he has told them definitively not only that Jesus' Sonship is historically verifiable but that this is "the consensus of New Testament scholarship." The only thing left is to do what anyone does on television: plug a product. In answer to a final question—"How would you best characterize Jesus: was he a legend, a liar, a lunatic, or a lord?"—Craig holds up a book called *Jesus Under Fire,* which he says deals with many of these issues and to which he is a contributor. Craig then answers the question tersely: "He's Lord."

Crossan—who by this time, one feels, has done little more than cause confusion—answers next. "I would admire William Craig's commercial message, however [I maintain that] 'Jesus is Lord' is an act of faith."

Rook tries one last time to nudge Crossan into the pigeonhole allotted for him. She prods: "So you would say in answer to the question, 'Man.' "

But Crossan won't go. "No, I would not." Rook looks pained;

Crossan tries a final time to make himself clear: "I would say 'man' is a historical answer. By faith you would say 'Lord' or 'divine' or 'Son of God.' "

Surprisingly, in a telephone conversation after the program, Crossan seemed to think he had come off very well. He had emphasized a point that has caused confusion for many people, Christians and non-Christians: his opponent's arguments were illogical.

Clearly, these men were playing different games. In Crossan's, fine distinctions are everything; he is an Olympic fencer, making light taps with a thin blade. But how many people understand the rules of fencing? Craig, on the other hand, comes across as a boxer, and everyone knows a good body blow when they see it.

Craig's presentation seems to reflect what Robert Funk crowed about in his speech at the Santa Rosa meeting of the Jesus Seminar: this new wave of historical Jesus research has spawned an organized opposition. The book that Craig held up is a collection of essays by conservative theologians that takes direct aim at the Jesus Seminar, but more broadly at all historical Jesus research. The authors believe that critical scholarship can prove the historical truth of the supernatural events described in the New Testament, and they set about to do so.

One author, R. Douglas Geivett of Talbot School of Theology, even tackles the big question: "Is Jesus the Only Way?" Geivett proves, first, that there is a God; second, that He created the universe; third, that He did so for the benefit of mankind. He then pulls everything together:

> So let us suppose that God does take an interest in the human condition. Would it not be puzzling if it turned out that the resurrection of Jesus Christ, a

> well-attested historical phenomenon, had nothing to do with God's interest in the human condition? When an event like the resurrection takes place in a world that owes its existence to the sort of God we have been describing, we should give some consideration to the possibility that God is up to something.[1]

Therefore, Jesus is the only way. If such language sounds more like that of medieval churchmen than modern scholars, it should, for it is theology. But where medieval theology based itself on what it saw as the bedrock—Aristotelian logic—this new type of theology tries to use history.

There is, of course, absolutely nothing wrong with discussing such an issue as whether Jesus is "the only way"; it is the very stuff of theology. But it is disingenuous to pass this off on the public as verifiable historical fact, and it seems to be part of a trend. A similar attempted coup took place over Christmas 1994 when the London *Times* announced an amazing discovery in a front-page article. Three fragments of an ancient papyrus copy of the Gospel of Matthew had been found to date to the mid–first century. Matthew, therefore, was nothing less than an "eyewitness record of the life of Christ."[2] *Time* picked up the story and gushed about "hard external evidence" that Matthew dates to the time of Jesus. Several conservative commentators quickly stepped forward to speculate on the profound implications of this find.

Meanwhile, biblical scholars around the world did a double-take. Was it possible that the entire field of New Testament scholarship in all its aspects—archaeology, paleography, the stratification theory of the gospels—was totally wrong? Then the scholars noticed that the fragments in question were not newly discovered but had in fact been housed at Magdalen College Library at

Oxford since 1901; they were well known to papyrologists and had been reliably dated to the end of the *second* century. What was going on here?

The man who made the sensational claims was Carsten Thiede, a German papyrologist who for at least ten years had been unsuccessfully trying to convince his colleagues that a fragment found among the Dead Sea Scrolls was actually a tiny piece of Mark's gospel. When Thiede made his mid-first-century claim to the *Times*, he promised to follow up with a detailed argument in a scholarly publication. But, as Graham Stanton of the University of London pointed out, the article, which appeared in the *Zeitschrift für Papyrologie und Epigraphik*—hardly a match to the *Times* or *Time* for circulation—didn't argue for a mid-first-century date at all, but *late* first century, which does away with the sensational claim that Matthew's gospel was an eyewitness account—the whole point of the news story. In a follow-up book, co-written with the *Times* journalist who reported the story of the fragments, Thiede settles on a date of about 60 C.E. Papyrologists who have since reviewed Thiede's arguments for even a late-first-century redating have found them tenuous,* but the media splash had already been made. Several scholars characterize the whole episode as "a ploy" to derail Jesus scholarship, at least in the public's mind.

One conclusion from all of this: New Testament scholars—in particular the Jesus Seminar, with its media-savvy tactics—have insisted on bringing their arcane subject into the wider world, and some of its opponents have decided that two can play that game.

But the fact that the most visible responses to Jesus research are of questionable merit doesn't mean that there are no good

*The argument is based on handwriting analysis. The fragments are written in biblical majuscule, a style of writing that is believed to have begun in the second century. Thiede's claim is based on a contention that other fragments, in a similar style, may date to the first century.

arguments against it. Consider that the whole field rests on one theoretical support: the idea that the four gospels contain discernible layers of tradition and theology that developed in the decades after Jesus' death. What if it could be shown that this premise is wrong? The whole meticulously constructed picture of Jesus that has been outlined in this book would fall to pieces. There would be nothing left to do but go back to considering the gospel portraits as more or less reliable. "Gospel truth" would revert to its traditional meaning, or be abandoned altogether.

William Farmer, professor emeritus at the Perkins School of Theology, Southern Methodist University, has long championed an alternative to the so-called two-source hypothesis that most scholars subscribe to, which holds that Matthew and Luke composed their gospels primarily from two documents, Mark and Q. Farmer believes instead that Matthew was the first gospel, that Luke came next, and that Mark is a truncated version of these two, a sort of Cliff Notes to Jesus' life. This was essentially the view of the early church fathers, and is why Matthew comes first in the Bible. Does it make any difference which gospel is seen as coming first? Yes. If Farmer is right, then we have only one independent version of events: Matthew's. Without the ability to compare and contrast, there is no means by which to peel away layers to try to get at the earliest stage. The field of historical Jesus research falls by the wayside. Matthew's Jesus—the host of the Last Supper, the teacher of the Lord's Prayer, the self-aware Messiah—becomes the historical Jesus, or as close as we can get to him. Critical scholars and all their fearsome tools are thus kept at bay.

Farmer first published his thesis in the 1960s and restated it in the 1990s. It has gained some attention in conservative circles but remains unconvincing to most scholars, who hold to the early dating of Mark not because of one overwhelming piece of evidence but for a variety of reasons: his is the most primitive account of events (he includes no virgin birth or resurrection); clues in Mark's gospel date it to just after the destruction of Jerusalem, while clues in Matthew and Luke put them at a further remove; and the placement of shared material is more easily explained if Mark is seen coming first.[3] But the priority of Mark is still only a theory, and Farmer's spirited assault on it indicates that it is far from bedrock.

Another attack on the two-source hypothesis comes from German scholar Eta Linnemann. The second source that the theory depends on is Q—the hypothetical document invented to account for non-Markan material that Matthew and Luke share. As noted, Q study has blossomed in the past twenty years, to the point where it has become a kind of religion of its own, with some scholars positing an entire Q community, lost to history for two thousand years, that had its own beliefs about Jesus. In their enthusiasm, these experts seem to have forgotten that there is no piece of parchment containing Q, that it exists only in their own abstraction-loving minds. Linnemann, a veteran German exegete who studied under the great Rudolf Bultmann, vehemently rejects the entire Q hypothesis. She points out that, unlike the Thomas gospel, which is attested in ancient sources, Q has no ancient citations. Not the slightest reference can be found in any of the early church fathers to a written document or a community that followed Jesus in the manner that Burton Mack and others suggest.

More to the point, Linnemann maintains that the whole basis for assuming Q—the linguistic parallels between Matthew and Luke—is shaky. Her analysis of the relevant passages convinces her that only about forty-two percent of the words in the Q portions of those two gospels are identical to one another. She also argues that more than half of the parallel passages contain fewer than fifty words each, implying that these were short enough to be committed to memory by Jesus' hearers, which would do away with the need for a Q hypothesis altogether.

Along with other conservatives, Linnemann also attacks the primacy of the Thomas gospel, claiming that the evidence indicates it dates to the mid–second century, was dependent on the Synoptics, and represents a later offshoot from early Christianity, not one of its foundational groups.

Liberal scholars, Linnemann charges, have jumped onto the Q bandwagon, and insisted on the primacy of Thomas, in order to create a two-pronged attack on traditional New Testament scholarship, on the tradition of seeing the four canonical gospels as the base texts for information on Jesus' life and work. Why would they do such a thing? "The motive is clear," she wrote in *Bible Review*, one of the popular forums for New Testament scholarship. "Q (with Thomas's aid) gives a biblical basis for those who do not accept Jesus as the Son of God, reject his atoning death on the cross, and deny his resurrection."[4]

That's a strong charge, a charge of widescale intellectual dishonesty, and the arguments behind it might seem compelling to a layman. Is it possible that what we have here is a de facto conspiracy of secular academics to pull the rug out from Christianity?

Stephen Patterson of Eden Theological Seminary, an authority on the Gospel of Thomas and a proponent of the two-source hypothesis, doesn't think so. "The verbal agreement thing is just a smoke screen," he says of Linnemann's argument. "That's not the basis of the Q hypothesis. It grows out of the Markan priority. If you accept the hypothesis that Matthew and Luke made use of Mark separately, then you've got to have another theory for how they got the rest of the common material."

Patterson also points out that Linnemann herself was a champion of the Q hypothesis; her work as far back as the 1960s relied upon it, until her recent conversion to a fundamentalist brand of Christianity, whereupon she did a complete about-face and renounced all of her earlier writing.

What about Linnemann's charge that Q represents an anti-Christian conspiracy on the part of scholars? One problem with it is that many if not most scholars who accept the Q theory are Christian clerics. A conservative like John Meier not only supports Q but uses it as a basis for all of his work: "I accept the standard view in NT research today: Mark, using various collections of oral and possibly written traditions, composed his gospel somewhere around A.D. 70. Both Matthew and Luke, working independently of each other, composed larger gospels in the 70–100 period (most likely between 80 and 90) by combining and editing Mark, a collection of Jesus' sayings that scholars arbitrarily label Q, and special traditions peculiar to Matthew and Luke."[5]

Nevertheless, Meier and many others are uncomfortable with Q. It is a hole in the priority-of-Mark theory, a missing link. Those of a speculative nature can turn this missing document into the very root of Christianity, while more cautious minds see it as an embarrassing gap in the cherished theory of contemporary exegesis. Arguments such as Linnemann's, while not shared by most authorities, nevertheless highlight the tenuous nature of this work.

Such arguments against historical Jesus work are matched, on the other side of the spectrum, by a small but steadily repeated refrain of a very different sort. Through the decades, the claim has repeatedly been made that there never was a Jesus at all. At first blush this suggestion seems ridiculous, what with all the fuss being paid over the man in the gospels, canonical and otherwise, the writings of Paul and others, the public spectacle he made of himself in Jerusalem, Pilate's execution order, and so on. But consider that the earliest non-Christian mentions of Jesus—by Josephus and the Roman historian Tacitus—date from 93 C.E. and after 100 C.E., or more than sixty years after his death; that there is no record of his birth and nothing preserved about his sentence and execution under Pilate.

One scholar who put forward the nonexistence theory in a series of popular books was G. A. Wells, a professor not of New Testament but of German. Wells based his argument on the fact that the earliest writings about Jesus are the letters of Paul, who never knew Jesus during his lifetime but became the fountainhead of the Christian movement after experiencing a vision of him. How, Wells wondered, did Paul know it was Jesus? Had he seen pictures of the man? Wells argues that Paul had a mystical experience of *some* being, who called himself Jesus, and afterward, as he began to convert others to the cult of Jesus, a biography slowly came into being, which reached its final form in the written gospels. Supporting this idea is the fact that Paul's copious writings contain almost no details of Jesus' life.

Needless to say, mainstream scholars give little or no credence to Wells's argument. For one thing, it's a kind of scorched-earth approach to history. "If you're going to argue that, you'll also have to throw out people of the caliber of Julius Caesar and Cleopatra," says Robert Miller of Midway College. But it's also true that to take such a conjecture seriously would be professional suicide for any New Testament scholar; as much as any theologian or church official, these scholars have a vested interest in Jesus. Perhaps most people would side against this ultraminimalism on the grounds that it is too farfetched to suppose that such a saga, complete with such a lengthy cast of characters—Peter, Andrew, James, Judas, Mary Magdalene, etc., etc.—could possibly have been spun out of whole cloth. But if one chooses to be an ultraminimalist, if one is determined to undercut Christianity at its very roots, the meagerness of the records makes it theoretically possible. As with the conservative attacks, this radical one demonstrates that when the skeleton of the historical Jesus is exposed, it is found to be very frail indeed.

The best argument from the opposite end of the spectrum comes, not surprisingly, from a Christian cleric. N. T. Wright, Dean of Lichfield Cathedral in England and former professor of theology at Oxford University, is a major critic of most New Testament scholarship who challenges the whole idea of separating the gospels into discrete layers.

Dean Wright is the counterpart to Bishop Spong. Where Spong sits in a high institutional position within Christianity and argues in favor of a drastic rethinking of the New Testament, Wright, occupying a similar seat on the other side of the Atlantic Ocean, argues just as vociferously in support of the historical New Testament. Wright singles out Spong in particular as a deluded dabbler. Like Spong, however, Wright takes a crack at the "Who was Jesus?" question by grinding his own home blend of history and theology: "Among other beliefs," he writes, "I hold more firmly than ever to the conviction that serious study of Jesus and the gospels is best done within the context of a worshipping community."[6] Automatically, therefore, Wright finds a purely academic quest dubious. Like the other conservative critics discussed in this chapter, he doesn't believe in trying to peel away layers within the gospels to get at the root image of Jesus. He wants to accept the gospels more or less as written; rather than force the social scientific worldview onto them, he opts for reconfiguring what we mean by "truth" to accommodate both.

For anyone interested in seeing what dispassionate history can tell us about Jesus and then bringing that insight into the realm of theology, letting it interact with Christian faith, Wright is the wrong man to follow. But at the same time, he states the best argument of all against the historical Jesus model that has formed the basis of this book. One of the foundations of the scientific method is that a simple hypothesis is to be preferred to a more complex one. Ptolemaic astronomy became more and more complex as it tried to keep the earth at the center of the universe and still account for the movement of the stars and planets; finally, it collapsed under its own weight, and the Copernican model, which put the sun at the center of the solar system, eventually became accepted as a cleaner, simpler way to account for things.

Something similar is going on in historical Jesus study, according to Wright. Jesus scholars take it for granted that the gospel language about Jesus as redeemer of mankind is later overlay. This means that the historical Jesus, the figure beneath this overlay, was something very different from the one Christians have been worshiping for two millennia, and getting at that mysterious figure has involved an increasingly vast and bewildering toolbox of models and theories and suppositions. But suppose, Wright asks us, Jesus *did* see himself as the redeemer of mankind. What might that have meant?

To answer this, Wright explores the idea of apocalypse. He decides that Jesus was indeed an apocalyptic prophet who preached the coming End, but that for first-century Jews this didn't mean a coming earthly kingdom inaugurated by God, as Sanders believes, nor would it be an end to the space-time universe. Wright believes that the ancient Jews saw "apocalypse" metaphorically; he actually writes that they "knew a good metaphor when they saw one."[7] Speaking in a crisp Oxbridge to a gathering of the Historical Jesus Section of the Society of Biblical Literature Annual Meeting, he put his thesis this way:

> Apocalyptic is not the same as the end of the world. It invests the major events within history with theological significance. It looks specifically for the unique and climactic moment in, not the abolition of, Israel's long historical story. We must renounce naive literalism, whether fundamentalist or scholarly.[8]

According to Wright, Jews of the day were waiting for the man who would embody this climactic moment. Jesus decided that it was he. And once he decided this, it only makes sense that he would gather disciples, symbolically attack the Temple as he offered himself as its replacement, realize that he would be put to death for this, and host a final supper during which he would instruct his followers to go about the grunt work of setting up his kingdom. Then Wright makes his final, decisive move: "Why should such a person, a good first-century Jewish monotheist, not also come to hold the strange and risky belief that the one true God, the God of Israel, was somehow present and active in him and even *as* him?"[9]

This is bold stuff. Wright is trying to change the whole nature of New Testament scholarship so that it can encompass both historical truth and the storytelling truth of the Bible. He does this by attempting nothing less than a brand-new theory of human knowledge. "What I am trying to do," he says, "is a post-postmodern epistemology." He starts from the very compelling premise that the Enlightenment more or less began as an intellectual attack on the Catholic church's view of reality; how, then, can we expect it to do anything other than demolish the Christian worldview? Why even bother to do New Testament scholarship under these conditions? We know what the result will be: Robert Funk's "demotion" of Jesus.

Here, interestingly, Wright's critique of Jesus scholarship dovetails with the New Age perspective of Matthew Fox. "The movement from the Enlightenment's quest for the historical Jesus to today's quest for the Cosmic Christ names the paradigm shift that religion and theology presently need to undergo," Fox writes.[10] Both sides—the radical evangelical and the plain radical—seem to agree that we have to climb out of the box that our obsession with the scientific method has packed us into if we are to get anything meaningful out of Jesus.

Wright's new epistemology takes up a good chunk of his major work to date, *The New Testament and the People of God*, and it is difficult going. He insists that in his new theory of knowledge "truth" turns out to be something more subtle and complex than we're used to, so that it would be too simplistic to reduce him, like R. Douglas Geivett, to meaning "Jesus is the only way." On the other hand, he also says this: "Christianity and Judaism both make truth claims. Jews say the one God, who in the Old Testament is called the Lord or Yahweh, will be known and revealed to all the world in some great eschatological event. Christians say that event has in principle already occurred in Jesus. Those are competing truth claims. To my mind, the whole thing hangs on the resurrection. And if Jesus really did not rise from the dead, then I see no particular reason to embrace Christianity. And within that Jewish worldview, resurrection meant bodies coming out of tombs. It doesn't mean people having a nice religious feeling."

It sounds as though Wright wants to have it both ways: he wants to give "truth" a layered, up-to-date kind of meaning while also feeding us that old-time religion, which admits to only one ultimate truth. Perhaps by the time he completes his proposed five-volume study all will become apparent. In the meantime, anyone who finds it impossible to accept the New Testament accounts of Jesus as historically accurate won't be satisfied with Wright. But for those who are comfortable starting with the gospels as written,

Wright is doing something quite nervy: trying to make an evangelical Christian position sail along, not fight against, the twisting winds of "truth" that buffet the planet today. And he manages to raise a serious question about the whole historical Jesus enterprise: Might it not have too many parts—too many hypothetical documents, Greek crossover philosophies, and anthropological models, all held together with bluster and Scotch tape—for it to stand up? Isn't the neatest, cleanest way to explain the Jesus of the gospels by supposing that he really thought himself the Messiah? And, to nudge one step beyond this—a small step for a man of the cloth but a giant step for mankind—isn't it possible that he was right?

CHAPTER FOURTEEN

OPEN SPACES

At the end of the nineteenth century, at a spot on the northwest shore of the Sea of Galilee just south of Capernaum, excavators uncovered a fifteen-hundred-year-old mosaic floor. One part of it featured a garden of fancifully stylized plants and water birds, very beautifully and painstakingly rendered, but a separate mosaic proved to be the key to the whole place, for it showed a basket of loaves flanked by two fishes. This, according to tradition dating to the fourth century, is the very spot where Jesus of Nazareth multiplied the loaves and fishes to feed a hungry crowd that had come to hear him.

The elegant, spare limestone church one visits today that houses these artifacts was built in 1982, but it rests on the foundations of an ancient building. Clearly, pilgrims have been coming here for a very long time. The busloads of pilgrims today make a beeline for the mosaics, and stop to pray at and touch a rock that has become known as the exact spot where Jesus stood when he performed the miracle.

One of the nuns, who have come from all over the world to devote their lives to tending this holy place, is a young woman from the Philippines. She explained its significance to a visitor this way: "In this place, tradition has it, Jesus performed a miracle." She spoke simply, then went on to talk about the nuns who lived here, and the priest, who had written a monograph on the archaeology of the site. What leaped out, however, was the phrase she had put between commas: "tradition has it." She had come all this way, had given so much to this place, and yet she clearly didn't hold herself to the literal truth of that statement. It could have happened elsewhere, she was saying, or not at all. Hers, apparently, was a faith that could do without certainty on the details—that, perhaps, didn't have to rely on such things at all.

But there is more to it than that, for she had felt the need to add that clause. We have gone so far down the trail of modernism, or postmodernism, that even this nun is no longer an innocent, even *she* cannot simply believe, utterly and plainly. *Tradition has it.* She has lost what Paul Tillich called natural literalism: the straight, unreflective belief in the total truth of the Jesus saga, which virtually all Christians shared until the Enlightenment. Since that time, Tillich said, any Christian who professes a belief in the "literal" New Testament is engaging in a conscious literalism, is consciously affirming the biblical "facts" over those of science, letting the two war it out and declaring one the winner. There is no such thing, anymore, as historical innocence, except perhaps in children, for whom history and myth are the same thing.

So we give our historical muscle a workout, perhaps hoping that as it relaxes in exhaustion something more instinctual will take over. And a priest assigned as caretaker to one of the holiest spots in the Christian world devotes himself to writing an archaeological monograph.

For many, the search is on for a truly human Jesus. Behind this book is the hope that by pulling together much of the work being done in this field we might end up with—not *the* Jesus of history, and certainly not the true and complete object of a world religion—but a Jesus that somehow fits us.

The result is a fairly distinct figure, and that much is something: a first-century Galilean Jew who ventures south to the Judean wilderness, where he finds religion at the hands of an apocalyptic prophet. Perhaps he wholly adopted his mentor's philosophy at first, or perhaps he instantly blended it with other influences, such as Greek ideas he may have soaked in thanks to the nearness of a Greco-Roman center to his home. He came to use a phrase that almost no one had used before, "the kingdom of God." He talked of it coming soon, as eschatological prophets talked of the coming End Time, but also of it being present, within all things. As he communicated this, some people seemed to share his mystical awareness, and their acknowledgment of his special insight led to their being healed by him.

He also seems to have placed importance on shared meals as a practical way to bring about a change in his audience. These two acts—free healing and shared meals—evidently bothered the local authorities. And by talking openly of a *basileia,* a coming "Empire," he seems to have gotten the attention of both Jewish and Roman rulers. At the Passover of 30 C.E., he staged a protest in the Temple, perhaps because he had come to believe that the end of history was at hand, and this act led to his arrest and execution.

Is this a Jesus for our time? He appears to be quite human,

which is apparently what many of us want. There is evidence of inconsistency, of a changing, evolving viewpoint. And he is not all serene and laudatory. He suggested that his followers, good Jews all, learn to hate their fathers and mothers. He seems not to have cared for Gentiles. He is imperfect, contradictory, difficult. If the desire that motivates this whole enterprise is to isolate a human being who stands behind the edifice of Christianity, one could argue that it has been fulfilled.

But this picture will satisfy only the most ruthlessly reductionist among us, only those who want to strip the painting down nearly to bare canvas. Others might like to emphasize certain parts of the reconstructed image. This historical Jesus was, after all, by all accounts, a prophet of remarkable vision. Somehow, perhaps by mixing outside influences in with his Jewish traditions, he forged within the smithy of his soul an astonishing new ethic, one that involved a reversal of conventional values that, for all its improbable idealism, people have tried to imitate ever since.

But this leaves us merely admiring a teacher. Is *that* enough? How far do we go without sacrificing our commitment to critical objectivity? Or is there something wrong with that question? Was there ever such a commitment to begin with? Haven't we learned by now that all scholars—all searchers—start with a staggering load of presuppositions that frame their inquiry right from the start?

Appreciating the truth of this is perhaps the first step out of the maze. Any portrait of the historical Jesus is bound to be full of holes—nothing more than educated guesswork. But this may be fortunate. Whole worlds can fill those open spaces. Scholars and theologians as diverse as the neo-evangelical N. T. Wright, the reductionist Robert Funk, and the Roman Catholic Edward Schillebeeckx come together on one point: that critical inquiry can take one so far, but to rely on it exclusively will only wound the wielder. The open spaces are where we breathe. "The New Testament," writes Schillebeeckx, "is set in a 'story-telling culture,' not in one like ours that has replaced a narrative innocence with historical disciplines. However, we cannot ignore either." He goes on to say that we have to "pass through" history and return to " 'story-telling innocence,' which itself then recoups its critical power from scholarship and criticism."[1] In other words, our best hope is to go back and forth, from history to story.

This isn't a method that applies only to Jesus. If we didn't do something like this with other figures, letting the critical and the reverential play off one another, we would probably have no heroes left—they would all be slashed to pieces by our sharp methodologies. Wright's "post-postmodern epistemology" seems to be saying that science gives us a tool for grasping the external reality we feel certain is out there, but that to get to the deeper pools, the pools of human interconnectivity, the realm where love breeds awe and awe drops off into a welling silence, we need to supplement this with other tools. Crosses. Hearts. Water. Bread. Blood. As Funk says, we need parables to break down the walls of common sense, so that we are even able to see that the pools are there. We need stories.

And that is why, having come to the end of a piece-by-piece dismantling of this set of first-century stories, the wisest next step might be to put them back together—or rather to let them flow back together, like atoms of a molecule that have been artificially pried apart. We may play with facts like children with building blocks, but we tamper with story at our peril. Or perhaps the trick is to figure out a way to do two things at once: digging into history with one hand while tolling the beads of story with the other.

Then again, perhaps we aren't so much caught between the facts of history and science on the one hand and the myths of the past on the other but caught between two kinds of storytelling. Maybe, in time, through some mysterious alchemy, we will find that the story the historians seem to be uncovering has come to match up with the story that Christians have long told each other. Or maybe we will wake up one day and suddenly realize that one of them has become unnecessary.

NOTES

CHAPTER 1

1. Meier, John, *A Marginal Jew: Rethinking the Historical Jesus,* vol. 2 (New York: Doubleday, 1994).
2. All taken from Funk, Robert, "Setting Jesus Free." Paper delivered to the Jesus Seminar (October 1995).
3. Ibid.

CHAPTER 2

1. Luke 1:26 (KJV).
2. Deut. 6:4.
3. Borg, Marcus, *Meeting Jesus Again for the First Time* (San Francisco: Harper San Francisco, 1994), p. 26.
4. Mark 13:30.
5. Fredriksen, Paula, *From Jesus to Christ* (New Haven: Yale University Press, 1988), p. 50.
6. Mark 14:27; 14:33.
7. Mark 6:50.
8. Mark 1:18.
9. Mark 1:42.
10. Mark 16:8.
11. On Papias, see Aune, David, *The New Testament in Its Literary Environment* (Philadelphia: Westminster Press, 1987), p. 66.

12. 2 Kings 2:8–14.
13. Aune, *New Testament,* pp. 40–41. See also Vermes, Geza, *Jesus the Jew* (Philadelphia: Fortress Press, 1973), p. 89.
14. Spong, John Shelby, *Born of a Woman* (San Francisco: Harper San Francisco, 1992), pp. 17–18.
15. Rom. 16:21–23.
16. Koester, Helmut, *Ancient Christian Gospels* (Philadelphia: Trinity Press International, 1990), p. 305.
17. Matt. 23:33, 23:23, 23:17, 23:31.
18. Isa. 7:14 (KJV).
19. Matt. 1:22–23.
20. Vermes, *Jesus the Jew,* p. 218.
21. See Meier, *A Marginal Jew: Rethinking the Historical Jesus* (New York: Doubleday, 1991), vol. 1, pp. 222, 243(n.71).
22. Isa. 7:16.
23. Fredriksen, *From Jesus to Christ,* p. 38.
24. Brown, Raymond, *The Birth of the Messiah* (New York: Doubleday, 1977), p. 226.
25. Ranke-Heinemann, Uta, *Putting Away Childish Things* (New York: HarperCollins, 1994), p. 43.
26. Isa. 7:14.
27. Meier, *A Marginal Jew,* vol. 1, pp. 212–214.
28. Brown, *Birth of Messiah,* p. 26.
29. Armstrong, Karen, *The Gospel According to Woman* (New York: Anchor, 1986), p. 82.
30. Matt. 1:19–25.
31. Matt. 1:16.
32. Matt. 1:2–6.
33. Brown, *Birth of Messiah,* p. 74.
34. Mark 6:3.
35. Meier, *A Marginal Jew,* vol. 1, p. 216.
36. See Meyers, Eric, and James Strange, *Archaeology, the Rabbis, and Early Christianity* (Nashville: Abingdon, 1981), p. 57.
37. Ibid., pp. 58–59.
38. Mark 6:3.
39. Matt. 13:55.
40. See Meier, *A Marginal Jew,* vol. 1, p. 280.
41. See Rousseau, John, and Rami Arav, *Jesus and His World* (Minneapolis: Fortress, 1995), p. 251.
42. Meier, *A Marginal Jew,* vol. 1, p. 284.
43. Meyers and Strange, *Archaeology,* p. 43.

CHAPTER 3

1. Josephus, *The Jewish War,* G. A. Williamson, trans. Revised ed. by E. Mary Smallwood (London: Penguin, 1981), p. 370.
2. On temple cultures, see Mack, Burton, *Who Wrote the New Testament?* (New York: HarperCollins, 1995), p. 20.
3. Wilson, Edmund, *The Scrolls from the Dead Sea* (New York: Oxford University Press, 1955), p. 108.
4. *New York Times* editorial, September 7, 1991. For a thorough account of the breakup of the scrolls cabal, see the Introduction to Shanks, Hershel, ed., *Understanding the Dead Sea Scrolls* (New York: Random House, 1992).
5. Josephus, *Jewish Antiquities.* Trans. L. H. Feldman. Loeb Classical Library (Cambridge: Harvard University Press, 1954), vol. ix. 18.63–64, pp. 49–51.
6. Mark 2:5.
7. See Fredriksen, Paula, *From Jesus to Christ* (New York: Yale University Press, 1988), p. 105, and Vermes, Geza, *Jesus the Jew* (Philadelphia: Fortress, 1973), p. 67.
8. See VanderKam, James, "The Dead Sea Scrolls and Christianity," in Shanks, *Understanding Scrolls,* p. 188. Also Charlesworth, James, *Jesus Within Judaism* (New York: Doubleday, 1988), pp. 68–71.
9. The translation is from Schiffman, Lawrence, *The Eschatological Community of the Dead Sea Scrolls: A Study of the Rule of the Congregation* (Atlanta: Scholars Press, 1989), p. 53, as quoted by VanderKam, in Shanks, *Understanding Scrolls*, p. 195.
10. VanderKam, in Shanks, *Understanding Scrolls,* p. 201.
11. Mark 11:15.
12. Sanders, E. P., *Jesus and Judaism* (Philadelphia: Fortress, 1985), pp. 61–71.
13. On Tyrian shekels, see Borg, Marcus, *Jesus in Contemporary Scholarship* (Valley Forge: Trinity Press International, 1994), p. 114.
14. Segal, Alan, *Rebecca's Children: Judaism and Christianity in the Roman World* (Cambridge: Harvard University Press, 1986), p. 4.
15. Isa. 44:28.

CHAPTER 4

1. Jowett, B., trans. "Meno," from *The Dialogues of Plato,* vol. 1 (New York: Random House, 1937), pp. 356–357. Altered slightly.
2. Nietzsche, Friedrich, *The Birth of Tragedy* (New York: Vintage, 1967), p. 73. See also *Oxford Classical Dictionary,* "Dionysus."
3. Mack, Burton, *The Lost Gospel: The Book of Q and Christian Origins* (New York: HarperCollins, 1993), p. 57.

4. The story is taken from Philo, *de Vita Mosis* ii, 26–42, as translated in Barrett, C. K., *The New Testament Background: Selected Documents* (New York: Harper & Row, 1961), pp. 210–212. See also *Oxford Classical Dictionary*, "Septuagint."
5. Exod. 3:14.
6. Fredriksen, Paula, *From Jesus to Christ* (New Haven: Yale University Press, 1988), p. 14.
7. 4 Mac. 1:1.
8. Barrett, *The New Testament Background,* p. 208.
9. The influence of hellenism on Jewish Palestine during this period is elaborated on in great detail in Hengel, Martin, *Judaism and Hellenism* (Philadelphia: Fortress, 1974), especially pp. 32–78.
10. Freyne, Sean, *Galilee from Alexander the Great to Hadrian* (Wilmington: Michael Glazier, Inc., 1980), p. 140.
11. See Rousseau, John, and Rami Arav, "Cave of Letters," in *Jesus and His World* (Minneapolis: Fortress, 1995), p. 50.
12. Mack, *The Lost Gospel,* p. 57.
13. See Hengel, *Judaism and Hellenism,* p. 74.
14. 1 Mac. 1:21.
15. 1 Mac. 1:41–42.
16. 1 Mac. 1:43.
17. 1 Mac. 1:60–61.
18. Josephus, *Antiquities* 12:256.
19. 1 Mac. 2:27.
20. For more about the names of Jesus and his brothers, see Meier, *A Marginal Jew: Rethinking the Historical Jesus,* vol. 1 (New York: Doubleday), p. 207.
21. Eccles. 9:5. On the age of Ecclesiastes, see Ranke-Heinemann, Uta, *Putting Away Childish Things* (New York: HarperCollins, 1994), p. 229.
22. Dan. 12:2.
23. Wis. Sol. 5:15.
24. Josephus, *The Jewish War,* II, viii, 11. Quoted in Ranke-Heinemann, *Putting Away,* p. 235.
25. Ranke-Heinemann, *Putting Away,* p. 228–237.
26. Josephus, *The Jewish War,* G. A. Williamson, trans. Revised ed. by E. Mary Smallwood (London: Penguin, 1981), p. 35.
27. An alternate theory places the origins of the Essenes centuries earlier, at the time of the Babylonian exile of 586 B.C.E. To further complicate matters, Lawrence Schiffman, one of the most respected scroll scholars working today, argues that the people of Qumran were not Essenes at all but renegade Sadducees. The major arguments are put forth lucidly in Shanks, *Understanding the Dead Sea Scrolls* (New York: Random House,

1992), and are regularly amended and debated in the pages of *Biblical Archaeology Review.*

28. Hengel, *Judaism and Hellenism,* p. 245.

CHAPTER 5

1. Smith, Morton, *The Secret Gospel: The Discovery and Interpretation of a Secret Gospel According to Mark* (New York: Harper & Row, 1973), p. 78.
2. *National Catholic Reporter* (June 1993).
3. Josephus, *The Jewish War,* G. A. Williamson, trans. Revised ed. by E. Mary Smallwood (London: Penguin, 1981), vol. 1, pp. 159–165.
4. On the weights of the stones, see Charlesworth, James, *Jesus Within Judaism* (New York: Doubleday, 1988), p. 119.
5. Borg, Marcus, *Jesus in Contemporary Scholarship* (Valley Forge: Trinity Press International, 1994), p. 102, relying on Gerhard E. Lenski, *Power and Privilege: A Theory of Social Stratification* (New York: McGraw Hill, 1966), and John H. Kautsky, *The Politics of Aristocratic Empires* (Chapel Hill: University of North Carolina, 1982).
6. Crossan, John Dominic, *Who Killed Jesus?* (San Francisco: Harper San Francisco, 1995), pp. 39–41.
7. Sanders, E. P., "Jesus in Historical Context," *Theology Today,* vol. 50 (October 1993), p. 445.
8. Borg, *Jesus in Contemporary Scholarship,* p. 103.
9. Mack, Burton, *Who Wrote the New Testament?* (New York: Harper Collins, 1995), pp. 26–29.
10. Josephus, *The Jewish War,* pp. 117–121.
11. Haas, N., "Anthropological Observations on the Skeletal Remains from Giv'at ha-Mivtar," *Israel Exploration Journal* 20 (1970), pp. 38–59. Tzaferis, Vassilios, "Crucifixion—The Archaeological Evidence," *Biblical Archaeology Review* (Jan/Feb 1985), pp. 44–53. Charlesworth, *Jesus Within Judaism,* p. 130.
12. Vermes, Geza, *Jesus the Jew* (Philadelphia: Fortress Press, 1973). On Bannus, see Meier, John, *A Marginal Jew,* vol. 2 (New York: Doubleday, 1994), p. 27.
13. Smith, *Clement of Alexandria and a Secret Gospel of Mark* (Cambridge: Harvard University Press, 1973), p. 208; note the importance Crossan gives to this passage in *The Historical Jesus,* p. 231.
14. Manual of Discipline 3:18. In Vermes's *The Dead Sea Scrolls in English.*
15. John 12:36. Modern translations have it "children of light." The Greek is the masculine plural, which could be rendered "sons" or "children."
16. Betz, "Was John the Baptist an Essene?" *Biblical Review* (December 1990), reprinted in Shanks, Hershel, ed., *Understanding the Dead Sea*

Scrolls (New York: Random House, 1992), p. 213. On Yadin, see Shanks, *Understanding the Dead Sea Scrolls,* p. 107.

17. Luke 1:80.
18. Quoted in Meier, *A Marginal Jew,* vol. 2, p. 70.
19. Crossan, *Who Killed Jesus?,* p. 46.
20. 2 Kings 2:1–12; 5:14.
21. Matt. 3:5–6.
22. Mark 6:2.
23. Matt. 3:13.
24. Davies, Stevan, *Jesus the Healer* (New York: Continuum, 1995), p. 57.
25. John 7:5.
26. Matt. 3:4.
27. Matt. 3:7–10.
28. Matt. 3:11–12.
29. See Crossan, *Who Killed Jesus?,* p. 44; for arguments against this interpretation, see Meier, *A Marginal Jew,* vol. 2, pp. 34–40.
30. Meier, *A Marginal Jew,* vol. 2, p. 22.
31. Mark 1:9.
32. Matt. 3:14.
33. Luke 1:44.
34. John 3:22.
35. John 3:26.
36. John 4:1.
37. Mark 1:10–11.
38. Ps. 2:7.
39. James, William, *The Varieties of Religious Experience* (New York: Modern Library, 1994), p. 252.
40. John 4:2.
41. Meier, *A Marginal Jew,* vol. 2, p. 122.
42. Josephus, *Jewish Antiquities.* Trans. L. H. Feldman. Loeb Classical Library (Cambridge: Harvard University Press, 1954), vol. ix, 18. 117–118, p. 83.

CHAPTER 6

1. Matt. 16:13–20.
2. Funk, Robert, et al., *The Five Gospels* (New York: Macmillan, 1993), p. 207.
3. John 1:42.
4. Quoted in Finegan, Jack, *The Archaeology of the New Testament,* rev. ed. (Princeton: Princeton University Press, 1992), pp. 109–110; see also Charlesworth, James, *Jesus Within Judaism* (New York: Doubleday,

1988), pp. 109–111 and Strange and Shanks, "Has the House Where Jesus Stayed in Capernaum Been Found?" *Biblical Archaeological Review* (November/December 1982), pp. 26–37.

5. Mark 2:1. Fitzmyer's response to "Whose House in Capernaum?" in *Biblical Archaeology Reader* (January/February 1993), p. 68.
6. See Meier, John, *A Marginal Jew,* vol. 2 (New York: Doubleday, 1994), pp. 317–322; Funk, *Five Gospels,* p. 290.
7. Sanders, E. P., *Jesus and Judaism* (Philadelphia: Fortress, 1985), p. 228.
8. 1 Thess. 4:16–17.
9. Gos. Thom. 113:4, as given in Funk, *Five Gospels,* p. 531.
10. Matt. 13:33.
11. Matt. 16:6 (KJV).
12. Luke 13:18–19.
13. Matt. 13:44.
14. Luke 16:1–9; translation of Funk, Robert, et al., *The Parables of Jesus* (Sonoma: Polebridge Press, 1988), p. 32.
15. Translation of Funk, *Parables,* p. 66.
16. Funk, Robert, *Parables and Presence* (Philadelphia: Fortress, 1982), p. 17.
17. Schillebeeckx, Edward, *Jesus: An Experiment in Christology* (New York: Seabury, 1979), pp. 156–157.
18. Scott, Bernard Brandon, *Hear Then the Parable* (Minneapolis: Fortress, 1990), p. 57.
19. Gos. Thom. 97; translation of Funk, *Parables,* p. 61.

CHAPTER 7

1. 2 Edras 13:26.
2. These and other attempts at explaining away the miracles of Jesus are summarized in Schweitzer, Albert, *The Quest of the Historical Jesus* (New York: Macmillan, 1968), pp. 52–53.
3. Isa. 26:19, 29:18–19.
4. Matt. 11:4–5.
5. Matt. 15:31.
6. Schillebeeckx, Edward, *Jesus: An Experiment in Christology* (New York: Seabury, 1979), p. 189.
7. Ranke-Heinemann, Uta, *Putting Away Childish Things* (New York: HarperCollins, 1994), p. 82.
8. Strack, Hermann, and Paul Billerbeck, *Kommentar zum Neuen Testament aus Talmud und Midrash,* p. 529; quoted in Ranke-Heinemann, *Putting Away,* p. 83.
9. Crossan, John Dominic, *The Historical Jesus* (New York: HarperCollins, 1991), p. 324.

10. Sanders, E. P., "Jesus in Historical Context," *Theology Today* (October 1993), pp. 429–446.
11. John 9:2–3.
12. Matt. 10:34.
13. Matt. 10:5.
14. Luke 14:26.
15. Matt. 11:23.
16. Luke 4:34.
17. Davies, Stevan, *Jesus the Healer* (New York: Continuum, 1995), p. 23.
18. Davies, Stevan, "Whom Jesus Healed and How," *The Fourth R* (March/April 1993), p. 8.
19. Mark 2:1–12.
20. Funk, Robert, "Report: The Jesus Seminar," *The Fourth R* (March/April 1993), p. 15.
21. Meier, John, *A Marginal Jew,* vol. 2 (New York: Doubleday, 1994), p. 680.
22. Meyers, Eric, and James Strange, *Archaeology, the Rabbis, and Early Christianity* (Nashville: Abingdon, 1981), p. 58.
23. DSM-III-R: *Diagnostic and Statistical Manual of Mental Disorders, Revised Edition* (Washington, D.C.: American Psychiatric Association, 1987), p. 257; quoted in Davies, Stevan, *Jesus the Healer* (New York: Continuum, 1995), p. 70.
24. See Davids, Stacy, "How Did Jesus Heal?" Paper presented to the Jesus Seminar (October 1993), and " 'Heal the Sick . . . and Say to Them, the Reign of God is at Hand': Reconstructing Jesus as Healer." Paper presented to Society of Biblical Literature, Central States Region (April 1995).
25. Luke 14:12–14.
26. Borg, Marcus, *Meeting Jesus Again for the First Time* (San Francisco: Harper San Francisco, 1994), p. 56.
27. Mark 6:35–44.
28. Meier, *A Marginal Jew,* vol. 2, p. 966.
29. 2 Kings 4:42–44.
30. John 6:53–57.

CHAPTER 8

1. See Funk, Robert, et al., *The Five Gospels* (New York: Macmillan, 1993), pp. 290–293 and Meier, John, *A Marginal Jew,* vol. 2 (New York: Doubleday, 1994), pp. 317–323.
2. For the spectrum of arguments on the date of the Gospel of Thomas, see Crossan, John Dominic, *The Historical Jesus* (New York: HarperCollins, 1991), p. 427; Meier, *A Marginal Jew,* vol. 1, pp. 123–139; and Koester,

Helmut, *Ancient Christian Gospels* (Philadelphia: Trinity Press International, 1990), pp. 49–170.

3. See Mack, Burton, *The Lost Gospel: The Book of Q and Christian Origins* (New York: HarperCollins, 1993), p. 35.
4. Borg, Marcus, *Meeting Jesus Again for the First Time* (San Francisco: Harper San Francisco, 1994), p. 89.
5. Stone, I. F., *The Trial of Socrates* (New York: Doubleday, 1989), p. 19.
6. Mack, *Lost Gospel,* p. 237.
7. Ibid., p. 177.
8. Crossan, *Historical Jesus,* p. 82.
9. Ibid., p. 84.
10. Epictetus, *Discourses* 3.22:54; quoted in Crossan, *Historical Jesus,* p. 79.
11. Matt. 5:44, 5:39–40, 19:24.
12. Mark 6:8–9.
13. Crossan, *Historical Jesus,* p. 341.
14. Ibid., p. 421.
15. Sanders, E. P., *Jesus and Judaism* (Philadelphia: Fortress, 1985), p. 322.
16. Ibid., p. 232.
17. Cadbury, Henry, *The Perils of Modernizing Jesus* (New York: Macmillan, 1937), p. 141.

CHAPTER 9

1. Brown, Raymond E., *The Death of the Messiah* (New York: Doubleday, 1994), p. 15.
2. Neusner, Jacob, *The Midrash: An Introduction* (Northvale: Jason Aronson, 1990), pp. x–xi.
3. Luke 24:44–46.
4. Schmidt, Daryl, "The LXX Influence in Shaping the Passion Narratives," Jesus Seminar Papers (October 1995), p. 49.
5. For more on the application of Old Testament themes of suffering to Jesus, see Brown, *Death of Messiah,* pp. 1458–59.
6. Matt. 27:34.
7. Ps. 69:21; LXX 69:22 (translation of Brown, *Death of Messiah,* p. 1455).
8. Matt. 27:46.
9. Mark 14:50.
10. Brown, *Death of Messiah,* pp. 11–12.
11. Mark 9:31.
12. Mark 10:33–34.
13. John 7:5.
14. Fredriksen, Paula, "What You See Is What You Get: Context and

Content in Current Research on the Historical Jesus," *Theology Today* (April 1995), p. 93.

15. Sanders, E. P., *Jesus and Judaism* (Philadelphia: Fortress, 1985), p. 306.
16. Crossan, John Dominic, *Jesus: A Revolutionary Biography* (New York: HarperCollins, 1994), p. 129.
17. Mark 11:11.
18. Tob. 14:4–5.
19. Sanders, E. P., "Jesus in Historical Context," *Theology Today* (October 1993), vol. 50, p. 442.
20. Ibid.
21. Josephus, *The Jewish War,* G. A. Williamson, trans. Revised by E. Mary Smallwood (London: Penguin, 1981), p. 144.
22. Taylor, Joan, "The Garden of Gethsemane: Not the Place of Jesus' Arrest," *Biblical Archaeology Review* (July/August 1995), pp. 26–35.
23. Dibelius is the first I know of to argue it; see Schmidt, "The LXX Influence," p. 2, quoting John Donahue: Dibelius was "a pioneer in the discovery of the use of Old Testament allusions as a creative matrix in constructing the Passion Narrative."
24. Accounts of these parallels are found in Crossan, John Dominic, *Who Killed Jesus?* (San Francisco: Harper San Francisco, 1995), pp. 76–78, and Schmidt, "The LXX Influence," pp. 3–5.
25. Zech. 11:12.
26. Gos. Peter 11:48, in Maurer, Christian, and Wilhelm Schneemelcher, "The Gospel of Peter." In *New Testament Apocrypha,* rev. ed., 1991. Wilhelm Schneemelcher and R. Wilson, eds., vol. 1, p. 226.
27. Matt. 27:15.
28. Philo, Embassy to Gaius, 301–02; quoted in Pagels, Elaine, *The Origin of Satan* (New York: Random House, 1995), p. 10.
29. John 19:6.
30. Matt. 27:24.
31. Brown, *Death of Messiah,* p. 833.
32. Deut. 21:7.
33. Brown, *Death of Messiah,* pp. 837–838.
34. Lev. 20:9–12.
35. Robinson, James, "From Easter to Valentinus," *Journal of Biblical Literature* (101/1, 1982), p. 6; Finegan, *The Archaeology of the New Testament* (Princeton: Princeton University Press, 1992), p. 319.
36. Pagels, *Origin of Satan,* pp. 104–105.

CHAPTER 10

1. Tzaferis, Vassilios, "Crucifixion—The Archaeological Evidence," *Biblical Archaeology Review* (January/February 1985), p. 45.

2. Sloyan, Gerard, *The Crucifixion of Jesus* (Minneapolis: Fortress, 1995), p. 15.
3. Ibid., p. 16.
4. Josephus, *The Jewish War,* G. A. Williamson, trans. Revised ed. by E. Mary Smallwood (London: Penguin, 1981), 5:451, p. 326.
5. See Haas, N., "Anthropological Observations on the Skeletal Remains from Giv'at ha-Mivtar," *Israel Exploration Journal* 20 (1970), pp. 38–59; Tzaferis, "Crucifixion," pp. 44–53; Shanks, Hershel, "New Analysis of the Crucified Man," *Biblical Archaeology Review* 11, pp. 20–21; Charlesworth, James, *Jesus Within Judaism* (New York: Doubleday, 1988), p. 122.
6. Brown, Raymond, *The Death of the Messiah* (New York: Doubleday, 1994), p. 1463.
7. Ibid., p. 1462.
8. Quoting translation in ibid., p. 1463.
9. Matt. 28:19.
10. Translation from Brown, *Death of Messiah,* p. 1455.
11. Exod. 12:46; John 19:36.
12. Crossan, John Dominic, *Who Killed Jesus?* (San Francisco: Harper San Francisco, 1995), Chapter 4, and Koester, Helmut, *Ancient Christian Gospels* (Philadelphia: Trinity Press International, 1990), pp. 220–230.
13. Neusner, Jacob, *The Midrash: An Introduction* (Northvale, N.J.: Jason Aronson, Inc., 1990), p. x.

CHAPTER 11

1. 1 Cor. 15:3–5.
2. Luke 24:37–40.
3. Luke 24:41–43.
4. John 20:25.
5. Acts 22:6–8.
6. 1 Cor. 15:20.
7. 1 Cor. 15:35–50.
8. Luke 24:13–31.
9. Tertullian, *De Carne Christi,* Ernest Evans, trans. (London: S.P.C.K.), p. 19.
10. Pagels, Elaine, *The Gnostic Gospels* (New York: Random House, 1979), p. 6.
11. Ibid., p. xx.
12. Gos. Thom. 108: 1–2, as given in Funk, Robert, et al., *The Five Gospels* (New York: Macmillan, 1993), p. 529.
13. Robinson, James, "Jesus From Easter to Valentinus," *Journal of Biblical Literature,* (101/1, 1982), p. 6.

14. 2 Cor. 12–2; 1 Cor. 2:6–7.
15. Pseudo-Manetho, *Apotelesmatica* 4:198ff., cited in Hengel, Martin, *Crucifixion.* Trans. John Bowden (Philadelphia: Fortress, 1977), p. 9.
16. Schillebeeckx, Edward, *Jesus: An Experiment in Christology* (New York: Seabury, 1979), pp. 331–337.
17. Acts 4:11.
18. Charlesworth, James, *Jesus Within Judaism* (New York: Doubleday, 1988), pp. 124–125.
19. Aitken, Ellen Bradshaw, "Response to John Dominic Crossan, 'The Gospel of Peter in *Who Killed Jesus?*' " Paper delivered at the Intertextuality in Christian Apocrypha Seminar, Society of Biblical Literature Annual Meeting, Philadelphia (November 20, 1995).
20. Spong, John Shelby, *Resurrection: Myth or Reality?* (New York: HarperCollins, 1994), pp. 62–63.
21. Wilkins, J. Michael and J. P. Moreland, eds., *Jesus Under Fire* (Grand Rapids, Michigan: Zondervan, 1995), pp. 146–152; quote on p. 152.
22. Sheehan, Thomas, *The First Coming: How the Kingdom of God Became Christianity* (New York: Random House, 1986), pp. 135–146.
23. Mack, Burton, *The Lost Gospel: The Book of Q and Christian Origins* (New York: HarperCollins, 1993), pp. 180–181.

CHAPTER 12

1. Gallup survey, "Church Attendance—1993," "Religion in America: 50 Years: 1935–1985," p. 42.
2. Cox, Harvey, *Fire from Heaven* (Reading, MA: Addison-Wesley, 1995), p. 187.
3. Ibid., p. 225.
4. Gallup survey, " 'Born-again'—Recent Trend," 1995. For 1990 statistic, see Barry Kosmin and Seymour Lachman, *One Nation Under God* (New York: Crown, 1993), p. 235.
5. Gallup survey, "Church Membership: Seven in 10 Claim Church Membership," 1989.
6. Kosmin, *One Nation Under God,* p. 233.
7. Bloom, Harold, *The American Religion* (New York: Simon & Schuster, 1992), p. 32.
8. Ibid., p. 49.
9. Spong, John Shelby, "Did Christians Invent Judas?" *The Fourth R* (March/April 1994), p. 3.

CHAPTER 13

1. Wilkins, J. Michael and J. P. Moreland, eds., *Jesus Under Fire* (Grand Rapids, Michigan: Zondervan, 1995), p. 199.
2. London *Times,* December 24, 1994. See also Stanton, Graham, "A Gospel Among the Scrolls?" *Bible Review* (December 1995).
3. See Fredriksen, Paula, *From Jesus to Christ* (New Haven: Yale University Press, 1988), pp. 44–52, and Meier, John, *A Marginal Jew,* vol. 1 (New York: Doubleday, 1994), p. 44.
4. Linnemann, Eta, "Is There a Gospel of Q?" *Bible Review* (August 1995), p. 18.
5. Meier, *A Marginal Jew,* pp. 43–44.
6. Wright, N. T., *Who Was Jesus?* (Grand Rapids, Michigan: Eerdmans, 1993), p. ix.
7. Wright, N. T., *The New Testament and the People of God* (Minneapolis: Fortress, 1992), p. 333.
8. Wright, N. T. Paper Presented to Historical Jesus Section of Society of Biblical Literature Annual Meeting, Philadelphia (November 1995).
9. Wright, *The New Testament,* p. 103.
10. Fox, Matthew, *The Coming of the Cosmic Christ* (San Francisco: Harper San Francisco, 1988), p. 78.

CHAPTER 14

1. Schillebeeckx, Edward, *Jesus: An Experiment in Christology* (New York: Seabury, 1979), p. 156.

BIBLIOGRAPHY

Modern Works

ARMSTRONG, KAREN. *The Gospel According to Woman.* New York: Anchor, 1986.

AUNE, DAVID. *The New Testament in Its Literary Environment.* Philadelphia: Westminster Press, 1987.

BAMMEL, E., AND C. F. D. MOULE, eds. *Jesus and the Politics of His Day.* Cambridge: Cambridge University Press, 1984.

BARRETT, C. K. *The New Testament Background: Selected Documents.* New York: Harper & Row, 1961.

BLOOM, HAROLD. *The American Religion.* New York: Simon & Schuster, 1992.

BORG, MARCUS. *Jesus: A New Vision.* San Francisco: Harper & Row, 1987.

———. *Meeting Jesus Again for the First Time.* San Francisco: Harper San Francisco, 1994.

———. *Jesus in Contemporary Scholarship.* Valley Forge, Pa.: Trinity Press International, 1994.

BROWN, RAYMOND E. *The Birth of the Messiah.* New York: Doubleday, 1977.

———. *The Death of the Messiah.* New York: Doubleday, 1994.

CADBURY, HENRY. *The Perils of Modernizing Jesus.* New York: Macmillan, 1937.

CARLSON, JEFFREY, and ROBERT A. LUDWIG, eds. *Jesus and Faith.* Maryknoll, New York: Orbis Books, 1994.

CARROLL, ROBERT P. *The Bible as a Problem for Christianity.* Philadelphia: Trinity, 1991.

CHARLESWORTH, JAMES. *Jesus Within Judaism.* New York: Doubleday, 1988.

———, ed. *Jesus' Jewishness.* New York: Crossroad, 1991.

COHEN, SHAYE J. D. *From the Maccabees to the Mishnah.* Philadelphia: Westminster, 1987.

COLLINS, JOHN J. *The Apocalyptic Imagination.* New York: Crossroad, 1984.

COX, HARVEY. *Fire from Heaven.* Reading, Mass.: Addison-Wesley, 1995.

CROSSAN, JOHN DOMINIC. *The Historical Jesus.* New York: HarperCollins, 1991.

———. *Jesus: A Revolutionary Biography.* New York: HarperCollins, 1994.

———. *Who Killed Jesus?* San Francisco: Harper San Francisco, 1995.

DAVIES, STEVAN. *Jesus the Healer.* New York: Continuum, 1995.

DOWNING, F. GERALD. *Cynics and Christian Origins.* Edinburgh: T. & T. Clark, 1992.

FARMER, WILLIAM. *The Synoptic Problem.* New York: Macmillan, 1964.

———. *The Gospel of Jesus.* Louisville, Kentucky: Westminster Press, 1994.

FINEGAN, JACK. *The Archaeology of the New Testament.* Revised edition. Princeton: Princeton University Press, 1992.

FOX, MATTHEW. *The Coming of the Cosmic Christ.* San Francisco: Harper San Francisco, 1988.

FOX, ROBIN LANE. *Pagans and Christians.* New York: Harper & Row, 1986.

FREDRIKSEN, PAULA. *From Jesus to Christ.* New Haven: Yale University Press, 1988.

FREYNE, SEAN. *Galilee from Alexander the Great to Hadrian.* Wilmington: Michael Glazier Inc., 1980.

FUNK, ROBERT. *Language, Hermeneutics, and the Word of God.* New York: Harper & Row, 1966.

———. *Parables and Presence: Forms of the New Testament Tradition.* Philadelphia: Fortress, 1982.

———. *Jesus as Precursor.* Sonoma, California: Polebridge Press, 1994.

FUNK, ROBERT, BERNARD BRANDON SCOTT, JAMES BUTTS, and the Jesus Seminar. *The Parables of Jesus.* Sonoma, California: Polebridge Press, 1988.

FUNK, ROBERT, ROY HOOVER, and the Jesus Seminar. *The Five Gospels.* New York: Macmillan, 1993.

HENGEL, MARTIN. *Judaism and Hellenism.* Philadelphia: Fortress, 1974.

———. *Crucifixion.* Trans. John Bowden. Philadelphia: Fortress, 1977.

HORSLEY, RICHARD, and J. S. HANSON. *Bandits, Prophets, and Messiahs: Popular Movements in the Time of Jesus.* Minneapolis: Winston Press, 1985.

JAMES, WILLIAM. *The Varieties of Religious Experience.* New York: Modern Library, 1994.

KOESTER, HELMUT. *Ancient Christian Gospels.* Philadelphia: Trinity Press International, 1990.

KOSMIN, BARRY A., and SEYMOUR P. LACHMAN. *One Nation Under God: Religion in Contemporary American Society.* New York: Crown, 1993.

LUEDEMANN, GERD. *The Resurrection of Jesus.* Minneapolis: Fortress, 1994.

MACK, BURTON. *A Myth of Innocence.* Philadelphia: Fortress, 1988.

———. *The Lost Gospel: The Book of Q and Christian Origins.* New York: HarperCollins, 1993.

———. *Who Wrote the New Testament?* New York: HarperCollins, 1995.

MEIER, JOHN. *A Marginal Jew: Rethinking the Historical Jesus.* New York: Doubleday. Vol. 1, 1991; vol. 2, 1994.

MEYERS, ERIC, and JAMES STRANGE. *Archaeology, the Rabbis, and Early Christianity.* Nashville: Abingdon, 1981.

NEUSNER, JACOB. *First-Century Judaism in Crisis.* Nashville: Abingdon, 1975.

———. *The Midrash: An Introduction.* Northvale, N.J.: Jason Aronson, Inc., 1990.

———. *A Rabbi Talks with Jesus.* New York: Doubleday, 1993.

NIETZSCHE, FRIEDRICH. *The Birth of Tragedy.* New York: Vintage, 1967.

PAGELS, ELAINE. *The Gnostic Gospels.* New York: Random House, 1979.

———. *The Origin of Satan.* New York: Random House, 1995.

RANKE-HEINEMANN, UTA. *Putting Away Childish Things.* New York: HarperCollins, 1994.

ROUSSEAU JOHN, and RAMI ARAV. *Jesus and His World.* Minneapolis: Fortress, 1995.

RUSSELL, BERTRAND. *A History of Western Philosophy.* London: George Allen & Unwin, 1946.

SANDERS, E. P. *Jesus and Judaism.* Philadelphia: Fortress, 1985.

SCHABERG, JANE. *The Illegitimacy of Jesus.* San Francisco: Harper & Row, 1987.

SCHILLEBEECKX, EDWARD. *Jesus: An Experiment in Christology.* New York: Seabury, 1979.

SCHÜSSLER FIORENZA, ELISABETH. *Bread Not Stone: The Challenge of Feminist Biblical Interpretation.* Boston: Beacon Press, 1984.

SCHWEITZER, ALBERT. *The Quest of the Historical Jesus.* New York: Macmillan, 1968 (orig. pub. 1906).

SCOTT, BERNARD BRANDON. *Hear Then the Parable.* Minneapolis: Fortress, 1990.

SEGAL, ALAN. *Rebecca's Children: Judaism and Christianity in the Roman World.* Cambridge: Harvard University Press, 1986.

SHANKS, HERSHEL, ed. *Understanding the Dead Sea Scrolls.* New York: Random House, 1992.

SHANKS, HERSHEL, WILLIAM DEVER, BARUCH HALPERN, and P. KYLE MCCARTER. *The Rise of Ancient Israel.* Washington: Biblical Archaeological Society, 1992.

SHEEHAN, THOMAS. *The First Coming: How the Kingdom of God Became Christianity.* New York: Random House, 1986.

SLOYAN, GERARD. *The Crucifixion of Jesus.* Minneapolis: Augsburg Fortress, 1995.

SMITH, MORTON. *Clement of Alexandria and a Secret Gospel of Mark.* Cambridge: Harvard University Press, 1973.

———. *The Secret Gospel: The Discovery and Interpretation of a Secret Gospel According to Mark.* New York: Harper & Row, 1973.

———. *Jesus the Magician.* New York: Harper & Row, 1978.

SPONG, JOHN SHELBY. *Born of a Woman.* San Francisco: Harper San Francisco, 1992.

———. *Rescuing the Bible from Fundamentalism.* San Francisco: Harper San Francisco, 1991.

———. *Resurrection: Myth or Reality?* New York: HarperCollins, 1994.

STONE, I. F. *The Trial of Socrates.* New York: Doubleday, 1989.

TILLICH, PAUL. *Dynamics of Faith.* New York: Harper & Row, 1957.

TWAIN, MARK. *The Innocents Abroad.* New York: Penguin, 1980.

VERMES, GEZA. *Jesus the Jew.* Philadelphia: Fortress Press, 1973.

WARNER, MARINA. *Alone of All Her Sex: The Myth and the Cult of the Virgin Mary.* New York: Knopf, 1976.

WELLS, G. A. *The Historical Evidence for Jesus.* New York: Prometheus, 1982.

WILKINS, MICHAEL J., and J. P. MORELAND, eds. *Jesus Under Fire.* Grand Rapids, Michigan: Zondervan, 1995.

WILSON, EDMUND. *The Scrolls from the Dead Sea.* New York: Oxford University Press, 1955.

WRIGHT, N. T. *The New Testament and the People of God.* Minneapolis: Fortress, 1992.

———. *Who Was Jesus?* Grand Rapids, Michigan: Wm. B. Eerdmans, 1993.

Ancient Works

EUSEBIUS. *Ecclesiastical History.* Kirsopp Lake and J. E. L. Oulton, trans. Cambridge: Harvard University Press, 1932.

Holy Bible: New Revised Standard Version, with Apocrypha. New York: Oxford University Press, 1989.

JOSEPHUS. *Jewish Antiquities.* Trans. L. H. Feldman, Loeb Classical Library Cambridge: Harvard University Press, 1954.

JOSEPHUS. *The Jewish War.* Trans. G. A. Williamson, revised edition by E. Mary Smallwood. London: Penguin, 1981.

ROBINSON, JAMES, general editor. *The Nag Hammadi Library.* Third edition. San Francisco: Harper & Row, 1988.

TERTULLIAN. *De Carne Christi.* Trans. Ernest Evans, London: S.P.C.K., 1956.

VERMES, GEZA. *The Dead Sea Scrolls in English.* Third edition. Sheffield: Sheffield Academic Press, 1987.

Articles

CARROLL, ROBERT. "Israel, History of (Post-Monarchic Period)," in *New Anchor Bible Dictionary,* 1992.

DAVIDS, STACY. "How Did Jesus Heal?" Paper presented to the Jesus Seminar, October 1993.

———. " 'Heal the Sick . . . and Say to Them, the Reign of God Is at Hand': Reconstructing Jesus as Healer." Paper presented to the Society of Biblical Literature, Central States Region, Tulsa, Oklahoma, April 1995.

FREDRIKSEN, PAULA. "What You See Is What You Get: Context and Content in Current Research on the Historical Jesus," *Theology Today,* April 1995.

FUNK, ROBERT. "Setting Jesus Free." Paper delivered at Jesus Seminar, October 1995.

HAAS, N. "Anthropological Observations on the Skeletal Remains from Giv'at ha-Mivtar," *Israel Exploration Journal* 20, 1970.

KEE, HOWARD CLARK. "A Century of Quests for the Culturally Compatible Jesus," *Theology Today,* April 1995.

KOESTER, HELMUT. "Historic Mistakes Haunt the Relationship of Christianity and Judaism," *Biblical Archaeology Review,* March/April 1995.

LINNEMANN, ETA. "Is There a Gospel of Q?" *Bible Review,* August 1995.

MURPHY-O'CONNOR, JEROME. "The Damascus Document Revisited," *Revue Biblique* 92, 1985.

NOLL, MARK, et al. "Scandal? A Forum on the Evangelical Mind," *Christianity Today,* August 14, 1995.

PATTERSON, STEPHEN J. "The End of Apocalypse: Rethinking the Eschatological Jesus," *Theology Today,* April 1995.

———. "The Challenge of the Historical Jesus and the Promise of the Christ We Confess." Lecture notes, 1995.

PERKINS, PHEME. "Jesus and Ethics," *Theology Today,* April 1995.

PRINCETON RELIGION RESEARCH CENTER. Gallup surveys: "Religion in America: 50 Years: 1935–1985"; "Church Membership, 1989"; "Church Attendance, 1993"; "Born Again—Recent Trend, 1995."

ROBINSON, JAMES. "Jesus from Easter to Valentinus," *Journal of Biblical Literature* 101/1, 1982.

SANDERS, E. P. "Jesus in Historical Context," *Theology Today,* October 1993.

SCHIFFMAN, LAWRENCE. "Origin and Early History of the Qumran Sect," *Biblical Archaeologist*, March 1995.

SCHMIDT, DARYL. "The LXX Influence in Shaping the Passion Narratives," Jesus Seminar Papers, October 1995.

SHANKS, HERSHEL. "New Analysis of the Crucified Man," *Biblical Archaeology Review* 11, November/December 1985.

SPONG, JOHN SHELBY. "Did Christians Invent Judas?" *The Fourth R,* March/April, 1994.

STANTON, GRAHAM. "A Gospel Among the Scrolls?" *Bible Review,* December 1995.

STRANGE, JAMES, and HERSHEL SHANKS. "Has the House Where Jesus Stayed in Capernaum Been Found?" *Biblical Archaeology Review,* November/December 1982.

TAYLOR, JOAN. "The Garden of Gethsemane: Not the Place of Jesus' Arrest," *Biblical Archaeology Review,* July/August 1995.

TZAFERIS, VASSILIOS. "Crucifixion—The Archaeological Evidence," *Biblical Archaeology Review,* January/February 1985.

INDEX

Abraham, 38, 62, 85, 98, 180, 188
Absalom, 188
Acts of the Apostles, 42, 83, 102
Adam, 211
Aetheria, 113
Afterlife, 75–76. *See also* Heaven; Hell
Ahaz, 31
Ahithophel, 188
Aitken, Ellen Bradshaw, 226
Alexander the Great, 28, 68, 91
Allegro, John, 82
American Academy of Religion, 10, 14
American Religion, The (Bloom), 243
Andrew, 112
Angels, 79
Annunciation, 18
Annunciation, Basilica of the (Nazareth), 18–19
Antioch-at-Jerusalem, 72
Antiochus IV Epiphanes, 73, 75, 77
  suppression of Judaism, 73–74
Anti-religious sentiment, 242
Anti-Semitism, 190, 192, 194. *See also* Jews, blamed for Jesus' death; Matthew, Gospel of, anti-Jewish attitude
Antonia Fortress (Jerusalem), 201, 202
Apocalypse, 60, 63, 80, 93, 125, 146–47, 159, 177, 182, 214, 215, 265. *See also* End; End Time
Apocryphon of James, 120
Apostles, 63, 143. *See also* Disciples; *specific names*
Archaeology, 2, 18–19, 43–44, 53, 88, 92, 134, 136, 186, 199, 203, 270
Archelaus, 91–92
Aristobulus, 79
Aristotle, 68
Armstrong, Karen, 35–36
Augustus Caesar (Octavian), 28, 86, 87, 92, 110
Aune, David, 24

Bakker, Jim, 236
Baptism, 59, 84, 95
  of Jesus, 102–8. *See also* Jesus, baptism of; John the Baptist
Barabbas, 191
Barrett, C. K., 71
Beatitudes, 115. *See also* Sermon on the Mount
Belz, Otto, 95

Bethlehem, 20, 32, 42
Beutner, Edward, 36, 122, 136n
Bible. *See* Bible, Hebrew; New Testament; Old Testament
Bible, Hebrew, 24, 55, 56, 60, 61, 68–69, 124, 209
and gospels, 24
translation into Greek, 30–31, 68–69, 70. *See also* Septuagint
See also Old Testament; Prefiguration
Billig, Yaakov, 88
Birth of the Messiah, The (Brown), 39
Birth (of Jesus) narratives, 40–41, 171
Blomberg, Craig, 4, 192
Bloom, Harold, 243
Borg, Marcus, 15, 20, 90, 139–40, 150–51, 157, 160, 238, 241–42
Branch Davidians, 213–14
Brown, Raymond, 24, 33, 35, 39, 170, 174–75, 191, 192, 207–8
Bultmann, Rudolf, 127, 260

Cadbury, Henry, 163
Caiaphas, 174, 189, 225
Calvary (Calvaria), 201, 210–11. *See also* Golgotha
Capernaum, 109, 110, 112–13, 114, 135–36, 269
Jesus in, 113
Cephas, 112, 216. *See also* Peter
Charismatic churches, 234, 244
Charlesworth, James, 203, 225–26
Christ. *See* Jesus
Christianity
early, 21, 22, 26, 29, 34, 37, 42, 54, 55, 59, 60, 70–71, 80, 116, 123–24, 141, 142, 143, 193
and hellenism, 29
influences on, 27–28, 29, 55
and Judaism, 29, 55, 58, 59, 193
nontraditional, 15, 234–44
pluralism in, 244
in U.S., 1900s, 231–48
Christmas, 20, 28
Churches, traditional, decrease in membership/attendance, 12, 234
Cleopas, 42, 177
Coming of the Cosmic Church, The (Fox), 214
Communion, 239
Constantine, 215
Cox, Harvey, 235
Craig, William, 227, 251–53, 254, 255, 256
Creation Spirituality, 214
Crossan, John Dominic, 20, 39, 59, 98, 129, 130, 137, 139, 154–57, 160, 179, 185, 187, 208, 251–53, 255–56
Crucifixion and torture, 197–209. *See also* Jesus, crucifixion
Cults, 28, 35, 67, 91, 153, 213–14
Cynic philosophy, 155–57

Daniel, Book of, 75, 123, 141
David, 38, 77, 173, 180, 187–88, 206
Davids, Stacy, 137–38
Davies, Stevan, 100, 132–33, 136
Dead Sea Scrolls, 51–52, 53, 55–57, 59, 62, 78, 79, 111–12, 159, 172, 221, 258, 277n
analysis, 51–52, 55–57
discovery, 55
and End Time, 62
and New Testament, 60
publication, 51, 56
translation and transcription, 51, 52, 56
Vatican and, 56
See also Essenes; Qumran
Dead Sea Scrolls in English, The (Vermes), 52
Death of the Messiah, The (Brown), 174
Deformity. *See* Disease
Demons, 131, 132. *See also* Exorcism
Dialogues (Plato), 66
Dionysus, 67, 127, 128
Disciples, 20, 63, 104, 106, 111, 187, 224, 266. *See also* Apostles; *specific names*
Disease, 59, 129
and (sexual) sin, 59, 129, 130, 137

See also Healing
Dissociative state, 132–33
Divine birth, of Jesus, 27, 33, 36, 38
DNA analysis, 35, 49–52
Dome of the Rock (Jerusalem), 180, 204

Eating. *See* Food and meals
Ecclesiastes, 150
Edras, 124
Egyptian mythology, 28, 67
Elijah, 24, 93, 98, 164, 171
Elisha, 24, 98, 142, 164
Empty tomb tradition, 224–27
End, 23, 141, 158, 182, 184. *See also* Apocalypse; End Time
End Time, 61–62, 63, 125, 219, 224, 265, 271. *See also* Apocalypse; End
Enlightenment, Age of, 124, 266, 267, 270
Epic concentration, 126
Epictetus, 155
Epiphany, 127
Epispasm, 72–73
Eshel, Hanan, 11
Essenes, 53, 55, 59–60, 62, 69, 75, 77, 78–80, 95–96, 114, 172, 181, 278–79n
  baptism among, 59, 95, 96
  and End, 95
  founding of, 77–78
  vs. Maccabees, 77–78
  and Messiah, 59
  and Pythagoreanism, 78–80
  See also Dead Sea Scrolls; Qumran
Eucharist, 140
Evangelical churches, 234–36, 242, 244, 268
Evil, 65–66, 67, 95, 184, 194
Exodus, 186
  Book of, 98, 208
Exorcism, 128, 134, 135. *See also* Healing

Falwell, Jerry, 245, 246
Farmer, William, 259–60
Finegan, Jack, 19
Fire from Heaven (Cox), 235
Fish, 113, 140–42
Fitzmyer, Joseph, 113
Five Gospels, The (Jesus Seminar), 111
Flavius Josephus. *See* Josephus
Food and meals, 59–60, 138–44, 239–40, 271
Fox, Matthew, 214, 223, 267
Fredriksen, Paula, 15, 22, 31, 58, 70, 90, 160, 161, 178
Freyne, Sean, 72
Funk, Robert, 13–15, 120, 160, 256, 266, 272–78

Gadara, 155
Galilee, 43, 45, 46, 100, 109, 110
  Sea of, 45, 109–10, 124, 142
Gehinnom (Gehenna), 76
Geivett, R. Douglas, 256–57, 267
Genealogy, of Jesus, 38–39
Genesis, Book of, 209
Gentiles. *See* Christianity
Gethsemane, 168, 186–87, 189
Gnostic Gospels, The (Pagels), 220–21
Gnosticism, 149, 215–16, 222, 223, 243
God, Jewish, 34, 67, 70. *See also* Yahweh
Golgotha, 201, 203, 204, 211, 225. *See also* Calvary
Good, 65–66, 67, 95
Gospel According to Woman, The (Armstrong), 35–36
Gospels, 25, 40–42, 58, 83, 102, 113–14, 116, 171, 224, 259–60
  baptism in, 102–5
  birth of Jesus in, 41, 42, 171
  chronologies in, 113
  differences among, 29, 32–33, 146–47
  early, 194–95
  first, 21, 23, 147, 259–60, 262
  history vs., 23
  Jesus in. *See* Jesus
  origins, 20–21. *See also* Gospels, sources
  passion, of Jesus. *See* Passion (Jesus) narratives

reliability, 23
resurrection in, 217–18, 219, 220
similarities among, 147–48
sources, 259–60. *See also* Bible, Hebrew; Old Testament; Prefiguration; Q
See also specific gospel names
Graham, Billy, 245
Greece. *See* Greek culture; Hellenism
Greek culture, 65–80, 150, 151, 154–157
mythology, 27–28, 34, 67
philosophy, 2, 20, 67, 69, 78
Griggs, Wilfred, 50

Hananim (Korean deity), 235
Hannina ben Dosa, 92, 93
Hannukah, 74
Hasmonean rulers, 76, 85, 86
Healing, 137–38 *See also* Disease; Exorcism; Jesus, as healer; Miracles
Heaven, 75, 76, 80
Hell, 76, 80
Hellenism, in Palestine, 2, 20, 27-28, 45, 46, 67, 68, 69, 71–73, 76, 78, 80, 87, 133, 163–64, 271, 278n
Jewish revolt against, 73–74
See also Greek culture
Hengel, Martin, 71, 78, 79
Herod the Great, 19, 32, 33, 86–90, 180, 190, 202, 203
building program, 87–90
death, 91
Jerusalem under, 87–90
Herod Antipas, 92, 98, 103, 107
Historical Jesus, The (Crossan), 154
Historical Jesus study, 2–4, 8, 11–16, 35, 61, 236–39, 254–56
beginnings, 11
development, 12
and Roman Catholic church, 13
See also Jesus; Jesus Seminar; Science
Holy places, 77, 224, 225
Holy Sepulchre, Church of the (Jerusalem), 204–5, 209–11
Holy Spirit, 30, 37, 102, 105, 106, 107, 132, 133
Honest to God (Robinson), 245–46

Illegitimacy, 39
Illegitimacy of Jesus, The (Schaberg), 37
Illness. *See* Disease
Immaculate conception, 38
Isaac, 38, 85, 180
Isaiah, Book of, 30–32, 61, 63, 123, 125, 173, 208
Israel Antiquities Authority, 56
Israel Department of Antiquities, 199

Jacob (father of Joseph), 38
James (brother of Jesus), 1, 41, 42, 74, 177, 228
James, William, 106
Jason, 72
Jefferson, Thomas, 124
"Jehohanan the Potter," 199–201
Jeremiah, 93
Jerusalem, 21, 53, 72, 77, 91, 93, 183
under Herod, 87–89
Temple, 21, 22, 52, 87–89, 94, 97. *See also* Temple
See also specific sites
Jesus, 1, 2, 8, 11
arrest, 168, 185, 186, 187
baptism, 99, 101–2, 105, 110, 121, 158
as baptizer, 104, 107
birth, 19, 32
career beginnings, 24, 25, 44, 110–11, 113–14
as carpenter/laborer, 41, 44, 45, 99
characterizations of, 15–16, 27, 46, 47, 131, 152–65, 176, 239, 271–72
childhood and youth, 2, 19–20, 29, 32, 40–41
conception, 18, 37–38. *See also* Virgin birth
crucifixion, 9, 110, 168, 169, 174, 197, 201, 205–6, 207, 208
and Cynic philosophy, 155–57

date of birth, 19
David, parallels with, 187–89
death. *See* Jesus, crucifixion
and/as divine, 36
education and language, 41, 112
family, 1, 19, 41, 42, 100, 177. *See also specific names*
as food, 144, 185
in Galilee, 110–11
genealogy, 38–39
as healer, 26, 59, 125, 128, 130, 132, 134–39, 144, 271. *See also* Jesus, as miracle-worker
historical study of, 2, 3. *See also* Historical Jesus study; Jesus Seminar
as Holy Spirit, 133–34
as human, 43, 131, 271–72
illegitimacy, 37, 39, 100. *See also* Jesus, birth *and* conception; Virgin birth
influences on, 20, 42–43, 45–46, 47, 59, 99, 162, 164, 271–72
and John the Baptist, 101, 107, 110. *See also* John the Baptist, and Jesus
last days, 168–95
as Messiah, 15, 30, 111, 179, 186, 188, 215, 268
as miracle-worker, 123–44. *See also* Healing; Miracles
name, 38
nonexistence, 262–63
and Pharisees, 58
place of birth, 32, 42, 43–44
as political figure, 26, 130–32, 139–40, 145, 164, 184
as prophet, 60, 63, 104, 123, 124, 126, 141, 160, 164, 177, 179, 271, 272
resurrection, 172–73, 190, 207–8, 216–18, 224, 227, 240. *See also* Resurrection
as scapegoat, 208
Socrates, parallels with, 144, 151–52
stories of, 21, 25–26, 40, 144. *See also* Birth narratives; Gospels; Passion narratives
as sufferer, 186, 206, 207
as teacher, 20, 26, 39, 46, 104, 108, 114–22, 151, 153, 228, 271. *See also* Parables
in Temple, 60–61, 63, 158, 159, 179, 180–85, 193
trial, 169, 189–92, 201, 203
words of, 9, 121. *See also* Gospels; Parables
Jesus the Healer (Davies), 132
Jesus and Judaism (Sanders), 61, 158
Jesus Seminar, 8–9, 13–14, 121, 131, 134–35, 136, 157, 159, 160, 169, 227, 248
on miracles, 134–35
opposition to, 8, 9, 10, 251, 256, 258
voting process, 9–10
Jewish Wars, 21, 22, 29, 52–53, 57, 71, 181, 198, 228
Jews, blamed for Jesus' death, 168, 169, 190, 193, 194
Job, Book of, 150–51
John, Gospel of, 95, 103–4, 106, 107, 171, 194, 195. *See also* Gospels
John the Baptist, 83, 84, 90, 93–108, 158
and apocalypse, 93, 95, 97–98, 101
baptism of Jesus, 94, 96, 99, 101–5
birth, 94–95, 96
death, 107
Essenes and, 95–97, 114
and Jesus, 93, 100–101, 110
as political figure, 107
as preacher, 99
Jonathan Maccabeus, 74, 76, 78
Jordan River, 98–99, 105, 106
Joseph (father of Jesus), 1, 2, 30, 37, 38, 39, 40, 44
disappearance, 39
paternity of Jesus, 37, 38
Josephus, 33, 52, 53, 57–58, 62, 73–74, 75, 83, 95, 96, 107, 110, 169, 184, 198, 199, 262
on Jesus, 57–58

on Judaism, 57–58
Joses (brother of Jesus), 1, 41, 74
Joshua, 98
Judaism, 27, 29, 46, 53–54, 55, 62, 63, 86, 157–59, 164, 193–94
and Christianity, 29, 58
and Greek culture, 71, 80. *See also* Hellenism
Second Temple, 54, 63
See also Pharisees
Judas (brother of Jesus), 1, 41, 42, 74, 246
Judas Iscariot, 187, 188, 189–90, 246
Judas Maccabeus, 74
Justin Martyr, 209

Kingdom of God, 22, 108, 112, 114, 116, 117–21, 122, 130, 138, 139, 143, 144, 145, 158–59, 163, 164, 185, 266, 271
Kingdom of heaven. *See* Kingdom of God
Kinneret (Galilee), 109–10. *See also* Galilee
Kloppenberg, John, 150
Koester, Helmut, 11, 28, 187, 208
Koresh, David, 213–14
Kosmin, Barry, 243, 244

Lachman, Seymour, 243, 244
Language, Hermeneutics, and the Word of God (Funk), 120
Last Supper, 9, 60, 143, 144, 168, 178, 185, 239
Lazarus, 13
Leo X, 222
Life of Jesus Critically Examined, The (Strauss), 11
Linnemann, Eta, 260–62
Literalism and belief, 128, 236, 270
Luke, Gospel of, 18, 32–33, 40, 41–42, 125
Sermon on the Mount in, 114
Luther, Martin, 222
McCorvey, Norma, 84
Maccabees, 74, 75, 76, 77, 78, 92, 97
Mack, Burton, 68, 72, 91, 152–54, 157, 161, 228, 260
on Q, 152–54
Magicians, 58, 92
Manual of Discipline (Essene), 59
Marc Antony, 86
Mark, 22, 23
Gospel of, 21, 22–23, 24, 25, 28, 29, 41, 126, 156, 171, 177, 205–6, 207, 224, 225, 226, 228
as first, 147, 171, 176
Mary (mother of Jesus), 1, 18, 19, 35, 36, 37, 38, 40
cults, 35
purity, 38
See also Immaculate conception; Virgin birth
Mary Magdalene, 220, 224
Masada (Jerusalem), 53
Mattathias, 74, 76
Matthew, 28
Gospel of, 28, 29–34, 37–39, 111, 125, 257, 259
anti-Jewish attitude, 29, 146–47
Meier, John, 12–13, 14, 34, 42, 45, 102, 107, 108, 110, 134–35, 136, 141–42, 160, 262
Messiah, idea of, 80, 173, 186, 187–88, 233. *See also* Jesus, as Messiah
Meyers, Eric, 19, 44, 45, 136
Midrash, 24, 171, 173
Mind-body connection, 137
Miracles, 13, 24–25, 92, 123–44, 175, 247
explanations of, 124
of loaves and fishes, 140–41, 269–70
of water changed into wine, 127, 128
See also Jesus, as miracle-worker
Miryam. *See* Mary
Mithras, 28
Mohammed, 180
Moses, 24, 70, 78, 171, 172, 179

Mount Moriah, 180
Mount of Olives, 186, 188, 189
Mystery cults, 28, 67, 91, 153
Myth, role of, 36, 202
Myth of Innocence, A (Mack), 153
Mythology, 27–28, 67

Nag Hammadi, 120, 221
Names, Jewish, 74–75
Nature miracles, 128, 134, 141
Nazareth, 1, 17–19, 20, 32, 42, 43–46
Near Eastern religion, 66–67
Nebuchadnezzar, 180
Nero, 38
Neusner, Jacob, 171, 209
New Testament, 25, 26, 27
  and Dead Sea Scrolls, 60
  See also Gospels; *specific book names*
New Testament and the People of God, The (Wright), 267
Nietzsche, Friedrich, 67

Old Testament, 24, 70, 150, 169
  as source for Gospels, 23–25, 169–70, 171–72. *See also* Prefiguration
  See also specific book names
One Nation Under God (Kosmin and Lachman), 243
Origin of Satan, The (Pagels), 194

Pagels, Elaine, 194, 220–21, 222
Papal authority, 222
Papias, 21, 23, 113
Parables, 115–22, 139, 148, 159, 273
  Dishonest Steward, 119
  Good Samaritan, 119–20
  of kingdom of heaven, 117–19, 120, 121
  New Testament, 115–22
  Old Testament, 115
  See also Jesus, as teacher
Passion (of Jesus) narratives, 168–71, 174–75, 193, 205
Passover, 178, 183, 185
Patterson, Stephen, 261
Paul, 26–27, 95, 112, 116–17, 170, 216, 218, 219, 223, 229, 245, 263
  epistles, 26–27
  on resurrection, 218–20
Peasantry, Judean, 89, 90, 91, 130
Pentecostalism, 222–23, 234–36, 242, 244
Perils of Modernizing, The (Cadbury), 163
Pesher, 24, 172, 173, 174
Peter, 20–21, 22, 104, 111–12, 175, 225
  appointed successor to Jesus, 111–12
  Gospel of, 190
Pharisees, 54, 58, 117, 118, 193
Philo, 69
Pius IX, 38
Placebo effect, 137–38
Plato, 28, 66, 68
Pompey, 85–86
Pontius Pilate, 9, 92, 187, 189, 190, 191, 192, 194–95, 201, 202, 203
Possession, 132–33. *See also* Demons; Exorcism
Potasnik, Joseph, 251, 254
Prefiguration, 24–25, 142, 171, 173. *See also* Old Testament
Prophets, 58, 90, 92–93, 127, 133. *See also specific names*
Proverbs, Book of, 150
Psalms, Book of, 105, 173–74, 205–8, 209, 226
Ptolemy, 183–84
Pythagoras, 78, 79
Pythagoreanism, 78–79, 80

Q *(Quelle)*, 102, 148–50, 151, 152, 153, 154, 156, 157, 176, 228, 259, 260–62
Quest of the Historical Jesus, The (Schweitzer), 61
Quirinius, 33
Qumran, 53, 69, 78, 79–80, 95, 158, 181. *See also* Dead Sea Scrolls; Essenes

Rabbah, 209
Ranke-Heinemann, Uta, 33, 75, 76, 127
Rebecca's Children (Segal), 54
Reich, Ronnie, 88
Reimarus, Hermann Samuel, 11
Religious Right, 10, 15, 244
Resurrection, 219
 of Jesus, 142, 220–29, 247, 253
  physical, 218, 219, 220, 221–22, 228
  political significance, 221
  spiritual, 219
Robinson, James, 218, 223, 224
Robinson, John, 245–46
Roman Catholic church, 12–13, 115, 134. *See also* Christianity, early; Vatican
Roman Empire, 2, 26, 85, 89, 91, 155, 157, 193
 Christianizing of, 215
 conquest of Palestine, 21, 52–53, 54, 71, 85–86, 181, 183
 crucifixion under, 197–201, 203
 legal administration, 190–91
 presence in Palestine, 2, 74, 92
 taxation under, 89, 90, 129
Rome, ancient. *See* Roman Empire
Rook, Susan, 252–53
Russell, Bertrand, 79, 80, 155

Sacred Mushroom and the Cross, The (Allegro), 82
Sacrifice (animal), 54, 61, 77, 85, 93, 94, 183
Sadducees, 75, 77, 118, 193
Samuel, Book of, 187, 188
Sanders, E. P., 60–61, 63, 90, 116, 130, 157–59, 160, 161, 179, 181, 183, 184, 265
Sanhedrin, 94, 189, 225
Satan, 194
Sayings collections, 150, 175
Schaberg, Jane, 37
Schillebeeckx, Edward, 120, 126–27, 140, 224–25, 226, 227, 272–73
Schmidt, Daryl, 173
Schweitzer, Albert, 61
Science, 4, 12
 scientific method and research, 2, 35, 49–50, 265
 scientific truth, 4, 254
 See also Archaeology; DNA analysis
Scrolls from the Dead Sea, The (Wilson), 55
Second Coming, 160
Second Temple Judaism, 53, 63
Segal, Alan, 54, 62
Seneca, 199, 200
Sepphoris, 1, 2, 20, 49, 154
Septuagint, 31, 69, 70, 206
 Translation problems, 30–31
 See also Bible, Hebrew
Sermon on the Mount, 59, 114–15, 148
Sheehan, Thomas, 227
Sheol, 75, 76
Simeon (cousin of Jesus), 42
Simon (brother of Jesus), 1, 41, 74
Simon Peter. *See* Peter
Simon Maccabeus. 74, 78
Sin, 59, 129, 130
Sloyan, Gerard, 198
Smith, Morton, 82–83, 93, 130
Society of Biblical Literature, 10–11, 14, 265
Socrates, 66, 68, 151–52
Solomon, 77, 180
Spartacus, 200
Spong, John Shelby, 25, 140, 144, 226, 244–45, 246–48
Steinmann, Jean, 95, 97
Stone, I. F., 151
Storytelling, Jewish, 122. *See also* Parables
Strange, James, 10, 19, 20, 44, 45, 136
Strauss, David Friedrich, 11
Swaggart, Jimmy, 236
Synoptics. *See* Gospels

Tacitus, 169, 262
Taylor, Joan, 186
Teacher of Righteousness, 78, 79

Technology and Jesus study, 12. *See also* Science
Temple (Jerusalem; building and authorities), 60, 61, 73, 76–77, 85–87, 92, 93, 104, 129
  destruction of, 21–22, 44, 52, 54, 180, 182, 193
  treasury, 77, 183
  See also Jerusalem, Temple; Jesus, in Temple
Temple Mount (Jerusalem), 180
Thiede, Carsten, 258
Thomas, 217–18
Thomas, Gospel of, 40, 83, 121, 149, 150, 151, 152, 154, 157, 176, 222, 228, 260, 261
Tillich, Paul, 246, 270
Tobit, 182
Trance state, 132–33
Trial of Socrates, The (Stone), 151
Twain, Mark, 210
Twelve (tribes; disciples), 61, 63, 143, 159, 172

Upper Palace, of Herod (Jerusalem), 202, 203

VanderKam, James, 60
Varieties of Religious Experience, The (James), 106
Vatican, 12, 13, 56, 244. *See also* Roman Catholic church
Verhoeven, Paul, 8–9
Vermes, Geza, 25, 31, 52, 160
Via Dolorosa (Jerusalem), 201–4
Virgin birth, 25, 27–28, 30–32, 34, 35, 36, 38, 95, 247
  dubiousness of, 30–34
  mythological examples, 27–28
  origin of story, 36–37
  "translation error" and, 34
  Vatican and, 34–35
  See also Isaiah, Book of

Wailing Wall (Jerusalem), 87. *See also* Western Wall
"War of the Sons of Light Against the Sons of Darkness, The," 59
Way of the Cross, 201–4
Wells, G. A., 263
Western Wall (Jerusalem), 53, 87, 88
Wicked Priest, 78
Wilson, Edmund, 55, 56, 59, 221
Woodward, Scott, 50, 51
Wright, N. T., 264–66, 267–68, 272–73

Yadin, Yigael, 95
Yahweh (YHWH), 34, 67, 69, 73, 77, 98
Yeshu (Yeshua, Joshua). *See* Jesus
Yosef. *See* Joseph

Zadok, 77
Zadokite succession, 77, 78. *See also* Sadducees
Zechariah (father of John the Baptist), 96
Zechariah, Book of, 179, 189, 208
Zias, Joseph, 50–51

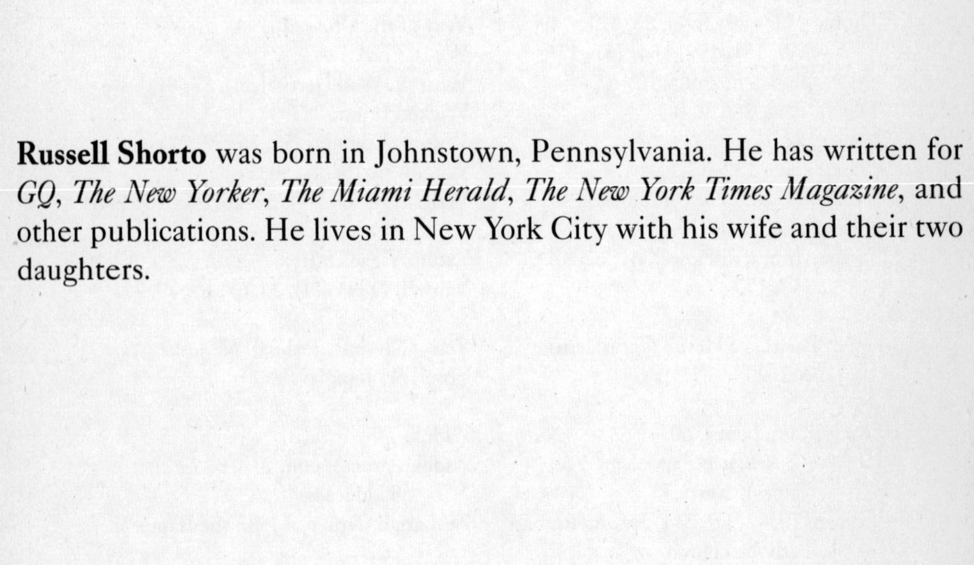

Russell Shorto was born in Johnstown, Pennsylvania. He has written for *GQ*, *The New Yorker*, *The Miami Herald*, *The New York Times Magazine*, and other publications. He lives in New York City with his wife and their two daughters.